The Siege of Derry

The Siege of Derry

CARLO GÉBLER

LITTLE, BROWN

A *Little, Brown* Book

First published in Great Britain in March 2005 by Little, Brown

Copyright © Carlo Gébler 2005
Maps © John Gilkes 2005

Endpapers: Captain Francis Nevill's map of Londonderry from *History of the Siege of Londonderry 1689*, Cecil Davis Milligan (Carter Publications, 1951).

A CIP catalogue record for this book is available
from the British Library.

ISBN 0 316 86128 6

Typeset in Bembo by M Rules
Printed and bound in Great Britain by
Clays Ltd, St Ives plc

Little, Brown
An imprint of
Time Warner Book Group UK
Brettenham House
Lancaster Place
London WC2E 7EN
www.twbg.co.uk

For Tyga

CONTENTS

ACKNOWLEDGEMENTS

I would like to thank Margaret Kane, Marianna Maguire and the staff of the Enniskillen Library; Rhys Griffith and the London Metropolitan Archives; Brian Lacey; John Milne; Glenn Patterson; Hazel Orme; Philip Parr; John Gilkes; Celia and Mike Levett; Richard Beswick; Vivien Redman; Linda Silverman; Jason Thompson; Edward Vallance; the editor of the *Irish Times* for permission to quote from Fintan O'Toole's article of Saturday, 12 May 1990; and Bloomsbury for permission to quote from *Loyalists* by Peter Taylor. All mistakes are my own.

I gratefully acknowledge the financial support of the Arts Council/An Chomhairle Ealaíon.

LIST OF ILLUSTRATIONS

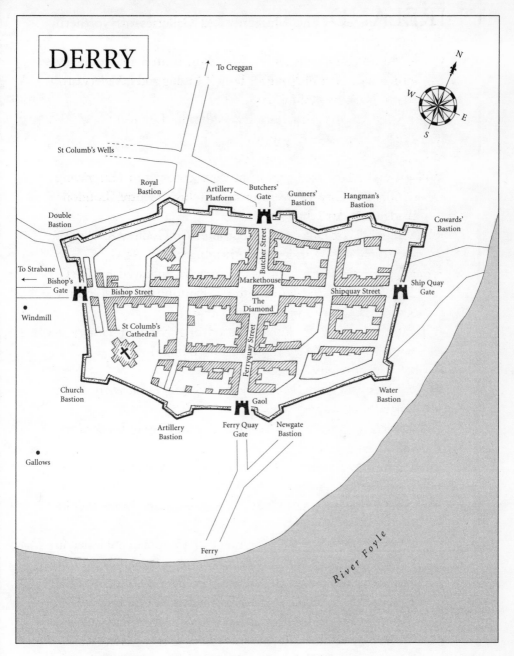

Derry, showing showing streets and fortifications (not to scale)

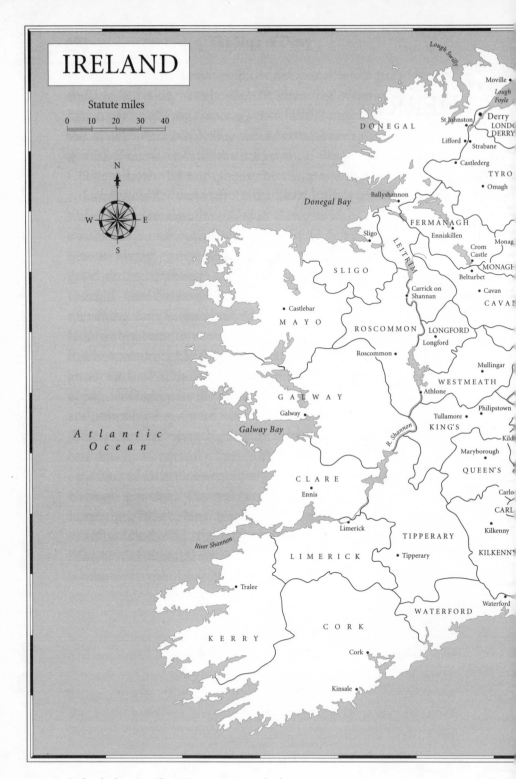

Ireland, showing showing counties and towns

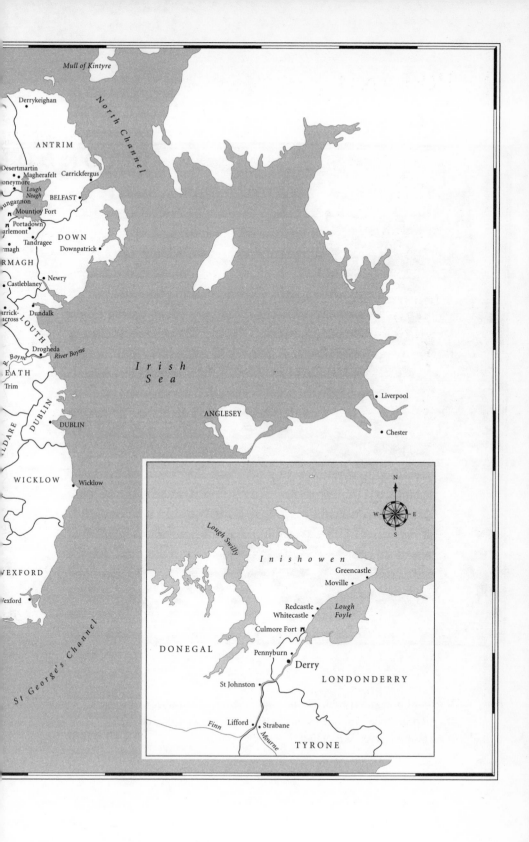

View of Londonderry during the siege of 1688–9, from an engraving after Romeyn de Hooghe from *The Siege of Derry in 1689*, edited by Rev. Philip Dwyer MA (Elliot Stock)

DERRY.

LONDONDERRY, MAP OF THE SIEGE, 1689.

A-B KIRKES FLEET   C IRISHMEN SURPRISED BY THE INHABITANTS OF INCH.   D ARRIVAL OF THE IRISHMEN.
E   SORTIE AGAINST THE IRISHMEN & THEIR DEFEAT F FRENCH WORKS INCOMPLETE. G, FRENCH APPROACHES H, FRENCH WORKS DESTROYED.
I.   FRENCH & IRISH FIGHTING   K CRUELTIES OF KING JAMES & D'AVAUX EXECUTED ON THE CLERGY

There is properly no history: only biography.

Ralph Waldo Emerson, *History*

In the lives of individuals and of peoples, too, the worst conflicts are often those that break out between those who are persecuted.

Amos Oz, *A Tale of Love and Darkness*

CHAPTER ONE

From Way Back to Back Then

This is a memory from the early seventies. I probably saw the advertisement in an Irish newspaper. It was for a school of driving. The female learner driver behind the wheel was the island herself – feet sprouting from County Kerry; hands emerging from County Galway; eyes, nose and mouth superimposed on County Donegal. The accompanying copy promised would-be drivers that they would master the art effortlessly. As an illustration, the hands and feet fitted well enough. The face, on the other hand, was much less convincing. The coastline of Ireland's top-left corner is tortuous and most unlike the profile of a face. There is also the small matter of the indentations behind the forehead, particularly Lough Foyle. This topographical detail gave the impression that Miss Ireland, the learner driver, had a hole in her head.

When I saw this, I was a student at the University of York. Like so many others of my generation, I saw Ireland's history primarily as a long list of bad things done to her by the English. And of all the places where bad was done, Londonderry or Derry – the city on the River Foyle, which fluttered like a kite's tail from the bottom of Lough Foyle – was surely where bad had happened (and continued to happen) in its most concentrated form. For a start, there was the name. This was an amalgam of London, from England's capital, and Derry, from the original Irish name for the site.* The issue of the name (endlessly recycled on news reports and documentaries) perfectly dramatized the Irish problem in the simple terms that the mass media adored. First, the strong power overwhelmed her neighbour. Then she forcibly tagged the name of her capital city on to an original Irish name. It was a very early example of rebranding following a hostile takeover, and it spoke volumes about colonial arrogance.

The media frequently discussed the city's name alongside a set of historical events, as if these had welded the name in place. The story, as television and the newspapers told it, went something like this. At the end of the seventeenth century, London-Derry, a walled city crammed with those who had been relocated to Ireland to hold the country for the Crown, was besieged by a Jacobite army. Though racially as well as religiously mixed, this besieging force, had it gained entry, would have returned the city to the indigenous Irish. Perhaps it would also have restored the original Irish name. But the siege failed and the loyalists inside held out. Their survival laid the ground for the Williamite triumph over the Jacobites, first at the Battle of the Boyne in 1690 – a victory still celebrated in Northern Ireland by Orangemen on 12 July every year – and then at the Battle of Aughrim, in 1691, which was the decisive encounter. The subsequent Irish surrender was followed by the Williamite settlement. This rewarded

---

*The place name Londonderry was and is a source of conflict. Loyalists cherish the term because it is a reminder of the British connection. Ditto (generally) Unionists. Republicans abhor the word for the same reason. Ditto (generally) Nationalists. When speaking, I use either Londonderry or Derry, according to who the listener is. It avoids tedious arguments.

In 1984, the city council, then Nationalist controlled, voted to change its name to Derry City Council. The official title of the city remains unaltered. BBC Northern Ireland news bulletins usually refer first to Londonderry in any item, and thereafter to Derry. This is a strategy I intend to emulate. Antagonizing everyone is at least even-handed. For the county, incidentally, I will use the full title.

English Protestant colonists and punished Irish Catholic natives. Also, it set Londonderry, the name, in stone. Over nearly three centuries that arrangement went unchallenged in Derry. The winners (Protestant, loyal, Unionist) held the city and enjoyed the benefits of ownership (power, wealth and privilege). The losers (Catholic, disloyal, Nationalist) lived outside the city walls in the so-called Bogside, a place for losers if ever there was one, and suffered the penalties of exclusion (powerlessness, poverty and insignificance).

By the late 1960s Derry had become a byword for squalor, inequality and corruption. The descendants of the original losers, although they now far outnumbered the descendants of the winners, seemed unable to do anything about their miserable conditions. Local elections were gerrymandered to such an extent that the Unionist minority always gained more seats than the Catholic majority. By holding on to power they also retained the best houses and the best-paid jobs. The Catholics often had no jobs at all. The Protestants were still gorging on the fruits of a victory gained 270 years before. The Catholics were still supping the bitter ashes of defeat.

Then something remarkable started to happen. Suddenly, after centuries of degradation, Catholics from outside the walls and Nationalists (two overlapping but not always identical groups), aided by Protestant egalitarians, decided enough was enough. They wanted houses. They wanted jobs. They wanted one man, one vote. They wanted an end to paramilitary-style police violence. They were tired of being second-class citizens in their own country on account of their religion. They wanted parity with the Protestants.

It was not going to be easy, but it fitted perfectly with the spirit of the times. All over the world the dispossessed were rising up and reclaiming what was rightfully theirs. This was the era of decolonization, and the media lapped it up. What could make a better story than wrongs righted and justice done after centuries of oppression? And the story of Derry was even more resonant than the others, because the continuity between past and present was so starkly visible. The walls still stood, separating the Protestant elite inside from the Catholics outside. They provided as potent a symbol of division as that other, much more recently erected wall in Berlin. The Bogside's squalid terraces cowering under Derry's northern wall seemed just as deprived as the concrete tower-blocks of the German Democratic Republic.

Throughout the early seventies, I followed on television and in print what was happening in this city. I saw for myself the reaction of the Unionists, the proxies of the British State in Ireland, to the laudable aspiration of the majority population to be accorded the same political rights as were enjoyed by everyone else in the United Kingdom. Night after night, I saw how policemen, some B-Specials (RUC special constables) and British Army soldiers repressed Catholics with indiscriminate violence. The low point came on 30 January 1972, in the course of a proscribed weekend march in Derry by the Civil Rights Association. Troops from the 1st Battalion of the Paratroop Regiment shot dead thirteen local people. After this, the Republican movement was able to argue that violence was the only recourse available to young Catholics. 'Bloody Sunday' famously encouraged more young Nationalists to join the IRA than any other event in Northern Ireland's unhappy recent history. From that fact (although all the new IRA members did not come exclusively from the city) arose Derry's mystique as the epicentre of violent opposition to the British State. In the popular imagination it became the Gaza Strip of the British Isles, the place where fury, expressed through violence, was found in its most concentrated form.

This is another memory, from 1974. A poster on a noticeboard at York University showed Britain as a squaddie. The head, under a steel helmet worn at a jaunty angle, was Sutherland and Caithness. The right hand, holding a truncheon, was Anglesey, and the left, holding a riot shield, was Pembroke. The victim was Ireland. She was being hit about the head of Antrim and weeping from the eyes of Donegal. There was to be a public meeting at which several speakers (socialists and Trotskyists, judging by the event's sponsors) would urge the withdrawal of the British troops then occupying the Province and the restoration of Northern Ireland to her true owners, the Irish.

My tutor at the time was from Ulster. He had seen the poster but didn't much care for the fixation of the English left wing with Ireland. He thought their grasp of history was wonky, and that all they really desired was the vicarious excitement of association with calamity. He also thought that, at heart, those revolutionaries didn't care a jot about the Catholic, Nationalist and Republican people. They merely wanted to strike a blow at Britain's governing classes and Northern Ireland's miseries were just the means to that end. He was on to something here. The fixation on Ireland had a self-regarding core. Though Ireland's woes were supposedly of such concern, it was what those woes would precipitate in Britain that really excited.

The radical thinking about Ireland common among those of us students who gave it any thought went something like this. Traditionally, England's difficulty was Ireland's opportunity. The early seventies had seen this reversed: Ireland – or, precisely, Northern Ireland – and her difficulties, especially those in Derry, were now to be England's opportunity. Unlike last time, the Irish were going to win, and their victory would precipitate revolution. What had happened in Russia after the Kaiser's army had defeated the Tsar's would be repeated in Britain. Distant events would create the conditions for a socialist revolution in England now.

My Ulster-born tutor thought this thesis was rubbish. The paramilitaries could push at the door as hard as they liked, he said: they would never force it open. They were just a few hundred men with small arms up against an army and a police force. Furthermore, the security forces were not the vicious incompetents the media usually made them out to be. They were learning from their mistakes and becoming more sophisticated by the day. Stormont might have been suspended, he agreed (direct rule by the Secretary of State was introduced on 24 March 1972), but the entity called Northern Ireland would survive because the majority wanted it to survive. The future, he predicted, was low-level, low-intensity, internecine strife between Loyalists, Republicans and the security forces, probably for decades to come, culminating, once exhaustion set in, in some sort of local arrangement with the border still in place.

He was proved right. Several decades and several thousand deaths later, by which time I was living in Northern Ireland, our paramilitary leaders magnanimously agreed to stop killing us. After thirty years of mayhem, they were finally worn out. So they mothballed their overalls and balaclavas, put on their Sabbath suits, set aside their old enmities (though these were not forgotten: no, that would have been a miracle too far) and began to practise politics.

CHAPTER TWO

A Short History of Conquest

I have driven from my home in Enniskillen to Derry many times. The journey begins with muddy lanes and wild hedgerows, small fields full of rushes and old cottages crassly modernized with brown pebble-dash, plastic windows and aluminium gutters. In France, there is a mythical line across the middle of the country which is said to divide the cold north from the sunny Mediterranean south. Houses on one side of the street are supposed to have slates while those on the other have terracotta roof tiles. En route to Derry, I always look out for a similar line separating boggy Fermanagh from the fertile lands to the north. I've never found it. Native terrain (as I class poor land) always shades into planter country before I realize the change has occurred. Suddenly, the fields expand, the rushes vanish, and the pebble-dash gives way to two-storey dwellings built of grey stone, with cast-iron spouting and impressive lawns.

Derry is a lovely, compact, prosperous-looking city (at least seen from the south) built on and around a miniature hill that rises to a mere 120 feet, while the River Foyle snakes around one side of its base. For most of its history (until air power became *the* power), this river would have been an impressive impediment to any foe.

And its efficacy as a defensive barrier was augmented by the stretch of bog or slob that, once upon a time, had encompassed the other side of the hill. The two watery barriers together formed a kind of moat. With such natural defences, it was inevitable that the hill should be identified as a good place to build. According to one version, Columcille, the great Christian proselytizer, was deeply involved in this process. He supposedly built a church there in the middle of the sixth century, but he was so attached to the forest of oak trees that stood on the site that he would not allow even one to be felled to make room for his buildings. These adored trees gave the place its name. *Doire* or *Daire*, meaning either an oak wood or an island covered by oak trees, which has come down to us today as Derry.

Over the following centuries, more churches, abbeys, monasteries and convents were established and flourished on the hill. And, of course, as was the way with such institutions in those times, they were also plundered: by Vikings, Anglo-Norman soldiers of fortune and, not least, by the Irish themselves. Derry's early inhabitants also had to put up with the depredations of nature. In 1146, according to early Irish historians, sixty oaks were blown down in a storm; in 1178 another 120 were toppled. Derry, in its early days, was beset by a series of disasters. Nevertheless, because of its location, settlers kept returning and rebuilding.

Sir John de Courcy, who plundered Derry twice, was one of the wave of Anglo-Norman conquistadores who streamed into Ireland in the reign of Henry II. He arrived in 1176 with Henry's deputy, William fitz Audelin, and for a while was part of the Dublin garrison. The next year, when Henry made his son, John, Lord of Ireland, de Courcy began his meteoric rise. He mustered 20 men-at-arms and 300 other soldiers. Then, without royal sanction, he led his forces into the kingdom of Ulaid, in north-east Ulster, hitherto hardly penetrated by the Norman forces. He seized Downpatrick, Ulaid's capital, expelled the native *ri*, or king and proclaimed himself ruler in the man's place. The Irish counter-attacked, but de Courcy rebuffed them, took the war out into the country and embarked on a process of conquest and colonization. To help the process along, like so many Normans in Ireland, he married wisely. His wife was Affreca, daughter of Godred, the Norse ruler of the Isle of Man whose dominions included the southern Scottish isles. Godred already exercised considerable influence in north-east Ulster.

Although he had his reverses, de Courcy eventually brought the entire province of Ulaid under his control. He then set about consolidating his position. One way he did this was by becoming a munificent patron of the Church and funding numerous ecclesiastical establishments. He also fostered devotion to the Irish saints, especially Patrick. He was canny. While Richard the Lionheart and King John ruled Britain, de Courcy served them in Ireland. He had run-ins with other, equally ambitious, Norman lords, but emerged as King John's trusted adviser when the latter visited 'his' properties in Ireland in 1210.

De Courcy and the Anglo-Normans never achieved total conquest. At first they were extremely violent. Later they made alliances and intermarried with the local population. During the Tudor period their descendants tended to be landowners or, less commonly, merchants and were most numerous in the provinces of Leinster and Munster. They were half English and half Gaelic. When Henry VIII changed religion they mostly did not. They saw no contradiction in maintaining the old faith and their loyalty to the Crown. They regarded themselves as English, but within England itself they were usually seen as Irish. The 'Old English' did not like this.*

Living alongside the Old English were those who had preceded them. They were sometimes known as 'Irish Enemies', 'Mere Irish' ('mere' here meaning original), 'Old Irish' or

---

*Before 1600 the usual term for those of English descent resident in Ireland was 'English of Irish birth'. 'Old English' came later. However, I hope I will be excused for using the term out of its time.

'Native Irish'. They comprised the Gaelic Irish, and were the over-whelming majority of the people living on the island. Most of them spoke Gaelic. Social coherence and identity were rooted in land not clan. You *were* your territory. Some Irish kings, like Venetian doges, even ritually 'married' their land. Each territory had its own system of political and legal administration. However, the predominant quality of Irish society was mobility. If he paid, for instance, a man could attach himself to a chieftain outside his home area. Authority was essentially temporary and inheritance was never guaranteed. Under Irish law, a man became a leader or chief and the owner or controller of his father's lands not because he was the first of his father's legally born male heirs but because he had the support and acclaim of the most subjects. With each new generation the foundations of authority and the ownership of property were redefined. This system looked like anarchy to English observers. Throughout the Tudor period Brehon (from the Irish *brethren*, meaning 'a judge'), the traditional system of law in Gaelic Ireland, and the new legal system of the English, which had come in with the settlers, were in conflict. On one level, the wars that punctuated the Tudor period were attempts to settle which system would prevail.

There was also a religious dimension to the conflict as authentic Irishness and Catholicism began to converge. (This should not be overstated, however; Irish Catholic nationalism on nineteenth-century lines did not exist in the sixteenth century.) The Counter-Reformation contributed to this, as did the presence in Tudor Ireland of a third, numerically small but extremely powerful group which abhorred the instability of Irish society. Following the Counter-Reformation, it identified exclusively with Protestantism. Later, its membership came to be known as the New English (as opposed to the Old English). Besides colonists (with land grants) sent over in connection with various plantation projects, the New English during the Tudor period included administrators, lawyers, soldiers of fortune and gentlemen adventurers in the de Courcy mould, and Protestant clerics. At their head was the Crown's representative in Ireland and the supreme New Englishman, the Lord Deputy (sometimes styled Lord Lieutenant, a title with more status). The Deputy presided over the Privy Council of the Chancellor and the Law Officers, the Common Council, formed by the addition of some Old English notables, and the Great Council, which comprised all of the preceding, plus representatives of the Dublin Parliament whose seats were within the Pale. More correctly known as the 'English Pale', this was the region that included parts of counties Dublin, Meath, Louth and Kildare where English norms in respect of language, culture, law, social structure and government were strongest while the influence of the Gaelic Irish was weakest. It was also where military power was concentrated, for the English State kept permanent garrisons in Dublin and in Dundalk in north Louth, near the Ulster border.

During Tudor times, but especially under Henry VIII and Elizabeth I, English customs were steadily introduced into Ireland. Irishmen joined the throng of European ambassadors at the Tudor court. One such was Young Hugh. He was a son of Red Hugh O'Donnell, the King of Tyrconnell, the territory in north-west Ireland known today as County Donegal. Young Hugh had been in Rome on a pilgrimage and in February 1511 was returning home. He broke his journey in London to attend King Henry VIII. The king was in a good mood that evening, following the birth of his son Arthur, and he knighted Hugh on the spot. The young Irishman thereby moved a rung or two up the caste ladder. But the ceremony was more significant than that. For as with hundreds of similar events in which the generosity of the English Crown was demonstrated, it represented the obeisance of the decaying, ossified Gaelic system to the vigorous, mercantile-minded, martial English system. Just by coming to London to accept his title, Hugh had acknowledged that power was shifting.

Among the many policy instruments used to effect this shift, and perhaps the most important, was the process known as 'surrender and re-grant'. The Irish or Old English chief gave his land to the Crown. The Crown then immediately gave it back to him. During the reign of Henry VIII forty of the principal Irish and Old English lords did this. At first glance it seemed that the lord lost nothing and gained an ally, while the Crown gained nothing. The deal also seemed to favour the lord because he remained firmly on his land in Ireland, while his feudal overlord was far away, across the Irish Sea. Over time, however, the policy assumed a complexion that was the very opposite of how it first appeared. All the major Irish landowners were now subordinate to the Crown. If they misbehaved, the English Crown could reclaim the land it had so generously gifted.

One must be careful not to overstate this process. It wasn't like the invasion of a weak modern state by a conquering super-power. It happened slowly, stealthily and amid considerable confusion. But it *did* happen, and as year followed year, Tudor officials (sheriffs, provost marshals and lawyers), Tudor styles and Tudor customs seeped into Ireland until it was eventually sodden with them.

As might be expected, this was a far from peaceful business. During Elizabeth's reign a Gaelic Irish uncle and nephew, Shane and Hugh O'Neill (the latter known also as the 2nd Earl of Tyrone or simply as 'The O'Neill'), successively launched bloody rebellions against their New English overlords. Ultimately, though, both were defeated, in part because the English realized the strategic importance of Derry for controlling the north of Ireland. They established a garrison there from which they could launch attacks against the rebels. The man responsible for this was Sir Henry Dowcra, who built two forts by the Foyle in the spring of 1600 close to where the city stands today. At times Dowcra's garrison was in dire straits, waiting in their wooden forts for supplies to arrive, surrounded by Tyrone's allies. But they held out courageously; and eventually, reinforced and resupplied, they emerged victorious to help force Tyrone's surrender in March 1603. Luckily for him, Tyrone capitulated shortly after Elizabeth's death. Had she been alive, given the trouble the Irishman caused her, she surely would have demanded his head. As it was, her successor, James I, was much more amenable: he forgave the recalcitrant earl his misdemeanours and returned all his property to him.

In the years that followed, Tyrone set about reasserting his preeminence among the Gaelic Irish. However, by 1607, the English had once again grown tired of his and his allies' plotting, and were set to move against him. Sensing this, Tyrone and some of his closest allies boarded a boat on Lough Swilly and fled to Europe, never to return, in what has become known as 'the flight of the earls'. Some disaffected Irish nobles remained on home soil, including a certain Sir Cahir O'Doherty. In the rebellion he launched the following year, through a mixture of surprise, force of numbers and neglected defences, he managed to overwhelm the garrison at Derry. Then he burned to the ground the two forts Dowcra had built. It was to be his last great victory: English troops defeated his army a couple of months later; O'Doherty himself was killed and decapitated, his head being displayed on a spike in Dublin.

With Tyrone and his allies having flown, and O'Doherty's forces in disarray, here, providentially, was an opportunity to 'civilize' Ulster, the power base of all the previous half-century's rebels. Their lands could be seized and then, in the language of the day, planted with Crown-approved subjects – loyal Protestants with military skills.

Plantation was not a new idea. It had been tried, for instance, in Queen's and King's counties in the 1560s.* Unfortunately, this scheme produced little more than two fortified settlements, Philipstown and Maryborough.† Here, behind their walls, settlers lived anxious, uncertain lives, surrounded by the original

---

*These were renamed Laois and Offaly by the Free State as part of its policy after partition to efface those traces of British rule that remained in the language.
†Also later Hibernicized to Daingean and Portlaoise.

inhabitants, Gaelic Irish as well as Old English. Plantation was supposed to transform into England the parts of Ireland it touched. All it achieved in Queen's and King's counties was to graft a fragile English twig on to a recalcitrant Irish tree.

However, with memories of the Ulster troubles still fresh, and with hundreds of thousands of acres of land suddenly available, it was inevitable the decision would be made to have another go. This time, though, the right people would be sent. The principal English and Scottish settlers (known as undertakers) would be given the largest tracts. Servitors (army veterans) would take smaller ones. Favoured natives would also get their cut, as would the Church and Trinity College. There would be binding agreements between the parties and the State. The planters would build towns, establish industries and drag Irish agriculture into the seventeenth century. The results of their virtuous effort would be permanent settlements that would transform the host, Ulster, into something amenable, governable and Anglicized.

Alas, the path of true plantation never does run smooth. Of the many things that went wrong, two are worthy of note. The English surveyors who supported the programme did not understand the Irish sizing system, which was based on yield rather than acreage. The surveyors' assessment of portions was often hopelessly inaccurate. As a result, impossibly small, and therefore useless, as well as improbably large tracts of lands exchanged hands, and both types of error compromised and hindered the project. There was also corruption: several adventurers shamelessly manipulated the sizing system to their advantage.

Even more serious, from the conquerors' point of view, was how awry the project went with regard to the Gaelic Irish. Apart from those areas that went to favoured natives, the plan was supposed to produce an independent, discrete settler block. This idea of separate existence was even enshrined contractually: all agreements specified that the Gaelic Irish could not live within planter settlements, or rent land from undertakers or servitors. In theory, settlers were supposed to deal exclusively with people like themselves: loyal, Protestant (preferably Anglican), good English subjects. However, as the settlers discovered on arrival in Ireland, this was neither possible nor practical. There simply were not enough of them, particularly at the lower end of the social scale. They needed bodies, so, in expropriated estate after estate, in lieu of any alternative, lands were let to the ex-proprietors, often at very high rents. The original landowners were willing to pay these premiums, and the settlers were delighted to charge them. In the long term, though, this arrangement was counter-productive. Plantation was not supposed to deliver a landlord class that exploited the original proprietors.

There was one exception to the pattern in the east of the province. There had always been toing and froing across the narrow waters separating Ireland and Scotland and in the early seventeenth century Scottish grandees settled thousands of Scots in Antrim and Down as part of a private plantation project. This flood of people was different from the English settler pattern in two ways. First, there were large numbers of covenanting dissenters in the mix; and second, there were many more artisans and yeomen. Contemporary commentators also observed that the Scots were tougher than the English and so more likely to endure. This was applauded, but their religion was not. The huge influx of awkward, fierce, mildly Anglophobic Presbyterians was far from what the devisors of the Stuart plantation had in mind.

In the spring of 1609 Sir Thomas Phillips, a redoubtable Welsh soldier of fortune who had fought Tyrone and settled in Coleraine after the end of the rebellion, visited London to advance his claim to some land. The Lord High Treasurer, Lord Salisbury, heard the soldier was in town and summoned him to discuss an innovative idea for a permanent settlement.

In the past the Crown had attempted plantation very much

alone. Salisbury's big idea was to do it in partnership. Why not try to persuade the powerful and prosperous City of London to act as a collective undertaker in the north-west of Ireland? Phillips liked the plan, and so, subsequently, did the king. The latter saw at once that an alliance with the City was going to be the best way of rooting English and Scottish settlers in the barbarous north-western corner of Ireland. These settlers would then civilize and Anglicize the terrain, and they would be the first line of defence in the event of another rebellion.

Once the idea had been floated there was rapid progress. Before 1609 had ended, the City of London was entrusted with the task. Responsibility then passed to the London guilds. The job was finally managed by the 'Society of the Governor and Assistants, London, of the new Plantation in Ulster, within the Realm of Ireland'. This was a consortium of City merchant companies who contracted with the government to carry out the plantation of Derry, Coleraine County and the barony of Loughinsholin in return for certain privileges. Perhaps the most onerous of the State's requirements was that a walled city be built somewhere in the vicinity of Dowcra's old establishment on the conical hill on the western bank of the Foyle. A future Sir Cahir O'Doherty would never be able to waste Derry again.

The site selected for the new establishment was slightly north-east of Dowcra's second fort, on the northern side of the hill that sloped to the edge of the Foyle. After numerous plans and surveys, the Society finally fulfilled its obligations and finished the walls of Derry (whose name they changed to London-Derry in respect of the new ties with the mother city) in 1618. These walls were twenty-four feet high and six feet deep, with a rampart of earth twelve feet thick and four gates let into them. On the north side there was Ship Quay Gate, which opened on to the Foyle. On the east was Ferry Quay Gate, which opened on to a path that led to the river bank. Here was located the ferry to the Waterside on the east bank. On the south-west of the city was the Bishop's Gate. This opened on to the road to Strabane and

Letterkenny. Finally, on the west of the city was the Butchers'
Gate. This overlooked the bog that was periodically flooded by
the waters of the Foyle. Later, this area would become famous as
the Bogside.

Today, the outline is so little changed – apart from the addition of new gates – that Nicholas Pynnar, one of Dowcra's
captains who surveyed the original shortly after completion,
would have no difficulty recognizing it. The same goes for the
layout of the town within the walls, which was marvellously
simple. In the middle was a central square (known as the
Diamond). From there, four roads, forming a cross, led downhill
to the four gates let into the walls. This is still the configuration
of the cityscape today.

The building work had not gone smoothly, and when the
walls were finally finished (by which time James I was dead and
his son Charles I was on the throne) there was an orgy of criticism. This mostly focused on what the London companies had
neglected to do. One of the loudest voices was that of Sir
Thomas Phillips. Although he was initially a supporter of the
City's participation (he had produced the paper on which
the City had based its official prospectus), he now had grave
reservations about the London companies' role. He felt that
their misjudgement and dereliction of duty were so severe that
he petitioned the king about them. Because of his status and
the strength of his views, Sir Thomas could not be ignored.
The government of Charles I appointed a commission to investigate and adjudicate between the Crown and the London
companies as to whether the latter had fulfilled their covenants.
Its report was damning.

Derry had been built in the wrong place. On the east bank, it
would have had the river as a buffer between itself and the west
(from where it was most likely to be attacked) and easy access to
roads running east and south, the direction from where military
reinforcements would come. But it was on the opposite bank,
and furthermore on the side of a hill that tilted towards the

Foyle. Warships could simply sail up the river and bombard the city at will. In addition, Derry was vulnerable to shelling from adjacent higher ground. And, as if that wasn't bad enough, the commissioners also criticized the fortifications themselves: the bastions were inadequate; there was insufficient ordnance and no storehouses for the provisions necessary to withstand a prolonged siege; finally, there were no billets for the thousand soldiers the commissioners believed was the minimum necessary to hold Derry in the event of war.

Partnership should have delivered a major fortress within which New English settlers could live safely. However, according to the commissioners, nine years of construction had produced a walled city that in all probability could not survive attack. This put the entire plantation project in jeopardy. Should Derry fall, all of Ulster would go with it, and the true religion (as the English regarded it) would be finished in the province. It was a dismal forecast.

CHAPTER THREE

Uncivil War

The troubles in Ireland that coincided with the English Civil War were long anticipated. Throughout the autumn and winter of 1640, wild rumours circulated. On 21 November, for example, the Lord Chief Justice brought to the notice of the House of Commons the testament of a Mrs Anne Hussy, a convert from the Catholic Church. She pointed the finger at an Irish priest named O'Connor who had told her that 'many thousands were preparing and in pay to cut all the Protestants' throats'. But it was another three months before the first whispers of actual conspiracy were recorded. In February 1641 Rory O'More broached the subject to Lord Maguire. Before midsummer other Gaelic Irish magnates, including Sir Phelim O'Neill, were enlisted. This trio was typical of the instigators of the rebellion. Their families had survived plantation and they had maintained their old connection with the land. They might have been heavily indebted, but they had not been dispossessed.

Throughout the summer and early autumn, the secret plotting continued; there was a lot of hot talk and high optimism. In September the conspirators, lay and clerical, met at Multifarnham Abbey in Westmeath, then occupied by a community of Franciscans. Henry Jones, the Anglican minister who investigated these events, produced an account of this meeting, having been given the details by a Franciscan friar who was present. There was, says Jones, considerable debate over what to do with the New English settlers who had flooded into all of Ireland, and especially Ulster, for three decades. Some speakers proposed slaughtering them. Others were for banishing them, like the Moors from Spain. Both courses were problematic. The first could provoke the neighbouring kingdom of England to wreak revenge; the second left the way open for the New English to return one day and once again relieve the Irish of their property. In the end, the delegates agreed to disagree: all were free to choose their own course; they could kill or not as they wished. A number announced that they would simply take everything the settlers possessed, except for their lives.

The Multifarnham delegates were much more united when it came to agreeing aims and how to secure them. They recognized the king, but sought a political identity for Ireland that was separate from that of England. They wanted religious tolerance in Ireland, and gave no hint of Catholic zealotry. What concerned them most was the issue of land. As things stood, Gaelic Irish proprietors had no security of tenure. If legal disputes arose between settlers and the Gaelic Irish, the State invariably sided with the former. It also blocked all routes to self-improvement for the Gaelic Irish: they could not even purchase uninherited properties. The conspirators wanted all of this abolished. More radically, they also wanted the plantation reversed, and Irish families restored to their former estates. In order to achieve these aims – laudable and logical from their point of view – they envisaged a series of disabling military strikes against key targets in Ulster and elsewhere in Ireland. Once these places were taken, they believed negotiations would follow and the government would comply with their demands. They planned a coup, not a war of liberation.

On Saturday 22 October two hundred men from different parts

of Ulster and Leinster were to filter into Dublin secretly. Early the next morning they would seize the administrative centre, Dublin Castle. Simultaneously, Phelim O'Neill was to fall upon Londonderry, while his brother Turlough and Sir Henry O'Neill were to seize Carrickfergus, and Sir Con Magennis and his brothers were to take Newry. Only Anglicans were to be attacked; Presbyterians were to be spared on the grounds they might prove to be allies in the future.

However, of the two hundred soldiers promised for the attack on Dublin Castle, only eighty or so had turned up by six o'clock on the Saturday evening. In spite of the disappointing turnout, Lord Maguire and his fellow-conspirators decided to attempt to take the castle with the forces they had.

Unfortunately for them, a certain Owen O'Connolly, a Catholic turned Presbyterian, had heard of the plot and ran to the house of Sir William Parsons, one of the two Lords Justices, where he told his story. Extra guards were laid on at the castle. Supplies were brought in. An abandoned well was recommissioned in case of a long siege. With the castle secured, the Justices went on the offensive. A party of soldiers hurried to Lord Maguire's lodgings. He was gone, but they found hatchets with cut-down handles, skeans (daggers) and hammers. The soldiers fanned out to search the city and surrounding suburbs, and Maguire was eventually found. The other conspirators in the city, including the eighty soldiers mustering to attack Dublin Castle, were more fortunate. When news of Maguire's arrest reached them, they slipped away to Wicklow or in the direction of Ulster.

However, outside the city, where there were no troops and no O'Connolly to warn the authorities, the story was different. On the evening of the 22nd, Sir Phelim O'Neill appeared at Charlemont Castle with his usual large retinue. Lord Caulfeild and his mother were at home, and the visitors were welcomed. At dinner, Sir Phelim gave the signal: his retinue overwhelmed the household and took them all prisoner.

Later that night, Sir Phelim seized Dungannon. One of his officers, Cormac O'Hagan, surprised Moneymore. The O'Quins took the fort of Mountjoy, the O'Hanlons Tandaragee, and Sir Con Magennis Newry. The MacMahons seized Castleblaney, Carrickmacross and Monaghan; the O'Kellys took Cloghouter Castle in Cavan; the Maguires and O'Farrells over-ran Longford and Fermanagh. When Moneymore town and castle in County Londonderry were taken, William Rowley escaped from that town and rode through the night to Coleraine with the news, thus saving it.

Although the Gaelic Irish leaders had envisaged something quick and sharp that would bring the State to the negotiating table, they had failed to anticipate that their military action would unleash emotions: in this case thirty years of accumulated Irish rage with regard to land and landownership. Those who bore the brunt of the fury, inevitably, were the settlers.

In the early days those settlers who lived outside fortified towns were particularly vulnerable. On 23 October, for instance, at Markane in County Fermanagh, Thomas Loisanie, a yeoman, had the misfortune to encounter the followers of Captain Rory Maguire. Although many of the men were known to him, they still robbed and stripped him. He survived, but his father Charles, who was caught by the same mob a few days later, was not so lucky. He and his two companions were dispatched with swords and skeans, to loud cries of 'English Dogs!'

Also on 23 October, Anne Ogden was at her home in Tatemagiar, County Fermanagh, when thirty Irish soldiers broke down the door of the house, entered and hacked her husband to death in front of her. The party then stripped Anne naked and put her and her children on the road to Dublin. The young Ogden children did not survive the journey.

Meantime, a hundred of Lord Maguire's men approached Castle Shanoge, County Fermanagh. At the gateway they were met by a party of six men, including the owner, Arthur Champion, and his brother Thomas. The Irish visitors overwhelmed the men at the gate and killed them. Then they spread through the estate and killed twenty-four of Champion's tenants or followers. Finally, they reached the castle. Arthur's wife Alice was at home. She was taken out of the building, which was ransacked and set on fire. She requested her captors' permission to bury the thirty or so dead who lay around the estate but was refused. She was told she must wait until dogs had eaten a quarter of the corpses.

Though it may not sound like it (after all, her husband had just been murdered), Alice Champion was luckier than most women. She was neither killed nor, the more common fate, stripped and driven out on to the roads to die of exposure. She was merely imprisoned for nineteen weeks. During this time, she was told many of the details regarding the campaign against the settlers. She later reported that when the Irish burned the castle of Lisgoole, County Fermanagh, there were ninety English men, women and children inside. 'How sweetly they do fry,' Alice claimed the arsonists shouted. Alice's captors also spoke of their long-term ambitions. Lord Maguire had sent them, they said, with clear instructions to kill her husband and all of his retinue. More ominously, they said that King Charles supported their rebellion, that Phelim O'Neill would be King of Ireland one day, and that an army of fifteen thousand Irishmen would be in England by Midsummer's Day to rescue the papist cause. Alice's experiences were not exceptional. The level of violence she witnessed was commonplace. One particularly gruesome incident involved eighty Protestants being hurled off the bridge over the River Bann at Portadown. If they didn't drown, they were shot or clubbed to death on the banks by Phelim O'Neill's soldiers.

The reason so much is known about what happened is that it was written down. The accounts of the attacks on the settlers – known collectively as the 'Depositions' – comprise four sets of documents: material collected in 1652 by the High Court of Justice in connection with the trials of those held responsible for the atrocities; statements taken from refugees and insurgents for intelligence purposes; statements taken in Munster by the English Parliament; and statements from refugees taken between 1641 and 1647 by a special commission. As the function of this commission was to help survivors to register claims for compensation, many testimonies include precise lists of the value of goods looted and properties destroyed. In this material, secular factors like indebtedness were played down and confessional violence was played up, perhaps because the commission was led by Henry Jones, a pious Anglican cleric.

Jones and his commissioners got to work within months of the start of the rebellion. They tracked down survivors (including Gaelic Irish victims who had suffered retaliation at the hands of Protestant settlers – they wanted to be even-handed) and interviewed them all under oath. The testimonies began to find their way into the public domain in England and Ireland even as the commissioners were gathering them. Some of the early statements were included in 'The Remonstrance', published in 1642, whose purpose was to solicit relief funds in England. The next year Jones included material from the Depositions in 'The Discourse'. He hoped revelations of Irish violence against Protestants would scupper the proposed truce between Royalists in Ireland and the Gaelic Irish. In 1646 Sir John Temple wrote *The Irish Rebellion*, or, as it was tellingly subtitled, *An History of the Attempts of the Irish Papists to extirpate the Protestants of Ireland Together with the Barbarous Cruelties and Bloody Massacres which ensued thereupon*. Sir John's book is based on Jones's original material but reconfigured into a nightmarish, if garbled, account of settlers cruelly massacred by the savage, Protestant-hating Irish. In 1649 John Milton made his contribution when he published his *First Defence of the State of England*. The poet put the casualties at two hundred thousand (which was clearly preposterous), then argued that the Irish should be made vassals of the English.

The message of these texts, combined with oral accounts

from the survivors now back in England, was that the Gaelic Irish were barbaric while the New English settlers were blameless. They had gone to Ireland peacefully; they had lived among the Gaelic Irish, shared their knowledge, culture and civilization with them. The Irish had affected amity towards the newcomers, but it had been a pretence for, without warning, they had turned.

Another theme of the Depositions was intimacy: victims usually knew their victimizers by name. They were often friends and neighbours. One can easily imagine the impression this made on contemporary opinion. If the victims knew their tormentors, then guile was involved, which made the Irish deeds still darker. And a further twist on the theme of Roman Catholic cunning was that initially, at least, all the victims of the Irish were Anglicans. The rebels spared the dissenters in the hope that they might later be allies.

The Depositions also catalogued numerous examples of religious intolerance. Edward Flack, for instance, claimed he was relieved of his Bible by a party of Irishmen, who laid it open face down in a puddle, leaped on the spine and shouted, 'A plague on this book, it has bred all this quarrel!' Alexander Crichton, of Glaslogh, County Monaghan, told of mass forced conversion. A certain Father Hugh Mac O'Dugan Maguire administered the sacrament to forty or fifty Protestants. He made the recipients admit that it was the body and blood of Christ, and that the Pope was the supreme head of the Church. Crichton also reports that the Irish burned three Bibles, some service books and church pews. He was assured that until the Anglican Church was put in its proper place 'and the plantation lands returned to their rightful owners'* – significantly, the two were connected – the Irish would not lay down their arms.

---

*Meaning here, Irish-owned land that had been expropriated and planted.

There was no doubt that settlers such as Crichton viewed these attacks as components of a holy war. The real goal was extirpation of the faith. It was scarcely countenanced that the Protestants were targeted because they occupied the land the Irish wanted back.

The slaughter of 1641 considerably reduced the number of settlers. Approximately four or five thousand were murdered between October 1641 and April 1642, with as many again dying while refugees. The massacres had more than immediate significance because of how they were catalogued. The Depositions, and the texts that used them as source material, created a climate that made possible Cromwell's Irish campaign and, half a century later, helped to shape the recalcitrant attitudes of those who manned the walls during the siege of Derry. Indeed, these materials conditioned and poisoned attitudes in Ireland, and towards the Irish, not just for decades but for centuries to come.

CHAPTER FOUR

War and Cromwell

It fell to James Butler, the 12th Earl of Ormond and Ossory, who commanded the Royalist forces in Ireland, to do what he might after the great calamity of 1641. He continued in command until 1644, when he was elevated to the post of Lord Lieutenant and became the Crown's representative in Ireland. Ormond, Old English but Protestant, was one of the great survivors of seventeenth-century Irish and English history. From 1633, when he entered the Irish Parliament, to 1685, when he retired from public life on the accession of James II, he was continuously active on the military and political stages. This span of over half a century, in an era of shifting alliances and murderous disloyalty, was all the more extraordinary because his fidelity was unswervingly to the House of Stuart. It was not an easy cause and his was not an easy life, but he had one advantage: he never wasted energy changing sides. The simplicity of his position, despite the awkwardnesses and dangers it entailed, was certainly one reason he lasted as he did.

When the crisis broke in October 1641, Ormond's resources were small, and he could do little to help the settlers. As the refugees began to struggle into fortified towns, or escaped to

Dublin and beyond, their version of events came to the fore: this was not a dispossessed, resentful citizenry attacking prosperous settlers, they said, but a religious war. Inevitably, comparisons were made with the massacre of Protestant Huguenots in France on St Bartholomew's Day, 1572. The Irish calamity, it was believed, was part of an overall pattern of Catholic terror against Protestants that had been ongoing for over half a century. This theory was supported by the fact that, in December 1641, Catholic Old English families joined the Gaelic Irish rebels.

In the north, Derry became one of the principal places of sanctuary for refugees. The city was put in the command of Sir John Vaughan, an old Derry hand who had served under Dowcra. In January 1642 he wrote to the Lords Justices in Dublin. His letter painted an ominous picture. The aid expected from their lordships and from England and Scotland had not arrived and the entire country had been burned, right up to the east bank of the Foyle directly across from Derry. 'We of the city are in extreme want of arms,' Sir John continued, 'for at the beginning of these troubles the best went into the country . . . and there is not 100 swords in the city among all our men.' This complaint would be repeated time and again in years to come. Similarly familiar would be the condition of those who had taken refuge inside the city walls. 'The miseries that daily threaten us are unspeakable', wrote Sir John, 'for so many unserviceable people are crowded into this city that, if we escape the enemy's sword, it is to be feared that famines and infections and sickness will seize on us.'

The authorities in Dublin were unable to respond to Sir John's appeal, but the London companies sent ships laden with food and winter clothing, as well as ammunition and arms, including some heavy ordnance. There was also traffic in the other direction. Richard Winter, chaplain to Colonel Sir William Stewart and his regiment in Derry, was one of several brilliant clerical propagandists associated with the city and her defenders during the seventeenth century. His tract, *Newes from the North of Ireland*, described 'the monthly achievements of the forces of the City of Londonderry (founded by the honourable City of London) since the beginning of the bloody and unparalleled rebellion in that Kingdom, until November, 1642'. It spoke of Derry's 'stately buildings, strong walls and bulwarks raised and erected by those renowned founders of hers, London', then told of the refugees, crammed behind those walls, who had narrowly escaped 'cruel murderers and thirsty shedders of innocent blood'. Next it related, in ringing words saturated with high self-regard, how the citizens fortified their ramparts, repaired their walls and placed 'many artificial and exquisite engines upon them, demolishing also a great part of the suburbs to prejudice the enemy's covert approaches, to their own great loss and damage'. It was a paean of praise to the tenacity of the place and the people, stressing how precarious was the position of the settler refugees and venerating their capacity for virtuous resistance.

Newes from the North of Ireland was published in 1643. Its polemical purpose was to emphasize Derry's importance as a place of sanctuary: without the protection of the walls, the set-tler refugees would have perished. Hence Winter's generous praise of the London companies that had built them. However, Derry was more than just a walled city where the forsaken hud-dled. Without it, the author argued, all of Ulster would have been be lost. Derry, in other words, was where the Irish tide was stopped.

Another telling text came from the opposite side. Donnell O'Kane, an Irish soldier, wrote a letter to his cousin Anthony in Dunkirk. From there, 'a well-wisher to the advancement of the Protestant religion' sent the letter on to London. It was pub-lished in 1643. The letter tells, in considerable and admiring detail, how Derry organized itself. All citizens swore an oath of loyalty to King Charles and the State, and vowed to defend the city to the death. All Gaelic Irish men and women were expelled and prohibited from settling within two miles of the walls. A league of captains was established to command the citizen soldiery, with each captain being given absolute responsibility for a section of wall. Citizen soldiers were expected to guard ordnance and gates, day and night. Their women and children were expected to remain indoors. The importance of these activities, as recorded by O'Kane, was that later defenders saw them as a template and re-enacted them. In Derry habits of defence, just like memories of the 1641 massacres, enjoyed extraordinary longevity.

Having overwhelmed most of the island, the Gaelic Irish and Old English now had to devise a plan to hold on to their conquests. Should they sue for peace with Ormond's Royalist forces? Should they do likewise with the army put into Ulster by the Scots in April 1642 to defend those of Scottish dissenter origin? And how should they react to the volatile situation over the Irish Sea in England? The various parties came together in Kilkenny and eventually formed the Catholic Confederacy. The parties were unlikely bedfellows. The Old English, as they had protested loudly for years, were loyal to King Charles. They had turned on the settlers, they claimed, out of loyalty rather than anti-settler animus. Naturally, they believed Catholicism and loyalty to the Crown were not mutually exclusive. The Gaelic Irish were not necessarily antagonistic to Charles themselves, though he had done them no favours. But they were certainly deeply unhappy about insecure land tenure, which rankled with the Old English, too. The Stuart Settlement had punished both groups. However, shared grievances could not alter the fact that the former did not care for the latter and never had. The Old English might be Catholics, but they were not the right sort of Catholics. The Confederacy was therefore an ineffective organization, but it was up against an equally hamstrung opponent. Ormond still lacked resources, with Charles otherwise occupied in England.

The Scottish army in Ulster was an added problem. None of the various forces was strong enough to win alone, yet none was so weak it could be wiped out. Alliances were made and broken; pacts and betrayals, promises and disavowals were all standard. It was a military mess.

Then in June 1647, further complicating the situation, the English Parliament, as it had long threatened, dispatched a force to Ireland. General Michael Jones arrived in Dublin with an army of two thousand men. Lord Lieutenant Ormond handed him Dublin and left the country. Royalists did not normally hand power bases to Parliamentarians but this was an exceptional circumstance. When explaining his actions later, Ormond reportedly said he preferred English rebels to Irish ones.

The parliamentary forces defeated the Confederacy forces commanded by Thomas Preston at Dungan's Hill in August, but Jones's small army was unable to impose its authority on the country. Sensing there were possibilities to exploit, Ormond, returned to Ireland and resumed negotiations in the hope of uniting Royalist, Old English and Gaelic Irish elements against Parliament. He succeeded, and on 17 January 1649 signed a peace treaty with the Confederacy, uniting Catholic and Anglican elements into a single bloc against the common enemy.

Now there were just two combatants in Ireland – Royalist and Parliamentarian – everything should have been straightforward. The execution of Charles I at the end of the month (to which Ormond, demonstrating his loyalty to the Stuart cause, responded by instantly proclaiming his son) should have consolidated the new situation. But it didn't and the situation in Ireland continued to be a bewildering period of shifting alliances and compromises, as it had been before Ormond's treaty.

Derry was the scene of one of the most bizarre episodes of the entire Civil War. In March 1649 Royalist forces under Lord Montgomery began to lay siege to the city. Sir Charles Coote was in charge behind the walls, holding Derry for Parliament. He had 800 foot soldiers and 180 horse under his command. Sir Charles was described by Lord Castlehaven as 'an hot-headed and bloody man, and as such accounted even by the English and Protestants'. He had been especially vindictive following October 1641, when, as Provost Marshal-General, he had been entitled by martial law to 'put to death rebels or traitors, that is, all such as he should deem to be so' and had performed the task 'with delight and a wanton kind of cruelty'.

The siege lasted twenty weeks, until Coote managed to make an agreement with the sometime Confederate general Owen Roe O'Neill, who appeared to have no qualms about dealing with him if the price was right. On the promise of money, gunpowder and cattle, O'Neill marched two thousand men to Ballykelly, about ten miles from Derry. Montgomery, notwithstanding the peace treaty agreed earlier in the year between Ormond and the Confederates, considered it prudent to withdraw. O'Neill pushed on to the east bank of the Foyle, opposite Derry. Sir Charles visited him there to offer his thanks to Derry's unlikely saviour. If Derry usually sees Presbyterians besieged by Catholics, here Presbyterians were in alliance with Catholics against the Crown. The Civil War in Ireland was a bizarre time.

This kind of confusion could not continue, and very soon a man arrived in Ireland who would put an end to it. Oliver Cromwell landed in August 1649. He was met by hard-line New English settlers who hailed him as their saviour. In the campaign that followed he would not disappoint them, but he made the journey across the Irish Sea primarily to crush Ormond's Royalists rather than advance the cause of the colonists. In September, after a fierce battle, his forces took Drogheda, then proceeded to slaughter many of the inhabitants – combatants (English-speaking Protestant Royalists mostly) and civilians (including many Catholic priests) alike. Three thousand or so people died in the course of one night.

Cromwell saw this carnage as payback for what the Gaelic

Irish had done to the settlers in the autumn of 1641. Through the 1640s the Puritan pamphlets published in England had described, in extravagant detail, atrocities such as those at Portadown bridge, and Cromwell was as vulnerable to their indoctrination as his troops were. Although, as he later admitted, some of the Drogheda dead were non-combatants, he was not a simple Hibernophobe in thrall to poisonous fantasy. He believed the violence he unleashed made military sense. And he had ample evidence of this. Post-Drogheda, demoralization spread through Ormond's forces. The garrisons of Dundalk and Trim deserted their posts, while further north Newry and Carlingford were captured without difficulty, as was Belfast. Sir Charles Coote secured Down and Antrim, and with that the north was Cromwell's.

This military success was achieved at a cost: Drogheda marked the start of the propaganda war against Cromwell in Ireland. No less a figure than Ormond described the sack as 'making as many several pictures of inhumanity as are contained in the *Book of Martyrs* or the *Relation of Amboyna*'. These were emotive comparisons. Foxe's book detailed the ghastly sufferings of Protestant martyrs at the hands of Catholics. The second work described the horrible treatment of English settlers in the East Indies by the Dutch in 1619. Both pieces were well known in England. Cromwell probably lost little sleep over the rebuke: he always saw himself among the oppressed rather than the oppressors.

Cromwell's work in Ireland was not yet done, though, and his next major target was Wexford. In October, after a tense, week-long siege during which demands and counter-demands shuttled between Cromwell and the town's garrison (some pertaining to freedom of religion for the Catholic inhabitants), the Parliamentarians breached Wexford's walls. As at Drogheda, the fighting was fierce and brutal: Cromwell's men slaughtered over two thousand of the defenders, both citizens and soldiers, and razed many homes to the ground.

In his account of the sack Cromwell gave no indication that he should have restrained his men. The Wexford dead had paid with their blood for 'cruelties which they had exercised upon divers poor Protestants!' He was thinking beyond 1641 this time, as he had apparently 'been lately acquainted with' more recent Catholic atrocities. Cromwell does not even seem to regret the depredation of the town's fabric, which was blinkered, since Wexford was supposed to provide his army's winter quarters. He saw the destruction wrought by his soldiers as part of a divine plan: God, he believed, had wanted extra retribution meted out by his agents on earth to the people of Wexford, and the destruction of the whole town was just that.

For the rest of his time in Ireland, Cromwell enjoyed a string of easy capitulations as town after town decided to surrender to rather than antagonize the man who had decimated Drogheda and Wexford. By the following May, when he departed, ten months after stepping ashore in Ireland, Cromwell had good reason to feel gratified. True, the country was not quiescent: Confederate and Royalist forces lingered on, especially in the notorious bogs and woods of Ulster, but Ireland was in a more amenable state than when he came. Only mopping up remained, then the next stage of the Irish project could proceed. Henry Ireton took charge, the fighting continued, but within two years the war was over. In the meantime, the Cromwellian Settlement had been established.

The cost of paying for the Irish wars was carefully considered in England. Obviously, since the Irish had started them and they had taken place in Ireland, it was thought only fair that the Irish should foot the bill. For the decade before Cromwell's Irish campaign, the English Parliament had allotted Irish land to English investors, known tellingly as 'adventurers', to raise the capital needed to prosecute the Irish wars. Furthermore, Irish land was used as security on funds, and offered to soldiers instead of pay. Cromwell's campaign added three million pounds (a colossal figure in the seventeenth century) to the existing debt.

And this increased, as the fighting went on, in the two years after he left.

The settlement, to raise the funds to meet this deficit, extended the principle of making the Irish pay. Following subjugation, the property of all high-caste landowners who had been allied with the Confederates was expropriated. (The inferior or landless rebel, the common foot soldier, was ignored.) The plan also stipulated what should happen to those who lost their land. They were to be corralled in Connacht, between the River Shannon and the sea, and given land seized from local Confederate proprietors.* Theoretically, this was to be in proportion to what they had lost, but in practice, of course, no expropriated magnate was ever properly recompensed. This relocation of landowners to a reservation in the west was a new and radical development of the old plantation idea.

The commissioners enacting the settlement relocated about two thousand families and their retinues to Connacht. It was a miserable operation, endlessly delayed by petitions and incomplete land surveys, demands by new settlers for land in the Gaelic Irish canton, and, most amazingly, by the presence of several ex-Confederates who were in the market for land as well. But eventually the transfers were effected, and 'adventurers' and Parliamentarian soldiers were settled on the land vacated by the Irish who had been sent west.

As in earlier plantations, notions of acreage were vague. Some adventurers received huge estates, while others were granted only smallholdings. Ordinary private soldiers were often owed such small sums that the land they were given was correspondingly paltry. Many therefore sold their portion immediately to their officers, to the latter's obvious benefit but to the detriment of the scheme. The settlement envisaged a wide social mix,

---

*The west was chosen for reasons of security not economy: at this stage Ulster, not the west, was regarded as the poorest area of Ireland.

which was particularly important given the ambitious plan to establish a yeomanry of Protestant veterans. This did not happen. Finally, not all of the land passed unencumbered from Irish to English hands. As in the last big plantation in Ulster, older inhabitants often stayed on as tenants, thus compromising the idea of a landscape free of the Gaelic Irish and Old English for which the scheme's creators had aimed.

Yet, despite the shortcomings and the obstacles, the changes wrought by the settlement were colossal. In 1641 about 40 per cent of the land area of Ireland was in the hands of the Crown or settlers. Catholic proprietors held the remaining 60 per cent. Post-settlement less than 10 per cent of the land was held by Catholics. The Cromwellian Settlement saw more land transferred than all the other plantation schemes combined. In addition to the staggering shift in landownership, the settlers packed the borough corporations introduced by the settlement. Revenge for the massacres of 1641 had been achieved by driving the Catholics to the brink of the ocean.

CHAPTER FIVE

Richard Talbot's Rise to Prominence

By the time Cromwell left Ireland, virtually every man on the island had been involved in the fighting to some extent. Enjoying more than his fair share was one who for the next forty years would be prominent in Irish, and especially Old English, politics: Richard Talbot. Born in 1630 into a family of Catholic Anglo-Normans that had emigrated to Ireland in the fifteenth century,* Talbot had first seen action against Michael Jones's Parliamentary army in 1647. Later, as a lieutenant, he had been among the defenders at Drogheda, where he was injured and imprisoned before escaping. According to Cromwell himself, Talbot was the only officer of that garrison to slip through his clutches.

In 1651 he was captured again, this time by Sir Charles Coote, veteran defender of Derry. In October the English commissioners ordered Talbot's exchange in return for Parliamentarian prisoners. Three years later he arrived in Madrid with his brother, Peter, a cleric. Under the Kilkenny Articles devised by Parliamentary

---

*Talbot shared a surname with the Earls of Shrewsbury, to whom he was distantly related.

Commissioners when they met in that town, ex-Confederate soldiers were permitted to leave Ireland and serve in continental armies. It was an old practice and one the government – busy with land reorganization – encouraged. It was better to export troublemakers to the continent than keep them in Ireland. Unfortunately, the problematic individual, once abroad, could not be restrained. Talbot was no exception. He left Madrid, gravitated to the court of Charles Stuart, and became active in the murky world of Royalist intrigue.

At this time the royal household was in Cologne. One of the court's notables was an ardent Royalist and veteran of an attempted insurrection in England by the name of James Halsall. A contemporary described him as a 'little black man with a round face'. There is a whiff of the comic, the dilettante and even the ridiculous about him. He was not always effective but he was a consummate survivor.

In the summer of 1655 he borrowed a pistol from Lord Gerard and said he would pay a hundred pounds for it if the Lord Protector, Cromwell, were not dead in three months. He had assassination in mind, and he had accomplices. One of them was Richard Talbot.

The Cromwellian intelligence network, however, was an efficient machine, and its agents soon heard of the plot. Several of the plotters, including Talbot, were arrested when they arrived in London but were then complacently released without charge. Naturally enough, Talbot sought out Halsall at his lodgings. Talbot pushed for the assassination to go ahead. Halsall stalled, pleading poverty. They would need cash to bribe Cromwell's bodyguards and they had none. Talbot claimed he had a lady's jewel worth £1,500 that he could pawn for £600. Under orders from the Stuart court, Halsall still demurred. The prevarication lasted for months until Halsall's manservant turned in his master. Talbot was arrested the next day.

The conspirators were brought to Whitehall, where Cromwell interrogated them personally. Halsall was economic with the truth and did not reveal the names of his associates. When Talbot was interviewed, he met Cromwell's wily offer of preferment (intended to soften him up) with stony silence and, when challenged directly, denied any intention of murdering Cromwell. Trying another tack, Cromwell intimated that Halsall had betrayed his colleague, and hinted that Talbot might be tortured to wring the truth from him, but Talbot stuck to this story that he knew nothing and was no assassin. He maintained his impersonation of a wronged innocent throughout the interview, after which he was put in a cell and told he was to be transferred the next day to the Tower. Calmly, he requested the return of £240 that had been taken from him when he was arrested. He was given only £20, with which he bought wine. That night he plied his jailers with it. Once they had drunk deeply, he took a rope (presumably delivered with the wine), opened the window and let himself down to the ground. He made his way to the Thames, where a riverboat was waiting. Ten days later, it reached Calais, and by 3 January 1656 Talbot was in Antwerp. He sent Ormond a letter suggesting that the other conspirators would be safe, as long as they said nothing.

However, this matter was not yet over. Back in London, one of Talbot's nephews, Robin Dongan, a fellow-plotter, was sprung from the Tower. He subsequently alleged that his uncle had betrayed the plotters, his reward being his escape. Talbot had to write several judicious letters to Ormond before his innocence was believed.

Though Charles Stuart had no power in his own land, he did command modest military resources, those loyal Irish and English soldiers, about six thousand of them, who were on the continent. They initially served under the French, but this arrangement had to end when Cromwell effected a new treaty with France. So, in 1656, Charles's ministers, including the indefatigable Ormond, came to an agreement with Spain. The English and Irish levies would now serve with the Spanish in their war against France.

These soldiers – among them Charles's younger brother James, Duke of York* – marched into Spanish-controlled Flanders and were reorganized into five new regiments. Talbot assisted in this process from his base in Antwerp and thereby met James, who would become his champion. When, a little later, a vacancy occurred in the Duke of York's regiment, Talbot got James to insist on his appointment to the post of lieutenant-colonel against the wishes of the regiment's colonel, Cormac MacCarty, who wanted to promote another man. With Talbot's acquisition of rank came a corresponding rise in his importance.

Cromwell's death on 3 September 1658 did not result in the immediate recall of Charles. Instead, Cromwell's son Richard was appointed Lord Protector. He lasted until May 1659, when he abdicated. The king in waiting, his brother James, Talbot and other members of Royalist households in exile now hastened to the coast, the quicker to answer the call when it came and sail to England. But no call came, and on 14 September the disappointed Royalists returned to Brussels.

James had more than his brother's restoration to occupy his mind. He had fallen in love with Anne Hyde, the vivacious and intelligent, but not especially attractive, daughter of Edward Hyde, the Lord Chancellor, and he promised to marry her. Once this had been agreed, the couple considered themselves man and wife. It would not be long before the consequences of this agreement became clear, and in February 1660 Anne Hyde learned she was pregnant. This put Charles in the delicate position of being a monarch on the verge of restoration whose chief minister's unmarried daughter was pregnant by his brother, the heir presumptive to the throne.

Early in March George Monck, general of the fleet and

_____

*The future James II of England.

effectively governor of Scotland, brought his army south and took London without firing a shot. Though he had a reputation for being secretive and unreadable, it was assumed he had launched Charles's restoration by his actions. Soon after, members of the Long Parliament voted to end its existence and a secret interview occurred between Monck and Charles's emissary, Sir John Grenville. The latter returned to Brussels on 30 March. He told Charles that, in Monck's opinion, the court must leave the territory of a nation with which England was at war. The next day Charles crossed to the Dutch town of Breda and shortly afterwards the English fleet appeared off the coast of the Netherlands. The Duke of York, accompanied by Talbot, boarded the sometime *Naseby*,* now tactfully renamed the *Royal Charles*.

Late in May, the squadron set sail with its cargo of Stuart exiles. Landfall was made on the 25th at Dover. The last time Talbot had been in England, he was a suspected assassin who had narrowly escaped imprisonment, torture and possibly even execution. Now he was a Gentleman of the Bedchamber to the Duke of York and a lieutenant-colonel of his regiment (and soon to be a full colonel of cavalry). For the sixteenth child of a minor Irish landed gentleman, this was remarkable progress. And he was still only thirty. For the next three decades he was intimately involved in the administrations of Charles and then his brother James. He was always adroit, and sometimes clever, but he also had an unhappy knack for making life difficult for himself.

Meanwhile, his sponsor, James, was suddenly a figure of enormous interest to ambitious members of the opposite sex. However, there was the small matter of his promise to Anne and her unborn child. James married her at a secret wedding on 3 September 1660. On 22 October she gave birth to a baby boy.

---

*The Battle of Naseby was one of the great Parliamentary victories of the Civil War.

The infant later died but two future British monarchs came from this union: Mary, who with her husband William would succeed her father after he was ousted, and Anne.

One of the thornier problems awaiting Charles and his chief minister after the restoration was Ireland, specifically the tangle of claims and counter-claims caused by the redistribution of land. On 30 November 1660 Charles signed a declaration in which he made promises to the adventurers; to the soldiers settled by Cromwell; to the officers who had served in the army in Ireland before 5 June 1649; to any Protestants not being rebels who had lost their land to soldiers or adventurers; to 'innocent papists' who had been relocated to Connacht; to those Irish who had faithfully served him on the continent; and to thirty-six named members of the Irish nobility and gentry, henceforth known as the Nominees.

There was a predictable outcry. The reference to 'innocent papists' was found especially alarming. Adventurers and soldiers were quick to organize a delegation to lobby on their behalf with the Privy Council in London. The Irish decided to do the same. They might have chosen Ormond – the most influential Irishman in London, albeit a Protestant – but instead they chose Richard Talbot, the well-placed confidant of the Duke of York. This led to trouble almost immediately.

Talbot knew that Ormond had opposed his lieutenant-colonelcy in the Duke of York's Regiment back in Flanders. At a Privy Council meeting at which the Irish land issue was under discussion, he turned on the older peer. His language was so extreme that Ormond wondered aloud whether Talbot was proposing a duel. Charles was present and he did not approve of duelling. Talbot was sent to the Tower in October 1661. From his cell, he wisely made an apology, which Ormond accepted. On his release, he was sent to Lisbon to secure an audience with the Infanta, soon to be Charles's queen.

Talbot returned to London in April 1662 and went on to Ireland, where he resumed working on behalf of dispossessed

Irish proprietors. In addition, he acted as a buyer for Englishmen who wanted cheap Irish estates. He profited greatly from his work for both parties. After a year he set sail for London. There he met his first wife, Katherine Boynton, maid of honour to the Queen, Catherine of Braganza, as well as the woman who would later become his second wife, Frances Jennings. The latter was a member of the Duchess of York's circle.

Enough time had elapsed since Talbot's stay in the Tower for him to resume lobbying at court for his Irish clients. But again he put himself on course for a collision with Ormond. He acted assiduously on behalf of one James Allen, who, by bribing witnesses to perjure themselves, had obtained a decree of restitution restoring his estate. Ormond was appalled and wanted a law passed that would annul all decrees of restitution obtained by bribes and perjury. Hearing this, and assuming it was directed at him personally, Talbot again threatened Ormond. Word spread to Charles and James, and on 22 December 1664 a warrant was issued for Talbot's arrest. He went back to the Tower, but was held for only a month before being released.

In December 1665 the Bill of Explanation received royal assent. In conjunction with the Act of Settlement (dating from 1662) this Act was intended to ameliorate some of the injustices suffered by non-Confederates whose lands had been unfairly expropriated. However, most Irish grievances remained, and, furthermore, soldiers and adventurers were alienated because they were forced to relinquish some of their gains from the Cromwellian Settlement.

In late 1668 or early 1669 Talbot married Katherine Boynton. Past misdemeanours were forgotten: on 3 April 1669 Charles instructed Sir George Carteret, Vice-Treasurer of Ireland, to pay £4,000 to the newly married man. Talbot continued to lobby against the Act of Settlement and on behalf of his co-religionists. A petition of aggrieved proprietors was drawn up, and on 18 January 1671 Talbot appeared before Charles to deliver it. The petition stated that the signatories had been dispossessed of their lands by the Commonwealth for their loyalty, that they had faithfully served the king and his father, and suffered for them at home and abroad, and that they were in extreme misery. One of the signatories was Sir William Talbot, Richard's nephew. As a direct result of the petition, it was decided to re-examine the Act of Settlement. The pendulum was swinging in the direction Talbot desired, and not just with regard to the land problem. Anne, Duchess of York, died at the end of March 1671. Shortly before her death she converted to Roman Catholicism and indicated that she wished her husband to follow suit. At some point he did as she desired. Talbot's chief protector was now a co-religionist.

Talbot returned to Dublin to collect evidence for the forth-coming Commission of Inquiry into the Act of Settlement. The city was abuzz, with huge excitement among the Old English who stood to gain, and great anxiety among the settlers who stood to lose. His work done, Talbot returned to England and in September 1671 gave evidence. Although he was busy acting as accredited agent for upper-class Irish Catholics anxious to retrieve their land and status, he did not neglect his relationship with the Duke of York. In May 1672 he joined the allied English and French fleets then off the coast of Suffolk under the command of James. Talbot boarded the *James* just in time to take part in the second Battle of Southwold (or Sole) Bay. The enemy Dutch fleet, burned the *James* (it was the only English ship that was lost), and Talbot was yet again taken prisoner.

The Catholics for whom he had lobbied for years seemed to do quite well in his absence. In August the long-standing rules against their admission into corporations in Ireland were relaxed. Henceforth, they were also to be accepted as justices of the peace. Nine or ten were elected to the Common Council of the city of Dublin.

Meantime, the Dutch exchanged their notable Irish prisoner, and on 20 October Talbot arrived back in Dublin. Early in 1673 money was collected at masses throughout Ireland to be used in

England to advance the Catholic cause. Talbot was entrusted with delivering it to England in March, but he arrived in a London bristling with anti-Catholicism precisely because of what had been happening in Ireland. The mood was further fuelled by the discovery of papists in high places and the suspicion that James was among their number.

King Charles had to quell the mob. On 8 March he cancelled a Declaration of Indulgence, even though it favoured dissenters more than Catholics. Twelve days later the Test Act was passed. This made repudiation of transubstantiation mandatory for all State servants, including the Duke of York. James refused to comply and resigned his offices. He had all but publicly acknowledged his conversion.

This, in turn, fomented more anti-Catholic hysteria. On 26 March the House of Commons petitioned Charles and asked for the maintenance of the Act of Settlement; the cancellation of the Commission of Inquiry; that 'Colonel Richard Talbot, who had notoriously assumed to himself the title of agent general of the Roman Catholics of Ireland, might be immediately dismissed out of all commands, either civil or military, and forbid all access to Court'; that no Catholics in Ireland should be judges, justices of the peace, sheriffs or mayors; that Talbot's brother, Peter, now Archbishop of Dublin, should be sent into exile along with all priests; that all Roman Catholic convents, schools and institutions should be closed; that permission to live in corporations (city boundaries) granted to Catholics be rescinded; and that all papists in Ireland should be disarmed. Finally, they asked that 'His Majesty should give further directions for the encouragement of the English planters and the Protestant interest in Ireland and the suppression of the insolencies and disorders of the Irish Papists, by whose practices, and particularly of the said Richard and Peter Talbot, the peace and safety of Ireland had been so much of late endangered.'

The monarch replied with a promise: no man, he said, would

have reason to complain. He dissolved the Commission of Inquiry and said he was committed to the Settlement of Ireland. He claimed he was resolved not to disturb what the Acts had confirmed. Yet, at the same time, he appointed another committee from the Privy Council to look into the Irish land problem. But it had little power. He added more cash to the fund set up to relieve the Nominees, the thirty-six specially deserving Catholic magnates. The monarch's reaction was revealing. He was, or had been, personally sympathetic to the Irish who had lost land, but in the current climate he could not follow his beliefs.

For the first thirteen years of Charles's reign Talbot had been able to achieve something for his co-religionists. That was now over: the injustices Roman Catholics suffered under the Settlement would remain for the rest of Charles's reign. And Talbot's personal position was to become more precarious than ever. He had been named in Parliament as a bad papist and his long-time protector the Duke of York was now in no position to help him, having just announced his intention to marry the Catholic Princess of Modena, Mary Beatrice of Este. In September 1673, for once choosing discretion, Talbot went to France. On the 30th James married Mary Beatrice, to the disgust of the anti-Catholic London mob.

Charles had no legitimate children.* James, his younger brother and heir, had two daughters, Mary and Anne, who were both being brought up as Protestants. Mary would succeed James if he didn't produce a son. Next in line to the throne was the fiercely Protestant William, Prince of Orange, a nephew of the two Stuart brothers through their sister. In 1677 William visited London to ask for his cousin Princess Mary's hand in marriage. James demurred,† but his older brother overruled his objections. Mary became Princess of Orange on 4 November

---

*Although, by a succession of mistresses, he had many illegitimate offspring.
†James had in mind the (Catholic) French Dauphin for his daughter.

1677. In the long term everything seemed set fair for a Protestant succession. The problem was in the short term: the immediate heir to the throne, James, was probably a Catholic, his wife was certainly a Catholic, and, should she produce an heir, he would, no doubt, be raised as one.

Late in 1677 or early in 1678 Talbot returned to Ireland. In March 1678, his wife Katherine died at their home in Luttrell's Town. A few months later, close behind this personal tragedy came a political one in the form of the so-called Popish Plot. Hysterical allegations that Catholics were planning a violent takeover of the kingdoms led to widespread arrests. Talbot was among those seized. He was at Dublin Castle, seeing his old adversary Ormond, who was by now the Lord Lieutenant of Ireland (again), and who presumably was delighted to give the order to imprison Talbot.

At the beginning of Charles II's reign, English policy in Ireland leant towards understanding and benevolence. Then, after the 1673 petition to the House of Commons, policy went the other way. The Popish Plot led to things being momentarily worse (though the excesses seen in England never reached Ireland). Ormond, though he arrested individuals like Talbot, was a bulwark against terror. Thereafter, as the animosities stirred by the plot began to ebb, he ensured anti-Catholic laws were not administered as zealously as they might.

Across in England, the effect of this diminution in tension had all sorts of interesting consequences. The Duke of York's stock rose. He returned from exile in Brussels to the Admiralty and the Privy Council. At the same time, the prestige of William of Orange began to wane. He was no longer the man on whom extreme Protestants pinned their hopes. Their current rising star was one of the many illegitimate sons of Charles II: the Duke of Monmouth.

After all their troubles, in particular those caused by the

Popish Plot which highlighted once again the danger posed by the mob, Charles and his brother began to consider how better to defend themselves. Their big idea was to transform their forces in Ireland from a garrison army that protected the settlers into a real army that could protect the Stuart dynasty. It would have to include Catholic officers. In seeing through this plan, James later earned the reputation of a zealot. This was unfair: the direction in which he took affairs had been determined while his brother was still alive. It just didn't get as far as it might have done then because Ormond was not amenable to the changes being contemplated. In order to reduce his influence, the Lord Lieutenant was recalled to London in 1682. He was made a duke in 1683 (preferment being an excellent means of controlling a likely recalcitrant), but the king had to use traditional strong-arm tactics, too. Charles did not allow Ormond to return to Dublin until he was good and ready. In the meantime Talbot had already landed, and was assisting in the creation of the new army. It is unclear if this was an official mission or a personal one.

In Ireland the amount of land in Catholic hands had risen to about 2.5 million acres out of a total 11 million. So Protestants still owned most of the land while Catholics constituted the majority of the population. This society was volatile. When Talbot reappeared in 1684, the New English viewed him as the harbinger of ill fortune; to his fellow-Catholics he looked like a champion who might restore their lost land. After all, he had advocated extensive redistribution of land before the Privy Council in 1671. There was no reason to think he had changed his mind in the interim.

With settler pessimism swelling and Irish optimism rising, Ormond was finally granted permission to leave London. By the time he reached Dublin he learned that Talbot had already been and gone, but he had stirred opinion. In a letter written a few weeks after his arrival in Dublin Ormond complained that his conduct was being criticized. Back in London, Talbot was now briefing against Ormond. He lobbied for changes to the Irish magistracy, army and council. He wanted to see all these areas opened up to his co-religionists. Of course, such actions would weaken the power of the settlers. Talbot's beliefs sprang from his identity: he was Old English and Roman Catholic, and he'd consistently advocated opinions that favoured these groups. The only difference now was that his arguments were being listened to by Charles and James. They wanted to consolidate the pre-eminence of the House of Stuart in the three kingdoms, and saw in Talbot a man who would help achieve this. However, over-lapping ambitions are not the same as identical interests.

Charles II died on 6 February 1685. For his successor, James, kingship came freighted with both potential and danger. Here was the opportunity to improve the position of Roman Catholics, but Protestant resistance had to be neutralized, and quickly. James was already fifty-two, his brother was fifty-five when he died; James had no reason to think he would be granted many more years. Also, his heir was a Protestant married to a Protestant, so James had to make sure his changes were bedded in before Mary and her husband took over.*

In Dublin Ormond proclaimed King James II on 11 February. It was to be one of his last official acts. He had been warned of his imminent recall and soon received the order. He left for London and en route read in a newsletter that his own regiment had been given to Colonel Talbot. It was personally chastening, and an ill omen for Ormond and his kind. Armies were not neutral: an army's religious disposition determined its behaviour, or so it was believed. A Protestant army would defend the Act of Settlement; a Catholic army would confound it. Talbot, a Catholic, had been given the ex-Lord Lieutenant's regiment. The wind was blowing in a new direction. James had formally

---

* At the time, it seemed unlikely that James's other daughter Anne would ever become Queen of England. Mary had not yet had any children, but she was only twenty-three. There seemed plenty of time for her to produce an heir. She never did.

declared he would do nothing against the Protestant religion, and the overturning of the Act of Settlement had never been one of his personal objectives, but the regimental reassignment suggested otherwise. There were murmurs that James could not be trusted.

The Ireland Ormond left behind was not so different from the country where he had started his career. The settler interest still held the bulk of the land, while the political influence of the new settlers through the borough corporations produced by the Cromwellian Settlement remained total. These arrangements, albeit unjust, were supposed to ensure that Ireland's civil wars were never repeated. But with a Catholic army, continued peace seemed a faint hope.

CHAPTER SIX

The Reign of James II

After the 'Popish Plot', confessional alignment in England assumed a new and, for James, dangerous form. Anti-court forces, who came to be called Whigs, and those who supported the court and came to be called Tories, cooperated to first resist and then depose James. The eventual triumph of this coalition represented a victory of English anti-popery over those who favoured emancipation – the king, his Catholic advisers and a few dissenters and Whigs who hoped to benefit from toleration.

Unlike today, faith was of interest to everyone in the seventeenth century: at stake was nothing less than the future of your immortal soul. Furthermore, your faith often determined your quality of life: Protestants tended to have better chances in this life than Catholics. Dissenters, those outside both Churches, lay uneasily between the two, sometimes hated, sometimes courted by their more powerful fellow-Christians. All denominations had done awful things to the others. All were blind to their own malfeasance but acutely aware of that of others. They saw themselves only as victims or potential victims.

A further complication was the merging of faith and national identity. England was predominantly Anglican (at least at the top) with a tiny Catholic minority. Across the Irish Sea, the Catholics were in the majority. Redress of ancient grievances was long desired there, especially by the Catholic Old English constituency. This ambition made beneficiaries of the Cromwellian Settlement anxious and fearful, so they looked back to their Anglican brethren in England for support and protection. Their entreaties, which suggested that an Irish St Bartholomew's Day Massacre loomed, fanned English paranoia, which produced anti-Catholic sentiment. As a result, the Irish grew fearful that Cromwellian atrocities would be repeated. Ireland was gripped by a climate of mutual suspicion, antagonism and fear.

James II was crowned on 23 April 1685. Frances Talbot, who had now become Richard's second wife, attended the coronation in Westminster Abbey as a Lady of the Bedchamber. Shortly thereafter her husband went to Ireland. On 20 June he was created Baron Talbotstown, Viscount Baltinglas and the Earl of Tyrconnell.* These titles signalled royal favour, but his precise function in Ireland had not yet been defined. He had the command of a troop of horse but no commission over the Irish army as yet. For the moment the king had more important matters to address.

First, he had to deal with his nephew, the Duke of Monmouth, who launched his bid for the Crown in June and July 1685. His rebellion was swiftly crushed. Monmouth was executed for treason and Judge Jeffreys was dispatched to run the 'Bloody Assizes' in Winchester, at which justice was meted out to Monmouth's followers. According to the official records, 320 were executed, and many hundreds more were transported to

---

*Henceforth he styled himself Tyrconnell, as shall I.

the West Indies and sold into indentured servitude (a regime they were not expected to survive, although, surprisingly, many did, and returned to Britain later). The king appointed Jeffreys Lord Chancellor on his return to London. He also decided that the militia was untrustworthy. He disbanded this body across Britain. In Ireland the task was given to Tyrconnell, who was delighted by this turn of events: most militia members were settlers.

The post of Lord Lieutenant was still vacant after Ormond's departure, and Tyrconnell coveted it. But, even if he wished it, James could not yet risk a Roman Catholic as his deputy in Ireland. Instead he chose Henry Hyde, the 2nd Earl of Clarendon, son of the old Chancellor and brother of James's first wife, Anne. Like his father, Clarendon was not known for his warmth of feeling towards the Irish or Tyrconnell. Settler spirits rose. On 29 August Tyrconnell wrote to James that 'Clarendon's nomination as governor of Ireland terrifies the Catholics.'

Clarendon left for Ireland in January 1686. As he headed west, Tyrconnell was journeying east. Clarendon expected to meet him at Holyhead, but Tyrconnell sailed straight on to Chester. When he reached Dublin, Clarendon wrote to his brother Laurence Hyde, Earl of Rochester and Lord Treasurer, in London: 'everybody here knows the wind was so fair that he might more easily have done it [pulled into Holyhead] than have gone to Chester'. The fact that he had not set the tone for the entire future relationship of the two men.

Though he bypassed Clarendon, Tyrconnell had not gone to England so much to avoid the Lord Lieutenant as to denigrate him, as he now did with great gusto. He also went because James II had summoned him. The King wished to discuss the army. The first step towards creating a strong force had been Ormond's removal. Ormond had combined civil and military authority in one person, but in the new order, James envisaged, Clarendon would hold civil power, Tyrconnell military.

Tyrconnell was appointed Lieutenant General in March 1686. Around this time, several of his relatives and allies of long standing were commissioned into the Irish army. Colonel Justin MacCarty, Colonel Richard Hamilton and Sir Thomas Newcomen would assist him with the Catholicization policy he was expected to finesse. The process by which the force would become a Jacobite instrument was now under way.

Tyrconnell, however, was in no hurry to start. He spent the spring of 1686 in Bath, taking the waters for his gout. He returned to London on 27 April and only then did he make preparations to go to Ireland. The night before he left, Tyrconnell met Rochester, recipient of his brother Clarendon's letters and champion of the Anglican section of King James's supporters. Tyrconnell wanted Patrick Trant, a Roman Catholic, made Vice-Treasurer of Ireland. Rochester demurred and there was a row. The next day Tyrconnell left for Ireland 'with full power to propagate the Roman Catholic religion there, and place and displace whom he pleases'. As always, if one community prospered it was at the other's expense.

Clarendon met Tyrconnell over several days in June 1686. They discussed those who had profited from supporting Cromwell during the Civil War. Tyrconnell said the new king wanted any of them who held public office removed, and demanded names. Clarendon refused to give them and changed the subject. Tyrconnell then attacked the injustice of the Acts of Settlement. Clarendon countered that surely the king would not be so unwise as to repeal them: that would precipitate rebellion. Tyrconnell proposed a compromise: those who had acquired land could give up a third, or even half, if the remainder were secured to them permanently. From what they surrendered, money might be raised to help those unfairly punished by the Settlement. Clarendon seemed amenable to this proposal.

Next they moved on to the army, and James's determination
to add Catholics to its ranks. 'We have here a great many old
men and of different statures,' declared Tyrconnell. 'They must
all be turned out, for the King would have all his men young and
of one size.' It was a striking conceit to clear out all the old
wrongly sized Protestants and replace them with properly sized
Catholics. Clarendon, knowing that what was really being suggested was the wholesale Catholicization of the army, said the
current soldiers could not be turfed out overnight. Tyrconnell
angrily suggested that they had enjoyed the king's pay for far too
long already.

Two days on from this awkward revelation of his (and the
king's) intentions, Tyrconnell returned to Dublin Castle. He had
inspected the Royal Regiment in St Stephen's Green and put its
new officers in their commands; he now wished to proceed to
the country garrisons. Still keeping the form of taking his orders
from the Lord Lieutenant, he asked 'when he should be dispatched into the country'.

Whenever he wanted, replied Clarendon. Conversation then
turned to the question of appointing Roman Catholic sheriffs,
justices and corporation members. Tyrconnell insisted the current Protestant incumbents were 'rogues and old Cromwellians';
Clarendon defended them as fine, upstanding men. Neither
could be persuaded by the other's arguments (and never would
be).

A couple of days later Tyrconnell took his leave of the Lord
Lieutenant 'with a thousand compliments of friendship' and
went home to Talbotstown, from where, the next day, he would
start for Wexford. His plan was to combine troop inspections
with a health cure for his gout. 'Whether my Lord Tyrconnell
will continue to be so terrible as he is at present,' Clarendon
complained to his brother, 'nothing but time will determine. At
present nothing can more dissatisfy honest men than the ranting,
swaggering way he is in, and the abominable insolent language
he treats men with.' But Tyrconnell's manner was neither here

nor there compared to the changes that had occurred in the pre-
ceeding weeks. A number of Roman Catholics had been
appointed to the Privy Council, including Tyrconnell himself,
Roman Catholics had been admitted into the corporations and
the army was already being transformed. Jittery settlers observed
these events and concluded that they were on the slippery slope
back to 1641. 'It is impossible to tell you the alterations that are
grown in men with this month,' continued Clarendon, 'but last
week . . . 120 people went in one ship from hence to Chester;
and multitudes are preparing from all parts of the kingdom to be
gone as fast as they can get in their debts and dispose of their
stocks.'

And Clarendon heard that he would soon be joining them on
the boat to England: a rumour was current that Tyrconnell was
in the process of angling for his removal from office.

On 19 July Tyrconnell returned from his troop inspections,
and two days later Clarendon invited him to Dublin Castle.
Clarendon announced that he had heard a rumour: apparently
Tyrconnell had said that only Roman Catholics were to be
admitted into the army in future.

Tyrconnell vehemently denied that he had made any such
statement, and on his next visit to the castle declared that 'he
could not imagine why the bringing in [of] a few Popish officers and soldiers should make such jealous tensions among
people that they must lose their lands and the Acts of
Settlement [be] broken'. He was mystified because 'it would
appear, after he had made all the alterations he now designed,
that there would not be a seventh part of the army Roman
Catholic'.

Clarendon felt he had to challenge this: of 2,300 new men
put in since Tyrconnell had arrived, 2,000 were Roman
Catholics. And Clarendon had heard another rumour: there
would not be an Englishman or a Protestant left in the army by
Christmas Day. According to Clarendon, this time Tyrconnell
offered no reply.

On 13 August various members of the administration, including Tyrconnell, met at Dublin Castle. The principal item on the agenda was a proposed Commission of Grace confirming the Settlement of Ireland for present landowners and indemnifying the original owners. Clarendon was emphatic that nothing less would calm the anxious New English. Tyrconnell – whose life's work had been restoration to rather than indemnification of the old proprietors – fiercely opposed the proposal. After three hours' wrangling the meeting ended with no agreement having been reached.

Three days later Tyrconnell ordered a vessel to be ready at an hour's notice to take him to England, 'to make projects for Bills'. Clarendon feared the worst: 'By the discourses he and his friends make here, they are such as will turn this kingdom topsy-turvy.' Here he was expressing the profound anxiety of his New English constituency, and they had good reason for fearfulness. The atrocities perpetrated on their behalf at Drogheda and Wexford, and during the Cromwellian Settlement, were still within living memory. If the vanquished reasserted their primacy (and they seemed about to), it could be as catastrophic for them as 1641. Or even worse. Forty-five years before, the Irish had not enjoyed the favour of the monarch. Now they did.

Tyrconnell spent the autumn in England, lobbying for Clarendon's post. On 8 October he was made a member of the English Privy Council, a sure sign that royal favour and his long-cherished aims were about to converge. After the New Year he got his wish, with just one minor disappointment: he was to be styled Lord Deputy, not Lord Lieutenant.

He arrived back in Ireland on 6 February 1687, and immediately sent his secretary to Clarendon with a letter from the king. Clarendon was to surrender the sword of office to Tyrconnell within a week. Six days later it was handed over in the presence of the Privy Council. The outgoing incumbent made a pleasant speech, mostly free from rancour, though he did allude to the 'feuds and animosities' that confounded the Irish, 'which I hope Your Excellency's prudence, with the assistance of so wise a Cabinet, will disperse'.

Clarendon's calm was not shared. Tyrconnell had arrived with full instructions signed by Lord Sunderland, the Secretary of State. He was to survey the army thoroughly and administer a new oath of loyalty. All who declined were to be cashiered. All arms confiscated from Catholics at the time of the Popish Plot were to be restored. Catholics were to be admitted as sheriffs and justices of the peace, and to all corporations and ports. Tyrconnell immediately proposed to city corporations, in surprisingly mild and diplomatic language, that members of both religions must be admitted. When this provoked the predictable protests he invoked the royal prerogative and issued an Order in Council recalling the charters. There was, in the end, as James II wrote later, 'no great trouble except at Londonderry (a stubborn people, as they appeared to be afterwards), who stood an obstinate suit, but were forced at last to undergo the same fate with the rest'.

Tyrconnell also issued an Order in Council warning churchmen of the penalties for making political speeches from the pulpit. The sermon was a primary source of information, and clergymen had both status and a captive audience. Protestant firebrands could mould parishioners into dangerous and committed opponents of official policy. However, trying to gag clergymen was a sure sign, from the minority point of view, that an anti-Protestant vendetta was under way.

In England the Protestants were growing similarly uneasy. The king celebrated mass, prohibited preaching against Catholicism and exempted Catholics from the Test Act. They were also admitted to offices of State. In response to the murmurs of disapproval these policies produced, James bulked up the army to twenty thousand, and garrisoned it on Hounslow Heath. Anti-Jacobites could not fail to understand the message.

In April 1687 James published a Declaration of Indulgence exempting Catholics (and dissenters) from penal statutes. He dissolved Parliament and sought to impose Roman Catholic fellows on the colleges. To some, James looked like a rigid papist planning to trample on the faith of the majority of his subjects.

In the summer, to test the waters for support for toleration, the king undertook a tour of the west and in August Tyrconnell joined his master at Shrewsbury, after which they spent two days in confidential conversation. Though there are no records to confirm it, they probably discussed the army. Tyrconnell returned to Ireland and continued to do his master's work. At fifty-six, he was now in late middle age, but he did not stint. He packed the army with friends and relatives, then packed the Bench with co-religionists, leaving only one Protestant, John Keating, Lord Chief Justice of the Common Pleas. Whatever happened in the other kingdoms, Ireland would be on side as far as James II was concerned.

In England the succession was again a focus for anxiety. The king had produced no male heir, but Mary Beatrice was still only twenty-nine: there could yet be a Catholic heir to the throne.* At the very end of 1687 James was told that his queen was pregnant again. He immediately ordered a day of thanksgiving. Public enthusiasm was muted.

In the year that followed James further provoked the majority English sentiment. He insisted on publicly receiving Count Ferdinando d'Adda as papal nuncio at Windsor. One Father Petre was openly sworn in as a member of the Privy Council. A convert to Catholicism was appointed Dean of Christ Church, Oxford. And there was Tyrconnell's policy in Ireland. Each of these might have caused only limited trouble, but cumulatively

---

*Even by the standards of the day, and this was a period of high infant mortality, the king and queen had been exceptionally unlucky: by 1687 they had lost five daughters and a son in infancy.

they gave the impression that worse was to come. Of course, this was exactly what James's enemies wanted, because it gave them the justification to act before it was too late. On 27 April James repeated his 1687 Declaration of Indulgence, which suspended the Test Acts, and ordered this to be read from all church pulpits in his realms. Protestant opinion, naturally, was inflamed.

Running in parallel with all these events was Mary Beatrice's pregnancy. Scurrilous pamphlets appeared, alleging that the child would be a false heir foisted on England to keep the Protestant princess – James's daughter Mary – off the throne. On 18 May a delegation of bishops addressed the king. They said they would not read his declaration from their pulpits. On 7 June James sent seven of them to the Tower.

On 10 June in St James's Palace Queen Mary Beatrice delivered a son and heir in the presence of a crowd of magnates. Nevertheless, rumours were almost instantly in circulation, including one to the effect that the baby had been born to another woman and then smuggled to the queen in a warming-pan, to be produced before the assembled crowd. Apparently the king's two daughters, Mary and Anne, believed this fable.

The bishops were acquitted on 30 June but the mood of fearfulness persisted: the Anglican hierarchy feared Catholicism in general as much as the possibility of a Catholic king. On the very day that the bishops were acquitted, Admiral Herbert left England for the Netherlands. Two months earlier, the Stadtholder of the Netherlands, William of Orange, had told some influential English visitors that he might be prepared to invade their country, if invited. Herbert carried the letter that contained the invitation.

The United Provinces (the part of Europe that is now the Netherlands and Belgium) had no absolute monarch in the seventeenth century. However, William of Orange was effectively its leader, a military commander and administrator appointed by an assembly of delegates from the provinces. Following his marriage to James's daughter, William had kept a close eye on events in England, partly because he hoped for assistance against Louis XIV of France, whose forces had occupied Dutch territory, including some of William's own estates in Orange, and whose fleet had imposed a blockade. After James's coronation, he tried to be reasonable towards his father-in-law: he exiled the Duke of Monmouth when James acceded, then attempted to dissuade Monmouth from mounting his ill-fated expedition. These actions were part of a larger project – the inveigling of Britain and Ireland into the League of Augsburg, the alliance William had fashioned against the French.

By 1688, though, William knew that James would probably never join a Protestant league against his fellow-Catholic Louis XIV. But now, suddenly, there was a new possibility on the horizon: the establishment, by armed intervention, of a free (i.e. anti-French) parliament. Louis could be forced to abandon his expansionist policies in the United Provinces, because France would have a new adversary in England. The scheme was brilliant, if it could be effected.

In England that August King James felt confident that the membership of a reconvened Parliament he'd been planning would be to his liking and he issued writs for it to meet on 27 November. Meanwhile, William was operating in a different political milieu. As Stadtholder, he had been appointed by and ultimately was answerable to the States of Holland, the other six Netherlands provinces, and to the States General, the decision-making body in which each province had one vote. But he was an adroit negotiator, and on 29 September the States of Holland passed a secret resolution giving full support for William's enterprise.

With invasion looking likely, James set about mollifying his subjects: he declared Catholics would not be eligible for election to the upcoming Parliament. However, he then cancelled the

Parliament and began to gather forces from Scotland and Ireland. His adversary was steely, patient and determined; but James seemed to be panicking. As they had been throughout his reign, his subjects were far from impressed.

CHAPTER SEVEN

The Closing of the Gates

Tyrconnell's remodelled Irish Jacobite army had been created for moments like this. A hostile foreign army was preparing to invade, and the kingdoms needed to be defended by soldiers loyal to the Crown. Tyrconnell had sent a regiment to England as early as March 1687. A second was called for in August 1688, a third in September. This had left the army in Ireland several thousand men short; Dublin was especially bereft. This troubled Tyrconnell because the city was packed with aggrieved and well-armed New English. The Lord Deputy had intelligence that some unhappy subjects had a coup in mind. He and the ordnance stored in Dublin Castle were vulnerable. As he needed troops around the capital, he decided to bring down the garrison from Derry. He issued the movement order in September 1688.

The commander of the regiment in Derry was William Stewart, Viscount Mountjoy.* He was

---

*He was no relation to the great Lord Deputy who had humbled the Earl of Tyrone. This Mountjoy was a descendant of Sir William Stewart, leader of the Lagganeers, who fought the Irish in 1641.

a brave soldier, an accomplished scholar, a zealous
Protestant, and yet a zealous Tory, was one of the very few
members of the Established Church who still held office in
Ireland. He was Master of the Ordnance in that kingdom,
and was colonel of a regiment in which an uncommonly
large proportion of the Englishry had been suffered to
remain. At Dublin he was the centre of a small circle of
learned and ingenious men who had, under his presidency,
formed themselves into a Royal Society, the image, on a
small scale, of the Royal Society of London. In Ulster, with
which he was peculiarly connected, the colonists held his
name in high honour.

It's a wonder Macaulay left out of this picture that Mountjoy's
father fought against Cromwell at Dunbar.

Mountjoy, precisely the sort of individual Tyrconnell would
normally have identified as an enemy, had given no indication of
disloyalty; and his regiment did not trouble Tyrconnell on that
score, even though its ranks contained many Protestants.
However, perhaps one reason they were moved to Dublin was so
that the Lord Deputy could keep a close eye on them.
Furthermore, the presence of Mountjoy's men would soothe
the agitated Protestant refugees who thronged the capital.

Once Mountjoy's regiment moved out, Derry would be left
without a garrison. To fill the gap, Tyrconnell selected the Earl of
Antrim's regiment, newly formed and largely Catholic. As with
bringing Mountjoy's forces south, Tyrconnell must have congratu-
lated himself for his cunning here. The Protestants of Derry were
awkward and potentially Williamite. If they proved troublesome
in the future, Antrim's regiment would be just the force to deal
with them. Tyrconnell could be certain of their loyalty and he
knew that, if needed, they would be zealous and unsparing. The
Earl of Antrim was ordered to be ready to march on 20
November, which ensured his troops had sufficient time to arrive
before Mountjoy's regiment left on the 23rd, as they had been

ordered by Tyrconnell. What the Lord Deputy cannot have known was that these orders would lead directly to the siege of Derry.

On 3 October Tyrconnell sent a letter to the king. He had no money to arm and equip the new forces he recognized he was going to need in addition to those he had already selected. While he waited for a reply he installed new governors in Cork and Limerick and gave them secret instructions: they were to obtain from sympathetic Irish nobles and members of the gentry lists of men suitable for this new army. Tyrconnell regarded this as a matter of urgency, since he presumed the invasion of England was imminent.

On 10 October William of Orange issued a declaration. It described the infant Prince of Wales as an imposter, yet emphasized that William had no desire to seize his father-in-law's throne (the crown only became an objective of William's at the end of 1688). It then went on to catalogue the crimes and abuses of James's reign but blamed evil counsellors rather than the king himself. The solution posited was a free Parliament in which wrongs could be set right. Sixty thousand copies of the declaration were printed and distributed throughout England.

By the end of the month the Dutch invasion force was ready. It comprised approximately twenty-one thousand men, including many regiments tempered by years of fighting the French, and it was well equipped with cannons, military supplies and horses. The Dutch calculated such a large force was essential if they were to succeed when they got to England. They had no idea resistance would prove to be as poor as it was. Taking such a large body of troops away from Holland left the country vulnerable to attack by the French, who might well calculate now was the perfect time to invade. Happily for the Dutch, though, Louis XIV's forces at this moment were heading north-east towards the Rhine in another act of aggression.

On 27 October prayers were said throughout the United Provinces. All denominations, including the Jews, prayed for the success of William's English adventure. The fleet sailed in fine weather three days later, then promptly ran into a storm. Perhaps as many as 1,000 of the 4,000 horses died. The fleet rushed home. It was refitted with alacrity and sailed again. The next day, all flags flying, it passed through the Straits of Dover. Spectators gathered on the white cliffs to watch. After their disastrous start the Dutch were now enjoying good fortune: the wind that sped them south and west had kept the English fleet penned up in its ports. When it finally emerged, the admiral in charge pursued the invaders slowly. The Dutch ships eventually anchored at Torbay on the Devon coast. A fisherman named Peter Varwell carried William to the beach and lodged him in his small house. It was (according to the old calendar that was still used in England) the day the Catholic Guy Fawkes had been foiled in his attempt to destroy Protestantism by blowing up Parliament.

William's troops disembarked with much pomp and ceremony. The Williamite standard was unfurled: a blue banner inscribed 'For the Protestant Religion and Liberty'. This would be a campaign where politics was disguised with a confessional gloss. The troops assembled into companies and marched to Newton Abbot. In the town bells were rung and William's declaration read aloud. On 9 November the Dutch reached Exeter, with flags flying and kettledrums pounding. This made a good impression, as did their purses: rather than help themselves, as soldiers normally did, they paid for everything. The army needed to reorganize and rest. Some West Country nobles came over to William's side and, as they did so, he heard good news from the North: York, Nottingham and Newcastle had fallen to his allies. On 20 November the Dutch set off again in dreadful weather. There was sickness in the ranks but William could not wait.

In the meantime, James's army had been heading west to meet the invader. The two sides encountered each other outside Axminster on 24 November. What James did next was inept, wrong-headed and self-destructive. He should have appealed to the national dislike of foreigners, roused the English against these Dutch usurpers and engaged the enemy. He should also have arrested potential traitors. He did none of these things. Debilitating nosebleeds and a growing sense that the tide was turning against him seemed to paralyse him.

The wily William took advantage of his father-in-law's indisposition. He sent a message to John Churchill, James's commander- in-chief,* quoting King David: 'If you come peaceably unto me to help me, my heart shall be knit unto you.' Churchill, who had long contemplated defecting at the urging of his wife Sarah and had committed himself to the Williamite cause in a letter to William in 1688, answered with another Old Testament passage: 'Thine we are, David, and on thy side, thou son of Jesse. Peace, peace be unto thee and peace be unto thy helpers, for thy God helpeth thee.' He switched sides, taking his regiment of grenadiers with him.

On 26 November, dismayed by the defection of Churchill, James withdrew towards London. His son-in-law did not hasten after him, but simply ordered more copies of his declaration printed, as well as a speech he had made in Exeter. Then he set off to hunt deer. His progress that day took him past a village where his vanguard had skirmished with Jacobites. To date, the death toll for both sides was fifteen. William wanted to keep the casualties low, so his strategy was to let panic rather than violence thin the Jacobite ranks. And his policy was working magnificently. When James arrived in the capital late on 26 November, he learned his younger daughter, Princess Anne, along with Sarah Churchill had left London to join their husbands and William.† No wonder, when the Williamite regime took charge a few weeks later, King Lear was banned from the theatre. The

---

*Churchill would later become the 1st Duke of Marlborough. He was a direct ancestor of Winston Churchill.

†Anne, a staunch Protestant herself, was married to another, Prince George of Denmark.

parallels between James's daughters and Goneril and Regan would have been a gift to satirists.

With Anne's defection, the king was finished. According to the author of *A Jacobite Narrative of the War in Ireland*, a near-contemporary account of the period from the Irish Jacobite perspective, James wrote to Tyrconnell after learning of it. He complained of betrayal by his army and the people of England. The letter revealed that he did not understand the depth of anti-Catholic feeling among his English subjects, or that his own religious practice was an affront. It was also heavy with self-pity and hurt.

Tyrconnell was of altogether different mettle. He was prone to neither self-pity nor disabling emotions (though he could dissemble and weep when the situation demanded it). On receiving the letter he immediately called a council and secured the agreement of every member to levy at once an army to maintain the king's rights, even though privately he had been exploring, in the event of an English revolt against James, the possibility of Ireland as a separate kingdom ruled by James's eldest illegitimate son, the Duke of Berwick. Because of the secret instructions he had issued to the Cork and Limerick governors, recruitment could start instantly. However, he still had no money to pay for it. This would hobble the Irish.

These were dangerous times for Catholic and Protestant in Ireland. The Williamite adventure threatened to topple Tyrconnell's patron and derail their project. But for the New English, William was far away, and if he were successful there might be an Irish reaction against them. This would be even more likely if the Irish Jacobite regiments or Catholics in England suffered in William's campaign. Many settlers, anxious to avoid a backlash, had sold up and fled to England or were in the process of doing so, but others had started to organize militarily, especially in the north (where they were most numerous and beyond Tyrconnell's reach).

Then, on 3 December 1688, in Comber, County Down, a letter was found in the street. It was addressed to a local

Protestant nobleman, Lord Mount-Alexander, one of Tyrconnell's adversaries. It was marked, 'To my Lord, this deliver with haste and care':

> Good my Lord, I have written to you to let you know that all our Irishmen through Ireland is sworn: that on the ninth day of this month they are to fall on to kill and murder man, wife and child; and I desire your Lordship to take care of yourself and all others that are judged by our men to be heads, for whosoever can kill any of you, they are to have a captain's place; so my desire to your honour is to look to yourself and give other noblemen warning, and go not out either night or day without a good guard with you, and let no Irishman come near you, whatsoever he be; so this is all from him who was your father's friend, and is your friend, and will be, though I dare not be known, as yet, for fear of my life.

The message was clear: on 9 December the native Irish intended to slaughter every Protestant in the land.

It is not known whether the writer of the letter was a Williamite seeking to galvanize the Protestant community into action or a Catholic hoping to scare them out of their wits. Whichever, the Protestants assumed it was genuine. It was immediately copied and circulated throughout Ulster, eventually reaching the town of Newtownlimavady, and the home of one Colonel George Phillips, a former governor of Londonderry. He was eighty-nine years old but still in command of all his faculties. As he listened to the visitor with the letter who told him of the coming Doomsday, he heard the tramp of marching feet. Outside the window the streets were swarming with soldiers in kilts. These were the Earl of Antrim's regiment – known as Redshanks because of their bare legs – all Highlanders, all Catholics, from the glens of Antrim or the Mull of Kintyre.

Colonel Phillips was not surprised by their arrival, just by its timing. He had been expecting them to pass through his town a fortnight earlier as he knew Lord Mountjoy's regiment had left Derry on 23 November, as Tyrconnell had ordered, and had headed for Dublin. However, Antrim's regiment had been delayed by the need to find men of a certain stature, lack of uniforms and reluctance among the ranks to report for duty. As a result, they were woefully late. Derry had been without a garrison for two weeks.

For all he'd been expecting them, Colonel Phillips now grew concerned about the Redshanks' presence. First, the Earl of Antrim, the seventy-seven-year-old colonel, had recruited as many six-footers as he could find. He was vain and believed a regiment of giants would reflect well on him. But in an age when the average height was five foot six or less, many tall men together looked unnatural and threatening. Second, Colonel Phillips had been expecting eight companies of soldiers (about four hundred men); but twenty-four companies had appeared. Third, they were only partially dressed in the king's livery and they were not properly armed: a few carried firearms but most were equipped with skeans and clubs. There wasn't the money for uniforms and firearms – as Tyrconnell had endlessly complained – but Phillips wasn't to know that. The lack of proper apparel gave an impression of ill discipline, while the weaponry suggested they were interested in skulduggery rather than regular battles. Finally, many Redshanks were accompanied by their women and children. Soldiers generally only brought their families with them in such numbers when they anticipated spoilation rather than fighting.

In other circumstances, Phillips might not have worried, but this evening marked the culmination of two years of drastic positive discrimination. Catholic sheriffs had been imposed; new charters had been foisted on most boroughs, creating Catholic majorities on the corporations; most of the recently appointed Privy Councillors and judges were Catholics; Protestant officers had been replaced in the Jacobite Irish regiments with Catholics. For forty years the New English had been dominant and the Gaelic Irish and Old English subservient. Now the positions were reversed. With the latter in the ascendant, inevitably there had been a degree of score settling. Tales of Catholics breaking into New English houses (on the pretext of looking for arms) and walking off with whatever took their fancy were rife. The few settlers who bothered to report such incidents found the law invariably sided with the Irish. But all that had happened so far was as nothing compared to what Phillips and others feared: the undoing of the Act of Settlement. And, from the opposite side of the divide, many Catholics who had lost land in the Cromwellian wars believed that the restoration of their property was imminent. They were therefore enthusiastic supporters of Tyrconnell, which only reinforced settler suspicion of the slippery Lord Deputy.

At some point in the evening Phillips sent a man to Derry with a message for an old friend, Alderman Samuel Norman. The alderman was to consult the sober people of the town and set out before them the dangers of admitting the Redshanks. The message was carefully worded to avoid creating panic. In the early hours of the following morning Phillips was still awake and troubled. An advance party of troops had mustered and left for Derry soon after his messenger. Phillips summoned a second man and gave him a new message: Alderman Norman was to shut the gates and admit no Redshanks. Phillips added that he would join the citizens of the city the next day, and that he would stand by them, even if it cost him his life or his fortune.

Seventeen miles away, the first messenger had already arrived at the Waterside, a settlement on the eastern bank of the Foyle. He boarded the ferry that ran to the city. Once on the other side he started up the path known as Ferryquay Street. The long eastern flank of the city lay in front of him, a curtain of stone augmented by four bastions, and pierced in the middle by the Ferry Quay Gate. In front of the walls he saw part of the dry ditch that encircled the city; it had silted up in places through neglect. When he reached the shadow of the walls the earth under his feet gave way to the wood of the drawbridge.* The gateway, towering above him, was topped with a battlement. He went through and continued up Ferryquay Street towards the Diamond.

Over half a century earlier commissioners had advised Charles I that in times of civil strife Derry would be the premier place of refuge for settlers and their families in the north. Now they were being proved right. Not all had arrived yet but a substantial number had: tens of thousands were already in the city, which only had adequate accommodation for about a thousand.

In the Markethouse Phillips' first messenger found an alderman called Tomkins reading a copy of the Comber letter to a group of people, including Alderman Norman, local clergymen and the city's bishop. The messenger said his piece. On hearing it, 'Norman and the rest of the graver citizens were under great disorder and consternation, and knew not what to resolve upon,' wrote George Walker, one of two clergymen who remained in Derry throughout the siege and later described it. To admit the Redshanks might be to court the massacre the Comber letter had warned Protestants to expect in two days' time. But locking them out could be just as bad. The troops were coming under order from Tyrconnell, the agent in Ireland of James II, who was still officially the monarch. If James saw William off, Derry might experience what the West Country had suffered after the Monmouth rebellion. Furthermore, he was a Catholic, and might be delighted to cull his Protestant Irish subjects if they gave him an excuse to do so. Finally, in spite of how much they distrusted it, there was the ingrained Protestant habit of obedience to lawful authority.

---

*Bishop's Gate also had a drawbridge. Butchers' and Ship Quay Gate did not.

While the worthies were struggling to make the right decision, the second messenger came upon the Redshank vanguard, about 150 men, two miles from Derry. He bypassed them unseen, took the ferry and delivered the new message: lock out the approaching Redshanks.

Tomkins needed to secure agreement but was having trouble with the clergy. James Gordon, a Presbyterian minister, insisted the gates be locked immediately.* Dr Ezekiel Hopkins, the Bishop of Derry, immediately contradicted Gordon. He said it was the duty of a subject to obey his sovereign in all things. Several apprentices listened to this debate. They were mostly men in their twenties and had none of their elders' anxieties: they wanted to shut out the Redshanks. This course of action had been urged on them over the preceding days. David Cairnes, a local lawyer who had just left the city, was among those who had recommended this. His twenty-five-year-old nephew, William, was one of the apprentices present. Horace Kennedy, a sheriff, was another supporter of the closed-gate policy with 'divers of those who made some figure in the town [and] wished the thing were done, yet none of . . . whom thought fit to be themselves active in it'. So said John Mackenzie, a Presbyterian minister, whose history of the siege rivals the other great account by the conformist minister George Walker.

As the town's notables continued arguing, the advance party of Redshanks was spotted on the quay at the Waterside. Word was passed back to the Markethouse. Towards midday on 7 December the first Redshanks disembarked on the western bank of the Foyle, a few minutes' march from the city walls. From this body a lieutenant and an ensign detached themselves, approached Ferry Quay Gate and were admitted to the city. They met John

---

*Gordon, a Scot, was a colourful character. He'd been forced from several former ministries after displaying an uncontrollable desire for the female servants. He was currently at Glendermot on the Waterside.

Buchanan, the Deputy Mayor, and the sheriffs, including Horace Kennedy. After producing their warrant they requested billets for their soldiers and forage for their horses. The document should have included the names of the officers to be billeted within the walls, but whoever had written it had omitted to do this. Without the names, the warrant was technically invalid. The sheriffs demurred, and an argument broke out between them and the two Redshank officers. Meanwhile, the rest of the soldiers were ferried across the Foyle. They mustered and approached the Ferry Quay Gate. Word of this reached the Markethouse.

The elders were still dithering, but the thirteen apprentices – 'the younger sort who are seldom so dilatory in their actions' – had heard enough.* They drew their swords and hurried to the main guard post. They seized the keys to the city from a couple of bailiffs and rushed to the Ferry Quay Gate. There they raised the drawbridge, slammed shut the gates and locked them.

Knowing nothing of the significance of what had just happened, the advance troops halted in confusion sixty yards away. Their lieutenant and ensign were inside with a warrant, and they would hardly have been admitted if Derry were planning a rebellion. However, if they assumed this was all a misunderstanding they were soon proved wrong. Behind the walls, the apprentices ran to the other three city gates and locked them.

The Redshank vanguard remained in Ferryquay Street, waiting to be allowed entry. James Morrison, a citizen sometimes known as the fourteenth apprentice boy, was standing on the ramparts at the Ferry Quay Gate. He cockily shouted down at the soldiers to be off. They did not move. Morrison turned and

---

*The thirteen original apprentice boys were Henry Campsie, William Crookshanks, Robert Sherrard, Daniel Sherrard, Alexander Irwin, James Steward, Robert Morrison, Alexander Cunningham, Samuel Hunt, James Spike, John Cunningham, William Cairnes and Samuel Harvey.

shouted, as if to someone standing behind him, 'Bring about a great gun here.' The waiting Redshank officers below could not know that this was a bluff. They ordered their forces to wheel about and march back to the quay. They reboarded the ferry and returned to the eastern bank.

CHAPTER EIGHT

Confusion and Clarification

Though the gates were locked and the Jacobite troops had withdrawn, the Redshank officers remained inside the city, with the Deputy Mayor, the sheriffs and a party of Catholic citizens. Undaunted by developments, these officers showed some initiative: they asked their party to take over the magazine and hold it until the full garrison was admitted.

When the apprentice boys heard of this, they rushed to the magazine, arriving first. The guard on duty was a Catholic named Linegar. As the apprentice boys approached, he fired his gun and hit Henry Campsie, the son of Derry's last Protestant mayor, John Campsie, and the apprentice boys' ringleader, on the arm. The other apprentice boys overwhelmed Linegar and dragged him to the jail.

The magazine lost, the Redshank officers gravitated to the Diamond, where they knew they would meet the apprentices and their supporters. For the rest of the afternoon they argued the case for admitting the regiment. This is the last we hear of them in contemporary accounts. According to Thomas Ash, another important eyewitness from within the walls, the apprentices were already in the ascendant at this point. He wrote:

we could not determine among ourselves what was best. While we were in this confused hesitation, on December 7th, 1688, a few resolute APPRENTICE BOYS determined for us. These ran to the gates and shut them, drew up the bridge, and seized the magazine. This, like magic roused a unanimous spirit of defence, and now with one voice we determine to maintain the city at all hazards, and each sex and age joined in the important cause.

Ash wrote with the benefit of hindsight. The closure of the gates certainly helped to swing the debate the way of those wanting to resist the Redshanks, as perhaps did the wounding of Campsie. Here was a foretaste of what would happen when the Catholics were in charge, it was argued. But the appeasers within the walls continued to put their case. However, by now they had a skilled debater against them: David Cairnes had arrived back in the city. He toured the walls and told everyone who would listen that his nephew and his friends had been right to close the gates. In the evening Cairnes and various town worthies, including Alderman Norman, gathered in the guardhouse to discuss the best way to defend the city. They wrote letters to potential supporters explaining their predicament and justifying their actions. Guards were posted on the walls. Meanwhile, in the Town Hall, there was an open meeting to discuss the situation, but only Protestants were admitted. Tomkins spoke first and claimed Lord Deputy Tyrconnell wanted to control the city and enslave its inhabitants. He urged the citizens to look to England to preserve their ancient liberties. The Deputy Mayor, John Buchanan, urged the contrary view: let the soldiers in, he said, and the people would enjoy peace and plenty. Alderman Gervais Squire dubbed Buchanan a traitor to the liberties of the people and the English Crown, from whom Derry, as a Protestant and now Williamite city, derived its charter and laws.

Bishop Ezekiel Hopkins spoke next. Nearly twenty years earlier, on 31 January 1669, the twentieth anniversary of the execution of Charles I, he had preached in Christ Church, Dublin, the following:

> If the supreme Majesty should abuse his sovereign power
> and command thee to do what God his superior hath
> commanded thee not to do . . . thou art not to resist, nor to
> raise tumults and seditions to depose him from his authority,
> but only quietly and meekly to appeal unto God, who alone
> is his judge and ruler, and to beg Him take thy cause into
> His cognizance and redress thy wrongs and thy cries.

Two decades on, Hopkins proved his consistency: Tyrconnell was the king's agent, he said, and to refuse his troops was treason. Derry would be besieged, then inevitably destroyed and her citizens would lose life, liberty and wealth. It must be remembered that at this point it was by no means certain that William would emerge victorious. If James clung on to power, the city could suffer as Drogheda and Wexford had suffered forty years before. Many in the audience feared this scenario, even if they did not dare say it openly.

There were, however, others in the Town Hall determined to resist James. One such was Alexander Irwin, one of the apprentice boys. Halfway through Hopkins' speech he shouted, 'My Lord, your doctrine's very good, but we can't now hear you out,' whereupon he left the meeting. In a single sentence Irwin had demolished the sensible caution of Hopkins and his allies.

Hopkins left the city the next day. He went quietly to Raphoe, his bishopric before his elevation to Derry, and then to England. He was not the only person to leave that day. Most of the town's Catholics, including a number of Dominican friars, left, or were forced to leave, too. And a large number of Protestant refugees also fled after hearing that the Catholics within Derry were going to set fire to the city.

There was also traffic in the other direction, as refugees entered. They brought ominous news from the Waterside: the Redshanks were angry; the food, warmth and shelter they had anticipated in their new garrison had been denied them. Now, in the time-honoured manner of soldiers the world over, they were venting their ill humour on the unlucky inhabitants of the suburb and roughing up the locals. Within the walls, there was only one conclusion to draw: if that was how the Redshanks treated the luckless people of the Waterside who had done them no harm, then those in the city could expect much worse on 9 December, the following day.

The magazine was forced open. Match, a barrel of powder and 150 muskets were removed. This left eight or nine barrels and about a thousand firearms, most in poor order. A census was taken with the object of arranging guards. There were no more than three hundred men capable of bearing arms, and only one gun for every two of them. These were hardly the resources with which to mount a robust defence.

That Saturday, as the citizens of Derry checked their weapons, King James's envoys met William at his camp in Hungerford. James was desperate: peers and influential figures were defecting to his son-in-law. He needed a settlement, but William had no need to negotiate. He could afford to wait and let everything come to him. Nothing was agreed.

Sunday 9 December dawned with the guards on Derry's walls watching and waiting. On the far bank of the Foyle no one stirred. The Redshank companies still quartered in the Waterside seemed uninterested in causing mischief. Indeed, in whatever direction the guards chose to look, the expected Jacobite Irish hordes were nowhere to be seen. As the day wore on it became clear that the dreaded massacre was not going to materialize.

But it was still a day packed with incident. With the post came the news that James's other son-in-law, Prince George of Denmark, had gone over to William. It was decided a celebration was in order, so instructions were issued that the two largest guns on the walls should be fired – although without balls, which were too precious to waste. There is a popular myth that when they heard these guns fired the Redshanks on the Waterside thought they were under attack and fled. The truth is more complex. As the guns sounded, fifty or sixty youths gathered on the Ferry Quay, marshalled by one George Cook, a butcher. They shouted abuse at the Redshanks on the far side of the river. The waiting soldiers concluded that the youths were Lagganeers, a militia famous for its victories over the Irish in 1641. Next, the guard on the walls fired across at the Redshanks. Then came the *coup de grâce* in this accidental sequence of events. A party of armed men on horseback appeared on a hill within sight of the Waterside. They were soldiers en route to Derry to augment the three hundred men within the walls who could bear arms. Their captain was the son of Alderman Tomkins, who had slipped out of Derry after making his stirring speech in the Town Hall and summoned them.

The Redshanks, recently mustered and never having seen action, deduced an attack by Williamites was imminent. They hurried back towards Newtownlimavady in disorder. About a mile down the road they met a coach and the rest of their regiment. Inside the coach sat the Earl of Antrim and Colonel Phillips. The Earl had arrived in Newtownlimavady the day before and found the bulk of his regiment awaiting him. He had made his way to Colonel Phillips' house as arranged,* thus preventing Phillips going to Derry as he had promised in his second message. The following morning, further complicating Phillips' plans, Antrim had insisted his host keep him company on the

---

*The commander of a mobile regiment generally billeted at the home of a local dignatory. In this case Antrim had arranged to spend the night as Phillips' guest several weeks before.

journey to the city. Looking through the coach window, Antrim now saw his soldiers hurrying towards him. Some had lost their coats, some their boots, some their firearms. Many had left behind their gear in their haste to escape what they feared was an attack.

On reaching the Waterside, Antrim asked Colonel Phillips to go across to the Foyle and ask who was in command of the city. When he arrived at the locked gate, Phillips gave his name and was reluctantly admitted by the nervous guard. Only when he reached the Markethouse was he recognized as the man whose timely messages had played such a crucial part in the decision to close the gates.

The man now in command in Derry was David Cairnes, the lawyer. Phillips explained what he had seen in Newtownlimavady and said that he wished to stay in the city. However, he continued, the Earl of Antrim was waiting on the far bank for news. Phillips was expected to go back to him, so, at his own request, he was 'publicly threatened with confinement' if he did not line up with the townspeople. As a further part of this subterfuge, Phillips wrote a letter to Antrim, explaining that he was detained against his will in Derry. He added there would be horrible bloodshed if the Redshanks forced their way into the city. The letter, rather than its author, went across the Foyle. Antrim read it and understood: he ordered his troops to return to Coleraine. The regiment made an about turn and marched back the way it had come, gathering the soldiers who had fled earlier.

Inside the city walls, with the agreement of Cairnes, Phillips was offered the post of Governor, which he'd last held under Charles II. He accepted, and the keys to the gates and the magazine were delivered to him. The Williamites were in the ascendant, but their triumph was by no means assured. Their likely saviour was on another island, while their prospective tormentor, Tyrconnell, was a mere 144 miles away in Dublin. Furthermore, Tyrconnell's master, King James, might still

prevail. In order to hedge their bets, the leaders of Derry tried
to neutralize Jacobite rage, but in such a way that, should
William emerge victorious, he would not take exception. They
attempted to achieve this balancing act with a sly letter to Lord
Mountjoy in Dublin. John Campsie, who had been Mayor
before Tyrconnell had established the short-lived Catholic
corporation, Samuel Norman and others signed it. The letter
explained, 'our rabble . . . had shut the gates against some of
the Earl of Antrim's regiment, which we then blamed them
for, though we could not restrain them'. However, it continued, in view of all they had learned since regarding the true
extent of Catholic malevolence, 'We cannot but think it a most
wonderful Providence of God, to stir up the mobile for our
safety, and preservation of the peace of the kingdom against
such bloody attempts as these northern people had formed
against us.' Thus, a bad deed had become a noble one initiated
by God. The writers entreated Mountjoy to take the letter to
the administration in Dublin.

As the letter was wending its way to Dublin, Derry advanced
along the path of military resistance. It was suggested to
Governor Phillips that David Cairnes go to London to represent the city and secure military supplies. The next day,
Monday 10 December, a letter was written for Cairnes to take
with him. It was addressed to the society that had funded the
building of Derry ninety years earlier, and it repeated the arguments put to Mountjoy. This time, though, those arguments
were couched in a way that would appeal to an English
Protestant reader. The 'younger and more inconsiderate' citizens, it explained, who feared for their lives at the hands of the
incoming papist garrison, had closed the gates against them.
'The next day,' the letter continued, 'we hoped to prevail with
those that assumed the power of the City, to open the gates and
receive the garrison' and might have done so but for 'the news
and intimations' now coming from the Waterside. The Jacobite
Irish troops had behaved so badly that the letter-writers

decided it had been right to close the gates; 'we then blessed God for our present escape, effected by means unforeseen, and against our wills'. Once again, divine intervention was being forwarded as the cause of the events in Derry.

On this same Monday John Cowan of St Johnston brought a company of foot into the city, while Captain John Forward and William Stewart brought in between two and three hundred horse. The troops were welcomed, but manpower was not as short as ordnance. That was to be the responsibility (among other things) of David Cairnes when he got to London. In the meantime, while the ship that would carry him was readied, Cairnes fashioned six companies from the enlarged pool of battle-ready men. He set sail for England on the 11th. He did not get far. The weather was so abysmal he had to return to Derry. He would have to wait until the New Year before it was sufficiently calm for him to set sail again.

Around this time, the Mayor, sheriffs and citizens prepared a declaration. It summarized events in much the same way as the letters had, then continued, 'we have resolved to stand upon our guard, and to defend our walls, and not to admit of any Papists whatsoever to quarter amongst us'. Confessional purity had been more or less established with the expulsions (although several Catholics remained) and now the authorities were committed to maintaining it.

In London King James could see his power slipping away. On 27 November he had summoned a council of peers and declared his determination to call a Parliament, dismiss Catholics from office and appoint envoys to negotiate with William. It was too little, too late. England was in the grip of anti-Catholic hysteria, partly the product of the so-called 'Third Declaration', which alleged a massacre of Protestants was imminent. Williamites had produced this inflammatory concoction, though it purported to come from William himself. It described the world as the anti-Jacobites wished it to be, and many subscribed to its values.

James was beleaguered. He sent his queen and the infant Prince of Wales to France. Then, on the night of 11 December, he sneaked out of the palace. As Tyrconnell had years before, he fled eastwards down the Thames, with the intention of going to the continent. At some point, he threw the Great Seal of the kingdom into the water.

In the capital the news spread rapidly that the king had gone. There was rioting, and the next day it was widely rumoured that disbanded Irish soldiers from the English army were killing Protestants. This, of course, was untrue, but the mob believed it. Property perceived as Catholic was attacked, as were individual Catholics. Peers and ministers of the kingdom, along with the Council of London, were appalled by the popular violence, and the peers decided to send a delegation to William. At the same time they endeavoured to find James and bring him home. The City invited William to London.

The hapless James had only reached Sheppey because his boat missed the tide. Although he had disguised himself, he attracted the attention of some sailors who assumed he was a Jesuit who had fled the London mob. They handled him extremely roughly, as did the crowd at Faversham where he was taken, and the treatment was in no way ameliorated when his identity was discovered. When the Earl of Ailesbury, who was sent to rescue James from the inn where he was held, arrived, he found the king close to breakdown.

On 16 December he was returned to London. At some point he held his last council meeting, when it was decided to replace Tyrconnell with the Earl of Grenard. An express messenger was sent to Ireland with these instructions but they were never effected.

James's father, of course, had been executed after a regime change, and James must surely have feared the same fate awaited him. But William was far too adroit to do something as coarse as execute his father-in-law. He didn't want James dead, just far away. Within twenty-four hours he had started the process that would achieve this end. On 17 December he ordered a detachment of Dutch Blue Guards to march on London and secure the approaches to St James's Palace, where James had re-established his court. That night, in pounding rain, the troops surrounded the building, and stood, match lit, ready to fire if need be, while their commanders counselled James's guard to leave. The guard chose discretion over valour and withdrew. Three envoys sent by William now entered. James was woken and apprised of the situation. He was also advised to with-draw, which he did under Dutch guard. Later that day he was lodged in a house facing the Medway estuary. From there he would soon make his second, and this time successful, escape attempt.

Although the king was out of the picture, old anxieties remained, especially with regard to Ireland, where the king's man, Tyrconnell, was still in charge. Some Irish nobles of the 'English interest' met in the Duke of Ormond's house in St James's.* They drew up an address which begged the Prince of Orange to demand Tyrconnell yield his sword of office and to arrest all Irish papists in London and elsewhere. Their thinking was that if the Irish knew their countrymen were held in England, they might be dissuaded from massacring Protestant settlers in Ireland.

William assented to both proposals. He sent a message to Tyrconnell demanding his capitulation, and every Irish officer from the Jacobite regiments in England on whom hands could be laid was seized. Although this pleased those who had demanded action, it was far from all that they wanted. From their point of view, the news from Ireland was dire and had been for a couple of years. Their ambition was nothing less

---

*Tyrconnell's old adversary was now dead. This duke was his grandson.

than the military subjugation of the island. This, in turn, would mean an emphatic reassertion of the settlers' position and a final settling of the land issue.

But William hadn't the resources necessary to deal with Ireland in this way; he was only just inside the door. Until recently the army in England had been against him, at least in theory: it was by no means certain that all of its officers and men would acquiesce to his elevation to the throne. And he certainly couldn't spare the army he had brought from Holland, which was needed in England until he reckoned he was secure. The Treasury was empty; the sailors in the navy were owed back pay. William was in no position to hire mercenaries to police Ireland. All he could do at this stage was show willing.

When the news reached Tyrconnell that the gates of Derry had been slammed in the faces of Antrim's troops, he was 'inflamed by the news almost to madness'. He reacted as he had after the Comber letter had come to his attention. On that occasion he had summoned 'the chief Protestants of Dublin to the Castle and, with his usual energy of diction, invoked on himself all the vengeance of heaven if the report was not a cursed, a blasted, a confounded lie'. Then, finding his oaths were not convincing his listeners, he had pulled off his wig and flung it on the fire. Now he repeated this presumably satisfying action. Tyrconnell had good cause to be angry, even if he was largely to blame for mismanaging the transfer of power from Mountjoy's outgoing garrison to the Earl of Antrim's incoming troops. Derry controlled the north-west. It was vital to regain control of it.

Tyrconnell calculated that Mountjoy was the man for the job. Though his regiment had arrived in the capital only three days before, and was exhausted after having travelled over a hundred miles in appalling weather, Tyrconnell ordered them to march straight back and secure Derry again. So Mountjoy and the regiment retraced their steps to Omagh. From there, Mountjoy dispatched Captain McCausland to Derry with a message: he wanted a parley in Raphoe.

When McCausland arrived in Derry, he was at a loss to know whom to approach. The corporation established by King James had fallen from grace, the more so since the Deputy Mayor, Buchanan, had strenuously argued for the admittance of Antrim's troops. People from the previous regime, Protestant and temperamentally Williamite, now staffed the semi-military administration. But, as they lacked legal authority, it would be difficult to make any binding agreements with them. In the end, Alderman Norman and John Mogridge, a city burgess, met Mountjoy at Raphoe. The commander offered a free and general pardon if they surrendered the garrison and their arms. Back in Derry, the deputation urged acceptance of the offer. It was rejected.

While Mountjoy had been marching north, Phillips had been hard at work. His efforts made compromise much less likely.

> The Governor had already formed 8 companies of good effectual men in the city, and armed them out of the stores, and with some management quieted all factions and tumults, and reduced all things to good order, so that all were unanimously resolved to stand it out till they received a return to the address sent into England.

The ever-patient Mountjoy suggested further negotiations. This time the venue was Mongavlin Castle, near St Johnston. Phillips and others were delegated to conclude an agreement with him. At the meeting they demanded that only Protestant troops could enter the city; their own armed companies would remain; and there would be a general pardon.

Obviously Mountjoy could not agree to this; instead he upped the ante. He intimated to the city's plenipotentiaries that he would move next morning to the gates of the city and demand entrance.

Phillips and the others returned to Derry, where their report made the citizens more combative than ever. But they acknowledged they were in a weak position: they had few arms and little powder. They also knew that Mountjoy, as Master of Ordnance, was aware of this. Furthermore, on an island full of enemies, why dismiss one of the few allies you have left?

The next morning, 12 December, Mountjoy did as he'd promised and appeared at Bishop's Gate. He found it closed. Inside the walls furious arguments raged. A new delegation – ten strong, including Phillips, and James Steward, one of the apprentice boys – was sent out to negotiate. This was the start of several days of hard bargaining, during which the Derry delegation simply reiterated their demands.

Meanwhile, on 13 December, sixty miles to the south, the people of Enniskillen – a village of about eighty houses clustered round an old castle – learned that two companies of Sir Thomas Newcomen's regiment were marching towards them. They decided to keep these soldiers out, just as the Derry citizens had kept the Redshanks out, and for the same reason. In a few hours a force was assembled. It numbered two hundred foot and about the same number of horse. Newcomen's companies, unaware of attitudes in Enniskillen, continued to advance. They had a supply of arms that they distributed to labourers and others who had attached themselves to the regular soldiers. These irregulars were less interested in fighting than in pillaging Enniskillen once the new garrison had gained entry.

Rather than wait to be attacked, the Enniskillen force sallied out and fell on the Jacobite troops at Lisbellaw on 16 December. At the sight of such a formidable and unexpected body of foot and horse approaching, the freshly armed camp followers quickly dispersed. The regular soldiers soon followed, fleeing to Cavan. Encouraged by their triumph, the victors set about devising plans for the defence of the whole district.

Gustavus Hamilton, an officer who had lost his commission during Tyrconnell's purge, was appointed Governor and Commander-in-Chief. Sympathetic local blacksmiths started forging weapons. Local country houses were fortified and Protestants enlisted. Catholics in the town were put under surveillance. Tyrconnell's ambitions for a subjugated Ulster had suffered another setback.

Back in Derry the negotiations between Mountjoy and the citizens at last bore fruit in the form of the 'Articles of Agreement'. This fastidious document indicates both the degree to which resolve had hardened and the depth of fear in those who wanted to keep out the Catholics. It was agreed that Mountjoy would, within fifteen days, publish a general pardon under the Great Seal for all offences against the law, murder excepted. Until then only two companies were to be quartered in the city, to be commanded by Mountjoy's second-in-command, Lieutenant-Colonel Robert Lundy, a Scottish Episcopalian. He had been a member of the Derry garrison since 1685. When the fifteen days were up, half of any other companies quartered in the city until 1 March should be Protestants. The citizens would keep their guards and watches and no stranger would be permitted inside the walls with firearms or swords, or allowed to lodge at night, unless authorized by Lundy and the two sheriffs. Before 1 March, if the soldiers of Mountjoy's regiment were ordered somewhere else, they would leave the city in the hands of its own levies and not admit another garrison. No soldiers of Antrim's regiment would be quartered in the city before 26 March. Provision was also made for inhabitants of the city and suburbs who wished to leave. There would be no embargo on ships leaving the harbour. Furthermore, if any ship that had sailed from Derry since 7 December was stopped in any port on account of the late commotion, it was to be released immediately.

The Articles bound Mountjoy to intervene on behalf of

named individuals who might suffer persecution later because they had openly supported William of Orange. Two of Mountjoy's own sons were resident in the city at the time, and the Articles stated that they should remain there as a pledge for the full enactment of all the proposals.

The Articles did not specify the composition of the first two companies who were to be under Lundy's command, but Mountjoy knew that the mood in Derry meant Catholic soldiers would not be welcome. He ordered Lundy to go to Strabane, quarter his six companies there, then purge all Catholics from the ranks and replace them with Protestants. The city – still distrustful – sent observers with him to verify this. The regiment's remaining four companies, 50 per cent Catholic, were quartered at Strabane, Newtownstewart and Raphoe until they too had been thoroughly reformed. Mountjoy clearly was acting in good faith. Phillips now resigned his post, and Mountjoy appointed Lundy in his place. In theory, James II was again in control of his city.

The Articles were signed on 21 December. The citizens had finally obtained a garrison congenial to their religious opinion. Had he known of this, Tyrconnell certainly would not have approved. Three days earlier he had written to Antrim, instructing him to have his regiment ready to march on Derry at an hour's notice. But once the Articles of Agreement, with their 'no Redshanks' clause, became known to him, he realized it was a fait accompli. Derry, for the time being, was a lost cause. Tyrconnell contented himself with issuing a summons: Mountjoy must return to Dublin at once. Friends pleaded with the latter not to go, but he was a good soldier: he obeyed orders.

Around this time, the full extent of the events in England were still unknown in Ireland. But those on both sides of the religious divide were starting to draw correct conclusions. A delegation from Enniskillen arrived and met Governor Lundy to petition his support for their action. He advised them to submit to the king's (that is, James's) authority. The delegation went to see Mountjoy, who was still at Newtownstewart. He offered the same advice.

> 'What, my Lord?' cried one of the emissaries, a man called Cathcart. 'Are we to sit still and be butchered?'
> 'The King will protect you,' replied Mountjoy, pedantically.
> 'If all we hear is true,' Cathcart famously replied, 'his Majesty will find it hard enough to protect himself.'

While Mountjoy was dispensing advice with which no Jacobite could find fault, he was simultaneously ordering that the Derry garrison's guns should be mounted on carriages and repaired. He also set other measures in motion that would improve the city's defences. Then he left for Dublin and what he expected to be a stormy interview with Tyrconnell. He was right to be concerned because Tyrconnell was furious when he heard of the assistance Mountjoy had given to Derry's defenders.

Meanwhile, on the Medway, the man who was still officially the king considered his future. It had not escaped his attention that the guard was somewhat lax. All the signs seemed to indicate that this time an escape would succeed. On 23 December James slipped from the house and headed for the continent. It was just what his son-in-law wanted him to do. If he had remained in England, James would have been a focus of opposition. He arrived in France and was reunited with his family at Saint Germain-en-Laye, a palace near Versailles, on Christmas Day 1688.

James's flight and the loss of Derry were, of course, separate events. However, the anonymous author of the *Jacobite Narrative of the War in Ireland* made an inspired and typically acerbic connection. James, he wrote, had been too trusting of his Protestant army in England and so had lost that kingdom. In Ireland, Lord Deputy Tyrconnell had similarly put too much faith in Irish

Protestants, 'and by that error lost Ireland, as the king himself had lost England'. And 'Londonderry proved to be the *prima mali labes*, the source of that kingdom's loss', concluded the writer. Derry, a poorly fortified city in the north-west corner of the island, was about to assume its central position in the history of Ireland.

CHAPTER NINE

Diplomacy and Skulduggery

The end of 1688 had been eventful. By contrast, the start of the following year was a time of consolidation as James and William, Tyrconnell and the citizens of Derry prepared their next moves.

In London, the path to the throne was clear, but the terms on which it could be occupied were not, and a technical difficulty impeded a solution. With no monarch to summon it (nor indeed a Great Seal with which to mark the summons papers), the Parliament that would be the forum for solving the dilemma could not assemble. On 26 December William convened an informal council of peers and sympathetic Members of the last Parliament. It was decided to follow the practice of the 1660 restoration: William would issue letters of summons, and a convention, rather than a Parliament, would meet on 22 January.

This convention decided that Mary, James's Protestant daughter, and William should reign in a dual monarchy. It also passed a Declaration of Rights, which was presented to William and Mary along with the offer of the throne. This was a comprehensive reassertion of old rights and liberties, as well as a retrospective criticism of James's reign. It was read at the start of the coronation ceremony on 13 February, but it was not a condition that William and Mary accepted in order to acquire the throne, as William made clear in the speech he gave. The Declaration became statutory as a Bill of Rights at the end of the year. The bill lacked the legal machinery required to enforce its provisions, such as regular parliaments – it was William's need for cash that would ensure these. The belief that it was the source of the British constitution remains a popular mis-nomer, but it certainly did debar Catholics from the throne. To contemporary Catholics, it sent an unmistakable message: they were not wanted, respected or trusted, and there would never again be a Catholic King of England.

Early in 1689, members of the old Derry Corporation – the one Tyrconnell had displaced – reassumed civic authority. A meeting of the Common Council was held in the Town Hall on 2 January. By unanimous agreement, they endorsed them-selves and among those who resumed authority were several members of the former Protestant Common Council, including John Campsie who was reinstated as mayor. David Cairnes left the city again, the weather having settled, and sailed for London.

In anticipation of the siege that was universally expected, another meeting was held in the same building around the same time to raise funds. Voluntary subscriptions amounting to £100 were raised. Now there was the cash to buy ordnance, of which there was still precious little within the walls. James Hamilton,* a merchant, travelled to Scotland and bought forty-two barrels of powder. When it was learned that a small barque sent from Dublin with thirty barrels of powder for Antrim's regiment was stuck on the coast of County Down, city officials arranged for its seizure. Simultaneously, local luminaries contributed supplies to be stored for use when the siege came. A committee then set about forging alliances with other pockets of resistance, notably

---

*Not to be confused with Captain James Hamilton, of whom more later.

that in Enniskillen, which commanded the principal pass between Connacht and Ulster, and so effectively blocked any advance on Derry from that side.

In Dublin the Lord Deputy was growing angrier by the day. The north-west, with Derry at its centre, was steadily extricating itself from his control and becoming a focus of dissent to his regime. Tyrconnell blamed Mountjoy. The Protestant officer was a dissembler who feigned loyalty to James while secretly aiding those who sided with William of Orange. Given all that had happened, it is not difficult to see how Tyrconnell came to this conclusion. He was anxious 'to remove the said Mountjoy . . . that he might not now take the occasion of heading the considerable numbers of Protestants, who in all likelihood would choose him for their general, as being the best soldier amongst them all, and the most leading Protestant of Ulster'. To achieve his exit Tyrconnell made 'a wise and sensible dissimulation to get him away'. When Mountjoy finally arrived in Dublin, having left his regiment in the north, he did so on the very day that news reached Tyrconnell of King James's flight. The Lord Deputy thought fast and told Mountjoy 'to go in his name to the King at Saint Germain-en-Laye, in France, to demonstrate to His Majesty the necessity of yielding Ireland to the Prince of Orange . . . The Lord Deputy joined with him in commissioning Sir Stephen Rice, a Catholic . . . to the end his design might be less suspected.' That 'design', of course, was Mountjoy's neutralization (and possibly elimination), which was to be achieved by means of a damning message Rice would deliver to the king.

Mountjoy, though, was puzzled. He suggested a Catholic would be a better choice for the job, as 'in all likelihood the King would sooner give credit' to a Catholic than to a Protestant. After further discussion, however, Mountjoy agreed to go, knowing he had no choice. Tyrconnell was at pains to dampen any suspicions or doubts the doomed Mountjoy might have.

On 10 January Mountjoy's relations with Tyrconnell were seemingly so cordial that he felt bold enough to submit to the Lord Deputy his proposals for the maintenance of peace in the kingdom. Among other things, he suggested a moratorium on all military organization until the king's will was known. (At this time, irrespective of the events in England, both Tyrconnell and Mountjoy regarded James as their king.) On the same day as he dispensed this advice (which the Lord Deputy received politely) Mountjoy sent a letter north. Tyrconnell, he said, had accepted his proposals. He added that he hoped his Protestant friends would not think, on account of the journey he was about to undertake, that he intended to betray them. He ended with a confident flourish: 'Let the people fall to their labour, and think themselves in less danger than they believed.'

Mountjoy and Rice left the same day for France. Once they reached the court in exile, Rice went immediately to James and delivered his secret message. Mountjoy, he explained, was a traitor, widely regarded by the Protestants of Ireland as their friend and leader. The rest of the island was staunchly Jacobite, and if James were to land there, preferably with a French army, they would rise in arms and support their king. Tyrconnell had skilfully dovetailed two elements. Mountjoy in France would weaken those settlers who sympathized with the Williamites, and weakened settlers made Jacobite triumph on the field of battle all the more likely. Even more astute were the further secret instructions Tyrconnell had given his emissary. Should James show any unwillingness about an Irish adventure, Rice was to secure a private audience with Louis XIV and offer Ireland to France as a province. In the event Rice had no need to see Louis because James was convinced and Mountjoy's duplicity was believed. The latter was escorted to the Bastille.

Dark thoughts must now have crossed Mountjoy's mind. The king had been told he was a traitor and he was in jail. Surely he was on his way to the block. But James could be generous, and he made it known that he did not wish the traitor punished. However, he also didn't want him in England or, worse, Ireland. James suggested he be exiled somewhere far away, but the French, who held jurisdiction, decided Mountjoy might prove useful in the future, so kept him under lock and key.

In England the news coming from Ireland, and especially from Derry, was bad. Members of the city's corporation had been bombarding William and Mary with letters. They wrote of slender resources and tremendous anxieties. But then from Dublin came several letters from William Ellis, secretary to Tyrconnell. The recipient was John Temple, eldest son of Sir William Temple, a former ambassador at The Hague and a man who owned property in Ireland. Temple had a wide range of connections that made him an ideal intermediary. In his letters Ellis implied that the Lord Deputy, having listened to the Protestant point of view over the past few weeks, might switch sides. English and Scottish Catholics had accepted William, so why not an Old English Irish Catholic, even if he had devoted his life to restoring land to his fellows?

Then the Irish Chief Justice, John Keating (the last Protestant judge),* reported that Tyrconnell would be willing to disband the army and abandon government if the new regime guaranteed that the status of Catholics would be as it had been at the end of the reign of Charles II. This letter was sent to Sir John Temple (the other John Temple's uncle), the Irish Solicitor General, who was in England at the time.

This seemed a tantalizing opportunity. If Tyrconnell really did want to join the Williamites, Ireland could be secured, with the English interest and the settlers protected. That, in turn,

---

*Keating would not stay Chief Justice for long. He was indicted for treason by William and Mary's administration and committed suicide in 1691.

would lock out the French. An army (which the Williamites could not spare anyway) would not have to be sent over the Irish Sea. Thousands of lives would be saved. Obviously, the envoy sent to persuade Tyrconnell to defect would have to be trusted by both sides. John Temple remembered Richard Hamilton, one of the Jacobite army officers seized the previous December and held on the Isle of Wight as surety against Catholic attacks on settlers in Ireland. He was a Catholic of Scottish stock who had lived in Ireland for some time, a favourite of Tyrconnell, and connected with the most important Irish family of the English interest: his mother was a sister of the 1st Duke of Ormond, the Lord Lieutenant who had served the House of Stuart so faithfully. Finally, and perhaps most importantly, he had made peace with the victors after his arrest. He seemingly bore the Williamites no ill will.

Hamilton was sounded out. Would he attempt to persuade Tyrconnell to surrender? And, if he failed, would he promise to return to England? When a gentleman gave his word, he was usually believed, and Richard Hamilton agreed to all conditions. Temple guaranteed his trustworthiness. William of Orange ordered the issue of a safe-conduct pass.

Hamilton sailed to Ireland in January. His arrival was later described to a committee of the House of Lords that had been appointed to look into Irish affairs. The witness was a Major Richard Done:

> hearing that a vessel was arrived from England at Ring's
> End, [Done] went . . . to see who the passengers were. He
> counted seventy men in red coats, and among them Col.
> Richard Hamilton, together with eleven other officers. The
> Colonel, whom he knew well, went with several others to a
> tavern, and from the next room [Done] heard plainly their
> discourse.
>   After salutations, the Colonel broke out into loud
> laughter, saying he could not forbear it, thinking how finely

he had shammed the Prince of Orange into a belief that he had interest and inclination enough to prevail with Tyrconnell to lay down the sword and submit to him.

Colonel Dempsey, who had come to congratulate him, replied, 'What interest could you have in the Prince, or how got you it, to persuade the Prince to believe you?'

Hamilton answered, 'I wanted not friends to persuade him into a confidence of me, on which account I got my liberty and this' – (pulling out a pass from the Prince, which he said was for himself, eleven officers, and a hundred and forty soldiers, which were all he could get account of to be in Liverpool, Chester, and Holyhead, else he believed he could have got a pass for seven hundred as well as seven score, adding, 'Had King James been so well advised as he might, he need not have come out of England for want of friends to support him.')

After much other discourse to the same effect, a coach came to the door with Sir Richard Nagle and Secretary Ellis. Hamilton said jokingly to Ellis, 'How, Brother Sham, are you there? The Kingdom of Ireland is beholden to you . . .'

Then turning to Nagle, he said, 'Could you think, Sir Richard, that Ellis could have such an interest with the Lord Deputy as to persuade him to lay down the sword and submit to the Prince?'

Sir Richard replied, 'It is a wonder to me that it could be thought or credited that he could do it alone, there being in England at that time many Irish gentlemen who . . . could have informed the Prince that Ellis's interest was not sufficient to do it.' After this they took coach and went away together.

For Major Done to have gone to see who had arrived seems plausible. But why did he then follow Richard Hamilton to the tavern? Was his testimony the truth?

It is important to remember that the major was talking to the winning side the year after the war had ended. He certainly knew what his questioners didn't want to hear: that Richard Hamilton owed his escape to Williamite naivety. It was much better to depict him as a cunning Irishman who had hood-winked the gullible English.

In fact, by the time Hamilton arrived, the task he had prom-ised to perform had become impossible. Tyrconnell had already set in motion a process that he could not control. The Irish believed that the Acts of Settlement were about to be set aside and that their lands were to be given back. The popular mood was set against conciliation and capitulation. Indeed, when rumours circulated that Tyrconnell was not averse to negotiating with William, the populace had been furious. The message came back to Tyrconnell that if he persisted, Dublin Castle would be burned, with him inside it, and Ireland would be offered to France. Tyrconnell was forced to issue a public statement: he had never intended to submit to the Williamites; he was trying merely to confuse them. In the month up to Hamilton's arrival positions had hardened still further. Tyrconnell couldn't turn now, even if he wanted to: the Irish simply wouldn't allow it. Hamilton's defenders always maintained that he travelled to Ireland in good faith. However, he quickly judged that his task was untenable, gave up on it, and, naturally, decided to join his co-religionists rather than go back to certain imprisonment in England. His Williamite critics never forgave him for not return-ing, though, partly because it was betrayal and partly because he provided a huge boost to Irish morale. In another testimony to the Lords committee, Sir Oliver St George reported, 'the Papists in Dublin made fires when Dick Hamilton came over, saying he was worth 10,000 men'.

In France the exiled James was telling his story to anyone who would listen. These notorious narratives, in which he betrayed little awareness that he was in any way implicated in his own tragedy, won him no friends. Madame de la Fayette observed that the more the French court saw of him, the less they pitied him for the loss of his kingdom. Nevertheless, the canny and ambitious Louis XIV saw that James in Ireland could divert a great deal of Williamite aggression that might otherwise be directed at the French in Europe. He agreed to send an observer to Ireland to assess the situation and explore the possibility of French aid for a Jacobite campaign there.

The Marquis de Pointis, Louis' ambassador, arrived five or so days after Mountjoy and Rice had left. With him travelled a Captain Roth, who carried a letter from James for Tyrconnell. In it James expressed the hope that 'you will be able to defend yourself and support my interest there till summer at least'. All that Louis had so far agreed was to send seven or eight thousand muskets, 'not being willing to venture more arms or any men till he knows the condition you are in'.

On 29 January the Lord Deputy replied to his king: 'I have been . . . in great disquiet not to have heard one word from your Majesty until the arrival of Monsieur de Pointis'. What particularly exercised him was James's request for information: 'I thought your Majesty very well informed, by my continual applications and care to inform you of every particular relating to [Ireland] since your accession to the crown.' He had gathered from de Pointis that Louis was prepared 'to succour us with arms and ammunition' but, unfortunately, he found the Frenchman 'indifferent upon that article which most concerns us, and of which we stand in greatest need, which is money'. Without cash, and he was emphatic about this, 'the Kingdom must be lost'. He could gather men, he continued, but 'having no money to subsist, all the order and care I can take will not hinder the ruin of the country, nor a famine before midsummer'. It was the timeless problem of all administrations trying to muster armies: without money for subsistence, the army would prey on the civilian population and destroy everything. What especially puzzled Tyrconnell was the parsimony of a Catholic monarch – Louis – towards a Catholic country in such dire need.

He next went on to enumerate the ratio of Catholics to Protestants in each area. Ulster had the fewest Catholics by virtue of having the highest number of 'Scotch Presbyterians'. The Catholics, he was adamant, were unanimously for James and against William, whereas, among the Protestants, 'generally tainted with the Principles of England, there are not in the whole Kingdom one hundred that may be relied on to serve your Majesty'. Indeed, in Sligo and several parts of Ulster they were in rebellion.

The coming conflict – and Tyrconnell was not afraid to say so – would be one in which the combatants would be aligned, more or less, along confessional lines. It would be nasty but there was everything to play for. For this reason Tyrconnell spent the balance of the letter denigrating the French for their lack of support and reiterating his desperate need for cash, for want of which he believed Ireland would be lost. He was careful, however, to end on a positive rather than a negative note. 'If, sir,' he concluded, 'Your Majesty will come hither and bring . . . arms, ammunition and some officers, . . . you shall entirely be the master of this kingdom and of everything in it.'

In February Tyrconnell sent another letter to James. Pointis had been and gone. He had been sent on his way with 'a note of the things of which we have immediate need in which I have been very modest for fear of turning away the King of France from the design of aiding us by asking too much at the beginning. [But] what I have asked is the least for our mere subsistence.'

At James's court in exile the letters had an immediate impact. So there was an army of forty thousand Jacobites assembled and more to be found. Admittedly, they were poorly equipped, being mostly armed with simple pointed staves that weren't even metal tipped, and they were woefully short of artillery. But they were at least vehement for the cause. The king knew he must travel to Ireland, and soon.

Vauban, the great French military strategist, now approved an expedition. The French agreed to commit a force sufficient to help James recover Ireland. This would comprise a small group of advisers to steer the Jacobite Irish in the right direction, plus five thousand or so French soldiers. In return, an equivalent number of (less accomplished) Jacobite Irish troops must take their place in France. With this commitment, small, peripheral Ireland became momentarily central in the great continental struggle for supremacy between France and her enemies.

When Vauban initiated the operation, the French endgame was not James restored to the throne in Britain but James pre-eminent in Ireland. Louis simply wanted to deflect William's limited military resources away from continental Europe. With James at his rear, William would have to keep a large proportion of his troops in England. The French offer was modest but, given the nature of their ambition, they believed their aid was pitched at the right level. Three of Ireland's four provinces were quiescent, and there was serious anti-Jacobite opposition only in Ulster. Derry was the core of this, but it could not hold out for long as a solitary Williamite island marooned in a Jacobite sea.

However, if French ambition was modest, James's was not. He viewed Ireland as a stepping-stone to recover his other kingdoms. This divergence between James and his French sponsor's ambitions was never resolved.

In the early spring of 1689 the king's forces bound for Ireland assembled in the Breton port of Brest. The English speakers who gathered there included James's illegitimate sons by Marlborough's sister Arabella Churchill, the Duke of Berwick and Lord Henry Fitzjames. The former would turn out to be brave and useful; the latter an incompetent drunk. There were also English notables who had followed James into exile, such as the Bishop of Chester and Lord Melfort, James's cranky chief minister. High-caste officers mingled with lower-caste soldiers, such as a certain Captain Talbot, who may have been Tyrconnell's illegitimate son. Among the French contingent, the most important was the Comte d'Avaux, the principal French adviser assigned by Louis to James. He carried with him half a million gold crowns but had been instructed by his crafty monarch to hold back two hundred thousand and to let no one know he had them. Next in seniority were Conrad, Count de Rosen, a professional soldier who was to be Commander-in-Chief, then Lieutenant-Generals Maumont (who also carried a secret stash of money) and Pusignan, Major-General Léry and the Marquis de Pointis, returning to Ireland as an artillery officer. The artillery was the weakest branch of Tyrconnell's army and the most in need of expert guidance. There were four hundred captains, lieutenants, cadets and gunners who would organize and train the Jacobite army in Ireland. The French also provided muskets for twenty regiments, with powder and ball to match, and, of course, the five thousand French soldiers. But the Jacobites were going to need more muscle, so Louis had granted facilities in France where continental Jacobite exiles could muster before following James to Ireland in a second fleet.

In Ireland Tyrconnell set about building up the army. Throughout the country Irish peasants abandoned their cabins and flocked to the colours. They believed the usurpers who spoke English and lived in fortified houses were to be crushed and that the old regime was to be restored, and with it their land. Catholic priests helped the recruitment drive: they exhorted parishioners to arm and prepare for the day when they would fight for the faith.

The Irish army under Ormond had comprised eight regiments. Under Tyrconnell, it would grow to forty-eight regiments. An army of this size needed thousands of officers, and commissions were granted without question. Cobblers, tailors and footmen, as well as gentlemen, as Macaulay put it, were given companies to command. In addition to the fifty thousand regular soldiers, there were a further fifty thousand irregulars. The administration disapproved of these, but found it could not suppress them.

The new Jacobite army was equipped with pikes, skeans and ash stakes. Every smith, cutler and carpenter in Ireland was put to work producing these weapons. For more sophisticated weapons and mounts, Tyrconnell turned to his traditional source of supply: the long-suffering settlers. Ultimatums were issued: either the settler coughed up or the newly enrolled and undisciplined soldiery would be sent in to loot the householder's property. Some firearms and horses were gathered in this way, but typically these were of poor quality.

Tyrconnell, as he continually emphasized, also needed cash – for ordnance, ships, materials and to pay his troops. First, he forbade the export of money, but this was not easy to enforce as many men of substance were leaving and taking their portable wealth with them. Then he made all newly commissioned officers responsible for feeding and clothing their soldiers for three months. He extended the liability to provide quarters for the new troops from tradesmen and innkeepers 'to all gentlemen of the best quality, if Protestants'. This allowed his new officers to impose themselves and their soldiers on settlers in the three provinces where the Jacobites exerted control. From Tyrconnell's point of view, these were sensible measures. Four-fifths of the population were Catholic, but four-fifths of all property was or had been in the hands of Protestants. The settlers, though, saw Tyrconnell's ordinances as granting permission to Catholics to steal from them. The results were predictably appalling. In West Cork, for example, the new levies marched around the country, stopping at empty Protestant houses and helping themselves to 'the property of the unhappy objects of their fury'. By rights, the settlers should have had redress in the courts, but they did not. At the Cork Assizes, Chief Justice Nugent described the depredations suffered by settlers as 'necessary evils'.

Along with property, livestock was another target. In the early spring – according to the lurid accounts in circulation – the Irish were wantonly slaughtering cows for their hides to make brogues, and killing sheep for their skins, leaving the carcasses to rot where they fell. Such poor husbandry boded ill for the future. If this was how animals were treated, how much worse would be the treatment meted out to people? Once again, with such tales the Ulster settlers had the materials to convince themselves that a repeat of 1641 was looming.

The fearful settlers in Derry were pinning their hopes on David Cairnes, who was in England acting on their behalf. Early February saw him secure an audience with the man who was shortly to be crowned King William III. The meeting was a prodigious success: the king directed that supplies must go immediately, in the *Deliverance* under Captain James Hamilton,* followed by troops. But it would take time before what had been promised could be effected. In the meantime, the settlers would have to fend for themselves.

By early spring, rumours were spreading through the north concerning Tyrconnell's expanding army. The Ulster gentry were 'with good reason, apprehensive, that this was not intended for their safety or advantage'. One John Hawkins, 'a young brisk zealous Protestant gentleman of good fortune and interest in the province . . . marched from place to place to stir up the Protestants to arm and assemble together for their own defence against the common enemy and abuses. And in a short time was so successful as to induce the whole province of Ulster to do so, except the towns of Carrickfergus and Armagh'. There were still Jacobite garrisons in these two towns. Protestant tenants were enlisted into newly raised regiments and armed with whatever weapons could be found. But to meet the threat Tyrconnell's

---

*The Hamilton family had Catholic and Protestant branches, and therefore members fighting on both sides. Captain James Hamilton was a nephew of Richard Hamilton, the man who had gone over to Tyrconnell, but James was a Protestant and a Williamite.

forces posed, ad hoc local arrangements were not going to be enough: a collective response by the settlers was needed. To this end, early in 1689, the gentry formed a Council of the North in Hillsborough, a village south-east of Belfast. Lord Mount-Alexander, to whom the Comber letter had been addressed, though he had no military qualifications, was chosen to command all the forces raised in Down, Antrim, Armagh and Monaghan.

Once established, the Council began to correspond with other leading northern rebels. They also drafted a letter to Tyrconnell's predecessor, Clarendon. They asked him to request 10,000 soldiers, 1,500 cavalry with mounts and 20,000 muskets with ammunition from William. If they had these resources, they promised to save Ireland for the Crown 'where unto we are willing to contribute with the hazards . . . our lives and fortunes'. The man selected by the Council to deliver this letter was Captain Baldwin Leighton. He had been a captain in Sir Thomas Newcomen's regiment. When news began to travel up from the south of what was happening there, Leighton had induced four other Protestant officers to resign with him and ally themselves with the resisters. One hundred and fifty other ranks followed this lead, and more would have done so had it not been judged safer to leave them in place. No wonder the letter Leighton carried spoke of him as one 'of whose sincerity to the Protestant and English interest we have a remarkable instance'.

In the middle of February good news arrived from London: William and Mary had been crowned king and queen. Council members were certain that Tyrconnell, seeing his position was hopeless, would switch sides or an army would come from England to tackle him. In light of this, Protestant military preparations were put on hold. The defectors from Newcomen's regiment neglected to train the raw levies raised by the Council. No efforts were made to stockpile weapons or supplies. A few companies were mustered but they were garrisoned haphazardly.

And the news of the coronation produced overconfidence as well as lethargy. The Council decided to attack Tyrconnell's garrison in Carrickfergus. The outcome was inconclusive, but in the aftermath both sides agreed that an account could be sent to Tyrconnell in Dublin. The man tasked with the job was a friar named O'Haggerty, who told Tyrconnell that the Protestants 'were untrained and had few experienced officers. The most part were without arms and, such as had them, their arms were . . . unfit for service.'

Armed with this information, Tyrconnell acted. On 7 March he issued a proclamation, promising a free pardon to all who laid down their arms and submitted. Those who 'still do persist in their wickedness by continuing in actual rebellion' would experience the full fury of Tyrconnell's forces. Mindful of the low esteem in which his own troops were held, he forbade them from using 'any violence to women, children, aged or decrepit men, labourers, ploughmen, tillers of the ground, or to any others who in these commotions demean themselves inoffensively, without joining the Rebels'. However, he placed Lord Mount-Alexander and nine others on a blacklist of arch rebels for whom there could be no pardon.* In tandem with the proclamation Tyrconnell issued orders to Richard Hamilton, now styled Lieutenant-General. He was to take a moderate army of about a thousand regular soldiers, two thousand new recruits and a few artillery pieces, head north, subdue the rebels and return Ulster to allegiance to James, whom, at any moment, Tyrconnell expected to arrive in Ireland.

James, however, had been delayed by the weather. He didn't step ashore in Kinsale until 12 March. According to his own memoirs, his Catholic subjects met him 'with all imaginable joy'. Being a cool soldier-statesman (as he liked to believe), he

---

*The others were Lord Kingston, Lord Massereene and his son Clotworthy Skeffington, Sir Robert Colville, Sir Arthur Rawdon, Sir John Magill, John Hawkins, Robert Sanderson and Francis Hamilton.

was unfazed by public rapture. His first concern was to land the arms, ammunition and money that had accompanied him from France, and lodge them in a fort. That done, he called to council Avaux and Melfort (who now exulted in the title Secretary of State for Ireland). The three men were addressed on the state of the kingdom by, among others, Sir Thomas Nugent and Lord Mountcashel. Orders were issued: local troops were to be re-formed into regiments, already enrolled dragoons were to be armed,* and the entire force was then to go to Dublin.

Meanwhile, Richard Hamilton and his forces were marching north. Like most seventeenth-century armies, they soon misbehaved and before long accounts of their misdeeds were circulating and provoking fear. For those who had declared for William, it looked bad: the Jacobites were coming for them and speeding ahead of Hamilton's army was a Presbyterian clergyman, Alexander Osborne. The day before Hamilton had received his marching orders, Osborne had been brought in front of Tyrconnell and told to carry the Lord Deputy's terms to the rebels. He proceeded to Loughbrickland, where he found the Council of the North in session. He informed them that if they surrendered to Hamilton, and handed over their arms and horses, they would enjoy a free pardon. If they demurred, they would be engaged in battle. They would also have to contend with the 'the country Irish (not of the army), men, women and boys, now all armed with half-pikes and bayonets, in the counties of Cavan, Monaghan, Tyrone and Londonderry', who would react badly to any resistance. They would 'immediately enter upon a massacre of the British in the said counties, which force and violence of the rabble His Excellency says he cannot

---

*At this time dragoons were mounted infantrymen. They rode to battle and fought on foot and got their name from their weapon, a short firearm called a dragon. Dragoons only became part of the cavalry in the eighteenth century.

restrain'. Osborne then described the approaching enemy: 'the Irish army, though their horses were good, yet their riders were but contemptible fellows, many of them having been lately cowherds et cetera'. He added that the Jacobites were short of ammunition. Finally, he counselled *against* accepting the Lord Deputy's terms. He based this advice on a simple observation: Tyrconnell had made promises to the Protestants in the three southern provinces and had broken his word. The consequences for the north, should they allow themselves to be similarly duped, would be disastrous. They would be reduced to 'Popery and slavery'.

It was a warning the Council was ready to heed. Captain Leighton was just back from England, and he bore a letter addressed to Mount-Alexander from William. The latter – while stressing that not all Catholics were hostile – said he approved of the measures taken by the Council. Furthermore, he promised, 'we are resolved to employ the most speedy and effectual means in our power for rescuing you from the oppressions and terrors you lie under'.

The Council's response to Tyrconnell was predictable, but couched politely. After all, there was no point in inflaming the Lord Deputy. The reply emphasized the Council's abhorrence of blood-letting and its determination to do all it could to avoid it. However, they could not lay down their arms. They would negotiate, but only if their lives, liberties and religious practices were guaranteed.

Meanwhile, Hamilton's army was closing in. A Council member, Sir Arthur Rawdon, took a small detachment to meet it. The two sides clashed at Dromore on 14 March, and the Ulster yeomen – untried, untested and undisciplined – fled in disorder. They were chased through the alleys of Hillsborough and into the countryside beyond. Protestant casualties were about one hundred, but the psychological impact of the collapse was huge: many Williamites immediately abandoned the ranks and went home. Later, they took 'protections' from Richard

Hamilton.* Mount-Alexander himself boarded an England-bound boat at Donaghadee and vanished from the story, leaving much more effective leaders of men and organizers of military resistance to take his place.

The best-known of these was the Reverend George Walker. He came from classic middle-ranking, middle-caste English stock that had gone to Ireland in the plantation era and prospered. In the early 1640s the Walker family, like thousands of other settlers, escaped the massacres and fled to England, to Yorkshire, where they had connections. While the wars raged in Ireland, the Walkers stayed away. After the restoration of Charles II the family returned. In 1662 George matriculated at Trinity College, Dublin, and then took holy orders. He married Isabella Barclay in about 1668 and became Rector of Donoughmore in the diocese of Armagh in 1674. He was still there in January 1689, aged forty-two or forty-three. As the news floated up from the south that Tyrconnell was creating a Catholic army, an apprehensive Walker reacted like many of his co-religionists: he raised a regiment (Lord Charlemont's) for the purpose of holding Dungannon against the Jacobites.

Of his early military exploits, Walker chooses to include only a single episode in his *True Account*, but it is a telling one. Like all the Ulster levies, Charlemont's regiment suffered from material shortages, which was bad for morale. Walker solved the problem by having a bag of mustard seed laid on one of the carriages. To his untrained soldiers, it looked like a bag of powder. Though deception was critical in war, it was unusual for an officer to boast about how he had deceived his own men. By doing so, Walker revealed an important facet of his character. He divided

---

*The householder who took protection agreed not to assist the enemy and in return received a guarantee that he would not be molested or ill treated by the Jacobite forces, in the form of a document signed by Richard Hamilton or other leading Jacobites that identified the bearer as a non-combatant and could be produced when necessary.

the world into two types: those who knew how to dupe and those who were duped. Walker believed that he belonged in the former category, and throughout his *True Account* he seeks to prove this. He seems unaware that he paints himself as condescending, self-serving and duplicitous. In his defence, it should be said he was also brave and he could write well. Given this mix of qualities, it is hardly surprising that he provoked strong feelings. Among his supporters he came to inspire unquestioning belief, while from his detractors he attracted a passionate hatred.

Walker's entry into the Derry story came on 14 March, when Governor Lundy ordered 'that the garrison at Dungannon should break up' and its troops fall back. Like most of his orders, this one provoked controversy. Dungannon had good natural defences and many provisions had been stored there in anticipation of the coming struggle. There were complaints, but orders were orders, and the garrison agreed to comply. However, the withdrawal, as predicted, led to most of the stores falling into Jacobite hands.

Around the same time the smaller garrisons of Monaghan and Cavan were also withdrawn. Wisely, the personnel burned everything before they marched off, in order to deprive the enemy of supplies. Lundy also ordered Lord Kingston to abandon Sligo, though the garrison there knew that without Sligo the north was open to invasion from the west, but they were duty bound to obey. Eventually the troops would withdraw and Kingston would sail to England. However, before doing this, he would see with his own eyes and hear with his own ears the consequences of Lundy's military mismanagement.

Some, such as George Walker, came to view Lundy as a closet Jacobite. How else could one explain his orders? The withdrawal from Dungannon, for instance, was seen as a ruse to ensure that the stores fell into Jacobite hands. And the withdrawals from Cavan, Monaghan and Sligo led to the concentration of all the Protestants and Williamites in Derry, presumably the better for Hamilton's army to eliminate them in one fell swoop. However, these theories about Lundy's motivation took no account of the precarious position in which he found himself. Back in December Mountjoy had persuaded Derry to accept Lundy and his troops as an alternative to the Redshanks. At that time, Lundy was technically in the commission of James II. The deal delivered Derry a garrison purged of Catholics, yet the fiction was maintained that authority still resided with the (Catholic) monarch. Since December Derry had changed radically. The Catholic corporation, imposed by Tyrconnell, was gone. The new administration was emphatically anti-Catholic and anti-Jacobite. The large number of refugees who flooded into the city reinforced its temper in this respect. As they saw it, this was now a confessional war, with the Jacobites on one side and the Williamites on the other. Allegiance was mostly organized along religious lines. The citizens, though they may have recognized the weakness of their position, could see no room for manoeuvre. With their hearts hardened by everything Tyrconnell's regime had done, or that they had heard his regime had done, they believed they had no choice but to fight. The alternative was annihilation.

For Lundy, the situation wasn't quite so clear cut. He was a professional soldier with limited resources and a city to maintain. He accepted the Williamite colour of those he had fallen among because he had no other choice, but he could not have been happy. There was a Jacobite army coming and Derry would be hard to defend: the city's fortifications were poor; its resources – powder, firearms, cannons – were meagre. And England, from where reinforcements could come, was far distant. Nor did he share the mood of his charges: he hadn't slammed any gates or openly rebelled. He didn't see his future as inevitably anti-Jacobite. Technically, he had been installed in Derry to hold the city for James, not William. If he crossed to William now and his old master prevailed, he would certainly be executed for treason. But if he failed to cross to William and James won, then he would be in just as much trouble. The paucity of communications at the time meant he never had the luxury of knowing the whole picture. When he ordered the Dungannon garrison to fall back, he did so to avoid a clash with Hamilton's more powerful army. He felt he needed to consolidate. However, had he been in possession of the full facts, he might have acted differently, as he would have known his position was less militarily precarious than he believed.

To start with, Captain James Hamilton, with his shipload of supplies, was already making his way across the sea. Furthermore, David Cairnes' lobbying had secured the promise of 'So considerable a body, as (by the blessing of God) may be able to rescue the whole kingdom and resettle the Protestant religion there'. In addition, when Cairnes left London for Derry on 12 March, he carried a letter with a message from William of Orange that was exactly what a hard-pressed commander such as Lundy would want to hear. As well as the conventional exhortations to encourage resistance with more than 'ordinary vigour' in order 'to keep out that deluge of Popery and Slavery' that threatened the city, the letter also confirmed that William had recommended the cause of Ireland to the two Houses of Parliament and was certain they would soon sanction the recovery of the whole kingdom, not just the city. To this end, Cairnes was instructed to perform an audit of men, arms and ammunition in Derry, and to investigate whether the surrounding hinterland could support a large body of troops.

At the time Cairnes had set sail, four regiments under the command of Major-General Percy Kirke were earmarked for Derry. However, for reasons that aren't clear, Kirke's attachment to the adventure was delayed, and only two regiments were selected for the task, the 9th and 17th Foot (later known as the Royal Norfolk and the Royal Leicestershire, respectively), the first commanded by Colonel John Cunningham, the second by Colonel Solomon Richards. Technically, Cunningham was the junior officer, but as his regiment was senior, the orders were addressed to him:

> You are, without delay, to repair to the quarters of the regiment under your command, and take care that it be in readiness to march to Liverpool at such a time as you shall appoint.
>
> Whereupon you are to go to Liverpool, and to inquire what ships there are in that port appointed to carry over the two regiments, where of you and Solomon Richards are Colonels, to the town of Londonderry; and whether the frigate order for their convoy be arrived there. And as soon as the said ships and frigate shall be in a readiness to sail, and fitted with all provisions necessary for the sustenance of the said regiments in their passage to the said town and for their return from thence, if there be occasion, you are . . . to embark with all speed.

At Liverpool, the orders continued, Cunningham would find muskets, which he was to use to make good any deficiencies among his own men. The rest he was to take to Derry and distribute among the local levies. At Chester, he was to locate Matthew Anderton, collector of customs, who would hand him £2,000 sterling. This money was for his soldiers' subsistence 'and for the defence of the place, in repairing and providing what shall be defective therein, and to such other uses as you, with the Governor of the said city, with whom you are to entertain a good correspondence and friendship, shall find necessary for our service'. Once these logistical matters had been sorted and the troops were aboard, Cunningham, 'wind and weather permitting', was to proceed to Derry.

On his arrival, his first duty was to ensure the city was still held by Williamites. Then he was 'to land the said regiments and stores, and to take care they be well quartered and disposed of in the said city'. He was to assure Lundy and the citizens 'of further and greater succours of men, arms, and money and provisions of war, coming speedily from England for their relief, and for the security of those parts'. This was perhaps the most important message Colonel Cunningham had to communicate. In the meantime, though, he was 'to make the best defence you can, against all persons that shall attempt to besiege the said city, or to annoy our Protestant subjects within the same'. In addition, he was required to report regularly on the situation in Derry, estimate what foodstuffs could be found locally, so stores would not have to be needlessly dispatched from England, and provide information on how well Captain James Hamilton had discharged his mission. If he judged it unsafe to land at Derry, Cunningham was free, at his own discretion, to land at Carrickfergus or Strangford. Otherwise, but only as a last resort, he was to return to Liverpool.

At the last minute, a postscript was added to these orders. The customs officer Anderton was to hand over a further £2,000. Of this, £500 was to be paid 'to our trusty and well-beloved Robert Lundy, Esquire, Governor thereof, as of our royal bounty, in part of the reward we intend him for his faithful services'.

Unfortunately, Governor Lundy, busily ordering one retreat after another, had no idea that any of this was on its way.

CHAPTER TEN

James in Ireland

On 14 March, while Richard Hamilton's army crushed the Williamite forces at Dromore, and Lundy ordered the garrison at Dungannon to retreat, Major-General Léry was landing at Kinsale with five thousand French troops. As had been agreed, an equal number of Jacobite troops then went in the opposite direction. The royal party rapidly moved from Kinsale to the city of Cork, where they lodged in the Bishop's Palace. In addition to the Bishop of Cork, James met some of the local Protestant clergy. The next day he made further efforts to improve relations with his disaffected Protestant subjects, in this instance the people of Bandon.

Two weeks earlier news had reached the town that the Earl of Clancarty was on his way with reinforcements for the garrison already inside the walls. Captain Fortescue, a captain in Clancarty's regiment but pro-settler in sympathy, organized a coup. The townsfolk turned on the garrison, killed some of them, confiscated their horses and weapons, and shut the gates. They then proclaimed their allegiance to William and Mary. The Jacobites reacted quickly. Lieutenant-General Macarthy (later Lord Mountcashel) appeared with a body of troops. Bandon agreed to pay £1,000 for a pardon. The Jacobite troops then pulled down Bandon's walls, on their commanding officer's instructions, so the inhabitants could not rebel again.

Now some of the ringleaders from Bandon were brought before James. They knelt and their minister begged the king's pardon for turning on his soldiers. James graciously forgave them. A few years earlier, in the West Country, James's treasonous subjects had been treated with extreme brutality for supporting Monmouth, but now the situation was different, and James had two sound reasons for adopting this benevolent approach. First, if he wanted to regain his throne, he would have to win over Ulster, where resistance to his rule was most concentrated. Even a bluff military-minded fellow like James could grasp that cruelty to the people of Bandon would deepen the resolve of the refractory northerners. Second, he knew any action in Ireland affected public opinion in England. It would be madness at this moment to inflame the already entrenched anti-Catholic sentiment in England by persecuting Protestants in Ireland.

Yet even as James played to his English audience, his natural constituency in Ireland was following a different agenda. As a result of Tyrconnell's reforms, they now had the machinery (notably the law and the army) to do this, and the actions of these bodies undermined the image James was attempting to cultivate. There was, for instance, the example of 'a Protestant Magistrate, one Brown, a gentleman worth five hundred pounds a year' that the historian, the Reverend John Graham, included in his *History of the Siege*:

> Brown had been in arms against the Rapparees,* and, as the assizes were going on when the King arrived, he put himself on his trial, expecting that in the case of his condemnation, the royal visit would insure him a pardon. But in this he was

---

*From the Irish *rapaire*, a sort of pike. Depending on your point of view, rapparees were either outlaw bands that preyed on houses and travellers or dispossessed Catholics attempting to right previous wrongs.

sadly mistaken; far from being wise or humane enough to begin with such an act of mercy, if not justice, the deluded monarch gave an appalling proof of the cruelty of his disposition, by leaving the unfortunate gentleman to his fate, who was immediately hanged and quartered.

This account may not be true,* but it certainly tallies with the prevailing opinion of James in the Protestant community: they saw him as a heartless Catholic bully.

Despite the disaster at Dromore, there were still four thousand committed men under arms in the north. Arthur Rawdon was still at large too, beaten but unbowed. With Hamilton's forces in the area it was critical to regroup and retreat, so Rawdon collected his troops and began to move them towards Coleraine. Progress was awkward and difficult, but one officer proved exceptionally courageous and had a particular gift for leadership. He was Major Henry Baker, aged forty-two, from an English family who had come to Ireland during the reign of Queen Elizabeth and acquired land in County Louth. In December 1688 he went north to join his co-religionists.

As Rawdon and his forces fell back, word spread through the settler communities of their disaster at Dromore, and, worse, that Hamilton's army with its terrifying camp followers were on their way. Macaulay describes these memorably as 'unclean birds of prey, which swarm wherever the scent of carrion is strong'. Of Hamilton himself, he adds, 'whatever power he might be able to exercise over his soldiers . . . [he] could not keep order among the mob of camp followers'. This was true.

For weeks settlers had been burning their furniture, pulling down their houses and moving north. Now, post-Dromore, panic set in:

---

*The author was writing long after the event, and was fiercely partisan.

the flight became wild and tumultuous. The fugitives broke
down the bridges and burned the ferryboats. Whole towns,
the seats of the Protestant population, were left in ruins
without one inhabitant . . . destroyed so utterly that no roof
was left to shelter the enemy from the rain and wind.

On 15 March Rawdon, his troops and the great body of refugees
now attached to them made it to Coleraine. Fifty years earlier
the town's rickety defences had saved many colonists and now it
looked as if they might have to do so again. These defences had
changed little in the intervening years: there was a mud wall and
deep ditch on three sides, with the River Bann, spanned now by
a wooden bridge, on the fourth. Fortunately for Rawdon, his
troops and the refugees, Hamilton had not opted for hot pursuit.
He was moving slowly.

The next day, Governor Lundy left Derry for Coleraine,
where he was to meet with the commander, Gustavus
Hamilton,* to discuss what to do next. Those he left behind in
Derry 'were not altogether pleased with Lundy's management of
affairs' so far. This opinion of him reached Coleraine before he
did. When he arrived, the expectation was that Derry, as the
larger and stronger partner, would provide help to resist Hamilton's
army. But Lundy said he could not offer powder or shot. Moreover, he thought it 'advisable to quit the town as soon as it
should be attacked'.

Lundy's primary duty was the defence of Derry, and he had a
point, but to the defenders in Coleraine he seemed like a weakling who would not stand up for his co-religionists. Now, with
the Jacobites approaching and Lundy failing to impress, trouble
was inevitable. 'Immediately after the conference, Lundy walked
towards the bridge, but the mob there, already suspecting his

---

*This was not the Gustavus Hamilton who was in charge in Enniskillen.

fidelity, imagined he was about to desert and drew up the bridge, while the guard presented their muskets and pikes at him.'

Lundy, now locked in Coleraine, had further conversations with the military authorities there. It was agreed that Lundy should return to Derry and that Gustavus Hamilton should manage events in the field. This reassertion of the status quo would not necessarily be agreeable to the mob who had raised the drawbridge. Accordingly, the next day, 18 March, Lieutenant-Colonel Whitney and a troop of soldiers were positioned on the bridge, 'lest the townsmen should again draw up their bridge to hinder Lundy's going away', and this time the Governor of Derry was able to leave.

Back in Derry, another ugly rumour was going round that Rawdon and some other officers in Coleraine intended to defect to the Jacobites and, in expectation of this, Lundy had decreed that 'in case the forces were beaten at Coleraine, the town of Derry would not let them into their gates'. Of course, Rawdon and the other officers were not about to cross over and no such order had been issued. However, given the febrile ambience in the city – it was packed with refugees ready to see a sell-out round every corner – it was believed. This was a particularly dangerous rumour since it combined the idea of disaster abroad – that the officers in Coleraine, the first line of defence against the Jacobite multitudes, were about to defect – with that of hard-heartedness at home. Governor Lundy had to take steps to quash it. To effect this, a declaration was drafted:

> For the wiping of which aspersion . . . it is hereby
> declared, . . . by Colonel Robert Lundy . . . the said . . . Sir
> Arthur Rawdon, and other officers . . . are . . . absolutely
> resolved to oppose the Irish enemy . . . and to continue the
> war against them to the last . . . for their own and all
> Protestants' preservation in the kingdom . . . [All] . . .
> Protestant . . . friends shall be received into this city. And, as
> much as in us lies, be cherished and supported by us.

The declaration was signed by Rawdon, other alleged turncoats and Lundy on 21 March. On the same day, which should have lightened the gloom, Captain James Hamilton and the *Deliverance* arrived with 480 barrels of powder, arms, ammunition and almost £600. (This was all the cash Hamilton was able to collect in Chester.)

Lundy read his orders from the king: he was to distribute the weapons and ammunition; break down bridges, cut dykes and sluices, if this improved Derry's capacity to defend herself; ensure the city's gates, guns, gun carriages and fortifications were in good order; demolish any houses and fell any trees that he thought would compromise the city's defence; erect palisades; spend the cash as he thought fit; report on the condition of Derry from time to time; and administer the oath of allegiance to the new monarchs to all officers, civil and military, in the city and garrison. This last command was problematic: because, before he could give the oath, he must take it himself. Rawdon and several others were aboard the *Deliverance* as Lundy read these orders. It seems that Lundy suspected they were snooping on him, because, maintaining he had private business to conduct, he asked the visitors to go out on to the deck (it was raining). He then closeted himself in the cabin with Captain Hamilton, which 'was much wondered at'. The presumption was that Lundy did not want to swear the oath to William and Mary because his heart was elsewhere.* This caused Lundy's relationship with the citizens of Derry to deteriorate still further. It didn't matter that he was building a ravelin† outside Bishop's Gate and already demolishing the suburbs beyond the walls so the Jacobites would have no shelter when they attacked. The hardliners in Derry no longer trusted him.

---

*Lundy *did* take the oath, as Captain Hamilton testified some months later before a parliamentary committee of inquiry. There were other witnesses, too – Colonel Stewart, Captain Henry Mervyn and Captain James Corry.

†An outwork of fortification, with two faces forming a sharp angle.

Accordingly, the next day, 'the Committee of Derry, and the Officers . . . desired Lundy might take the oaths before them all, for their greater satisfaction'. Lundy 'absolutely refused . . . on pretence of having taken them on board the day before'. His manner, here, as so often, was high handed and disdainful, which was the reason so many people later took against him.

Events in the north delayed Tyrconnell in Dublin. As a result, it was several days before he could make his way to Cork to greet his old protector.

> The King . . . did him an honour which sovereigns rarely pay their subjects, for having perceived him, he advanced to meet him at the door of the chamber and embraced him. He gave him the praises due to the unshakeable firmness which he had shown in his service, and did him the honour not only to make him dine at his table, but set him at his right and the Duke of Berwick at his left. In a word, the King gave him all the marks and signs of satisfaction that were due to such a subject and testified his esteem creating him duke.
>
> After he had received an exact account of all the affairs of Ireland, His Majesty held a council, in which the new Duke had the honour to take part.

Tyrconnell did not stint with the truth. He believed he had enough soldiers to maintain the king against his enemies, and Hamilton had triumphed at Dromore, but the Jacobites did not yet control Ulster. Coleraine, Enniskillen and Derry must all be taken. Tyrconnell also repeated that the king's troops in Ireland lacked arms, cavalry mounts, artillery, powder, ball, experienced officers and cash. James had not brought nearly enough from France to meet these needs. And what he had brought was of poor quality. These shortfalls had to be made good or the Jacobite project would founder.

This depressing forecast notwithstanding, the royal party had to take to the road. In the seventeenth century being seen was a critical part of the business of being a monarch. James left Cork on 20 March and proceeded with his retinue towards Dublin. While settlers were fleeing through the mud in Cavan, a hundred or so miles to the south it was a different story:

> All along the road, the country came to meet his majesty with staunch loyalty, profound respect, and tender love, as if he had been an angel from heaven . . . he could not but take comfort amidst his misfortunes at the sight of such excessive fidelity and tenderness for his person in his Catholic people of Ireland . . .
>
> The King made his entry into Dublin, on the 24 March, being Palm Sunday that year. The newly made Duke of Tyrconnell bore the sword of state before his master, while the lord mayor, Sir Michael Creagh, judges, [and] heralds formed an impressive procession behind. A Te Deum was sung in thanksgiving. Irish harpers and pipers played 'The King shall enjoy his own again.'

This was the *Jacobite Narrative*'s version of events. The Protestant Reverend Graham presented a starkly different interpretation:

> James made his public entry into Dublin in a triumphant manner, attended by a long train of British, French, and Irish together with Count d'Avaux, the French Ambassador. The magistrates of the city, and the popish ecclesiastics, met him in their proper habits, with the host borne before them in solemn procession . . . He took an early opportunity of dismissing the only two Protestants of rank or distinction in his army, merely on account of their religion. He refused the gallant Sarsfield commissions for two of that officer's Protestant relatives, saying that he would trust none of their religion. And on coming out from mass, immediately after his arrival in the metropolis, was heard to say, 'a Protestant stunk in his nostrils.'
>
> He had now a second opportunity of manifesting the

cruelty of his disposition, and the rooted hatred he
entertained to Protestants. The wife of a man named
Maxwell, who had been condemned to death for defending
his house in the Queen's County against Rapparees . . .
appeared before the king in the most lamentable condition,
having four or five small children along with her, all in tears.
She delivered her petition on her knees, praying His Majesty
to pardon, or even reprieve her husband for a short time . . .
the reply of the brute was 'Woman, your husband shall die.'

This example added a stimulus to the fury of the Romish
soldiers against the Protestants, who were treated in the city,
and under the immediate eye of the government, in the
most barbarous manner.

Naturally, the settlers in the north believed reports similar to
Graham's. Their determination to resist strengthened. It was
buttressed by signs that William of Orange had not forgotten
them. On the contrary, they appeared to be close to his heart
and he seemed minded to help them.

On 25 March James was busy. He issued a summons for
Parliament to meet on 7 May in order that he might raise funds
for his campaign. He also chaired a council of war with
Tyrconnell, Melfort and Avaux. There was a report from
Richard Hamilton: he was on his way to Coleraine but feared it
might be too strong to take, so he was requesting more troops.
Avaux repeated what had become his mantra: send reinforcements to Hamilton. The others muttered agreement without
making any firm decisions. No troops were sent.

The council then discussed committing the king himself to
going north and leading his army there. Tyrconnell wanted James
to remain in Dublin because he needed royal assent to a series of
measures the Irish Parliament was eagerly preparing to subordinate settlers and return their property to its original owners. He
suspected that once James was restored to the throne in England
his interest in the grievances of Irish Catholics would evaporate.

Avaux was equally against a northern excursion, because of its risk. The French saw James's future exclusively in Ireland. They desired a Catholic kingdom ruled by a Catholic king, purged of settlers, and totally loyal to the Church of Rome and France. In effect, it would be a French satellite. Ranged against Tyrconnell and Avaux were the English and Scottish Jacobites, represented by Melfort. They saw Ireland as a stepping-stone to Great Britain. As the king himself wanted to reclaim Britain, he naturally found Melfort's arguments most appealing. From Ulster, once the settlers had been subdued, it was only a short voyage to Scotland and from there the launch of James's desired assault on London. Typically, Tyrconnell put up a stern fight against Melfort and his views, and argued vigorously against the king going north and joining the army in Ulster.

The Lord Deputy's vehemence caused such friction within the council, it was decided to remove him temporarily from Dublin and send him to the country. His task there was to inspect His Majesty's forces and to disband those units surplus to requirements. Although the cull had been Tyrconnell's idea, he performed the task with a great lack of enthusiasm. One reason for this was that he contracted black jaundice as he trundled round making his inspections. This sickness was so serious he would spend the rest of the spring and summer recuperating, either in his country house at Talbotstown, or at the vice-regal summer residence at Chapelizod. This explains why Tyrconnell, who had so much to do with the start of the siege and the early part of the campaign in Ulster and who, given his inclination to interfere, made no interventions in the conduct of events, is conspicuous by his absence from this point on in the story.

In the north Hamilton's army finally reached Coleraine early on 27 March. His soldiers had indulged in a little recreational looting along the way at Lisburn, Antrim and Massereene Castle. Their slow progress had given the Williamites the opportunity to consolidate.

Using hedges and ditches as shelter, Hamilton's troops advanced to within fifty yards of the ramparts. They set up two batteries, 'one of three guns which played upon the bridge and Blind-Gate, their design being to break down the bridge and hinder our escape'. These gunners enjoyed some success: they split one of the chains used to lower the bridge. This was refastened by a Captain Archibald McCullogh, with the enemy 'firing very warmly at him'. The second battery 'did little mischief but killing one man and battering down a few chimneys'. The nonchalance of this account is misleading: Jacobite triumph had been greatly feared by the townsfolk.

At about four it began to snow; at five the Jacobites started to retreat, abandoning two guns and much baggage. The garrison inside Coleraine longed to rush out and chase them, but they had blocked their gates on the inside with timber, earth and rubbish. A few hardy souls jumped down from the ramparts and some Jacobite laggards were taken prisoner. From them, the defenders learned that Hamilton had been so certain of Coleraine's capitulation that he had brought only two days' worth of supplies.

The following day the Jacobites returned and reclaimed the baggage and cannon they had left behind. Hamilton sent word to Dublin of what had happened. Clearly, as Avaux had persistently argued, reinforcements were required to get the job done. Major-General Pusignan was sent to collect two mounted regiments and six of foot. His orders were to move north and join Hamilton. Troops based in Dublin were also mobilized; they would go later. Finally, Hamilton would have the forces to smash the settlers. On hearing this, he decided to bypass Coleraine and press on towards Derry.

To block Hamilton's forces, the bridge over the Bann at Portglenone, twenty miles upstream from Coleraine, was smashed and detachments of pro-Williamite soldiers posted at several key points on the Derry side. From Coleraine itself, where Sir Tristram Beresford now commanded, two regiments of infantry and some horse sallied over the bridge to the left bank. Their orders were to shadow the Jacobites on the opposite side as they looked for a place to cross. For several days, the two forces marched and counter-marched, each having the other in view all the time. The weather was permanently stormy and the river frequently burst its banks. Fevers and dysentery were decimating both sides, but the Jacobites at least knew reinforcements were coming.

On 4 April the Jacobites drove the Williamites under Rawdon out of Moneymore. On 7 April Hamilton's troops came across some boats at Portglenone that the defenders had carelessly left intact. Finally, they could cross the Bann. Once across, Gustavus Hamilton, Governor of Enniskillen, reacted as Richard Hamilton had calculated he would: he recalled his outlying detachments from their positions down the Bann and ordered Beresford to pull out of Coleraine entirely, destroying the bridge after himself. All the Williamite troops were then ordered to fall back on Derry.

The passage west was not easy: the roads were clogged with settlers, many laden with what household goods they could carry, fleeing the advancing Jacobites. Other roads leading to Derry, from Antrim, Down, Armagh, Monaghan, Tyrone and Donegal, were similarly choked with refugees. But the fleeing throngs were wrong if they expected undisturbed sanctuary in Derry. Hamilton's Jacobites were now only two or three days away from the city. The reinforcements were closing in, too. And, back in Dublin, King James had decided he was going to lead a third Jacobite force personally.

Naturally, this decision inspired fierce debate. But James was convinced he could persuade the northern settlers to return to him. On 8 April, he left Dublin. With him went several highly experienced French officers, who would act as advisers, and more troops. Of the latter, the Comte d'Avaux observed, 'never have troops marched like this lot; they come like bandits and plunder all they find in their path'. But there was little left to plunder. The dismal terrain across which the travellers moved had been traversed many times recently by other soldiers with the same needs as James's force. They tramped on miserably, the only bright spark being the news from the north that the rebels had abandoned Coleraine. The king immediately sent orders ahead to Pusignan and Hamilton: they were to proceed to Strabane. James's thinking here was as follows. Derry was on the western bank of the Foyle. In order to lay siege to the city the Jacobites must cross the river. The nearest ford was at Strabane, where the rivers Finn and Mourne joined to become the Foyle, which then wound northwards, passing Derry on its way to the sea. Once across, the Jacobites could march down the left bank of the Foyle to Derry, then attack.

Within Derry, refugees brought news that the Jacobite noose was tightening. Inevitably, there was lively discussion as to what to do next with the resources available. Besides the garrison, Lundy commanded the remains of thirty regiments that had been raised in the north over the preceding months. In all, he had between seven and ten thousand men under his command. Faced with the Jacobite challenge, the defenders could either wait for the enemy to arrive below the walls, or they could hold the fords and prevent the Jacobites crossing. The latter strategy was attractive because they would only have to keep the Jacobites at bay until James's men ran short of provisions, after which the enemy would have to withdraw and re-provision. This scenario was perfectly possible as the defenders had been energetically wasting the north-west – burning all the corn and hay they could find – with the exception of the Laggan, the rich agricultural district that lay between the Strabane fords and Derry. If the Jacobites got across the fords and seized this district, it would supply them with provisions when they laid siege to Derry.

So Lundy's choice seemed straightforward: he had to hold the fords. If he could force the Irish to retreat, he would gain a breathing space and help from England might arrive in the interim. Unfortunately, although this was the sensible course to take, very little was being done at the fords to improve their defensive position. This was yet another oversight.

CHAPTER ELEVEN

Fear and Loathing

On 10 April David Cairnes, who had left London a month earlier, stepped back on to Irish soil some miles down Lough Foyle from Derry. The road was crowded with refugees and officers streaming away from the city. He asked some why they were leaving. Governor Lundy's vision for the future, Cairnes learned, was bleak. He thought Derry indefensible and had offered passes to any officers who wanted them. Several men under his command immediately suspected he made this offer because he intended to surrender Derry to the Jacobites. Being 'unwilling to stay, only to be betrayed into the enemy's hands', they took the passes and left. Many civilians, having heard rumours or noticing the exodus of military personnel, fled with them.

Cairnes believed the Williamite cause was just and that right would triumph. He also had news that went some way to confirming this belief. Real soldiers were on their way 'to rescue the whole kingdom, and resettle the Protestant interest there'. Furthermore, he carried the letter that spoke of William's commitment to Ireland, and especially Ulster. On the evening of Cairnes' arrival this letter was read aloud by Lundy to his council of war, a rather unwieldy body of sixteen officers, including James Hamilton, who had come with the *Deliverance* and had been promoted to full colonel, having skipped two ranks. He was having a good war. After the reading, Cairnes summarized the preparations under way in England for Derry's relief. He urged that no one else should be allowed to quit the city.

Encouraged by what they had heard, the council drafted some articles of war. The first article stipulated 'That a mutual engagement be made between all Officers of this garrison and the forces adjoining, and to be signed by every man. That none shall desert or forsake the service, or depart the kingdom without leave of a Council of War. If any do, he or they shall be looked upon as a coward and disaffected to the service.' The next articles dealt with practical matters. For instance, the garrison 'shall have the old houses about the walls and ditches without the gates to be levelled with all possible speed'. They further included the order 'That all persons of this garrison, upon beating of the retreat every night, shall repair to their several quarters and lodgings.' Article nine ordered 'a pair of gallows shall be erected in one of the bastions, upon the south-west of the city . . . [and] all mutinous or treacherous persons of this garrison shall be executed, who shall be condemned thereunto by a Court Martial'. The concluding articles provided some carrots after these sticks. The weekly ration for each man was set at '8 quarts of meal', four pounds of fish and three of meat. Every soldier was also promised 'a quart of small beer every day . . . until some money shall come to allow them pay'. The troops would not get fat on this diet, but equally they would not starve.

These articles agreed, James Hamilton suggested the drafting and signing of the mutual agreement described in article one. This promised that the signatories would 'stand by each other with our forces against the common enemy, and will not leave the kingdom, nor desert the public service until our affairs are in a secure and settled position'. Three or four newcomers had joined the meeting by this point and they signed alongside such familiar names as Lord Blayney,* Sir Arthur Rawdon and James Hamilton. John Campsie, the Protestant Mayor and father of Henry, the principal apprentice boy, was not among the signatories because he was mortally ill (records do not specify with what). When he died the following day, the man who had signed in his place – Gervais Squire – became the new Mayor. He held the post throughout the siege.

The next day, Thursday 11 April, this 'mutual agreement' was posted on the wall of the Markethouse, along with the articles: these were also read to the battalions on morning parade. The soldiers cheered when they heard them. Lundy had recovered from his bout of defeatism and intended to fight. But in a few short days this improvement in morale would be undone.

As already noted, the Reverend George Walker was a man who held himself in high regard. In his account of the siege he often describes occasions when his wisdom was ignored. One such diary entry came on 13 April: 'Mr Walker receiving intelligence that the enemy was drawing towards Derry, he rides in all haste thither, and gives Col. Lundy an account of it, but the Colonel believed it only a false alarm.'† His intelligence unheeded, Walker left for Lifford. Had he stayed in Derry, he would have enjoyed the rare satisfaction of being proved right. Later that day some citizens on Derry's ramparts that overlooked the Foyle saw Richard Hamilton's vanguard on the other side of the river. The troops were marching towards Strabane, where the Jacobite forces were massing.

Separated from his prize by only the width of the river, Hamilton seized the opportunity for a little theatre: he ordered a

---

*He had commanded Protestant levies in Armagh and subsequently retreated, as Hamilton's forces advanced, to Derry. Though present at meetings, he took very little part in the city's defence and died the month Derry was relieved.
†As will become apparent, Walker often referred to himself in the third person in his diary.

single ball to be fired across. It struck the Newgate Bastion next to the Ferry Quay Gate. Fire was not returned because the city's gunners hadn't been issued with ammunition: the Governor hadn't felt it necessary, as the Jacobites had not yet reached Derry. The physical damage caused by that single Jacobite ball was minimal, but it made a huge dent in the Governor's reputation. Though he might have been right to hoard *matériel* until the Jacobites arrived, it now didn't look like prudence so much as one more example of his dilatory, even supine, attitude towards the developing crisis. The improved morale evaporated. In its place 'some discontents appear[ed] among the soldiers, who murmured especially against Col. Lundy, for taking no more care to put them into a posture of defence, and expressed great readiness to fight the enemy if they were led on'.

To assuage the volatile emotions of those inside the walls, it was necessary to give an impression of action. A council of war was immediately convened and it reached a unanimous decision. By ten o'clock on the morning of 15 April, 'all . . . that can or will fight for their country and religion against Popery shall appear on the fittest ground near Cladyford, Lifford and Long Causey as shall be nearest to their several and respective quarters'. Once there, the order continued, the troops must 'be ready to fight the enemy, and to preserve our lives and all that is dear to us from them'. Each man was further instructed to bring a week's rations and as much fodder for the horses as he could carry.

The council also heard from Major Stroud. Among other proposals, he suggested 'that harrows should be thrown into the fords, and for want thereof, the instruments called round-heads, which would have answered the same purpose'. This was to stop the enemy's horse crossing. The Governor dismissed this idea and he was proved correct: in the event the rivers were so swollen by rain that the Jacobite horses had to swim across.

With his mobilization orders, Lundy hoped that the citizenry would be convinced that matters were in hand. Far from everyone was, including the tireless David Cairnes, who wanted the forces dispatched to the fords at once, not in two days' time. Twice he visited Lundy, 'pressing him to take some speedy effectual care for securing the passes of Finn water, lest the enemy should get over before our men could meet', and twice the Governor demurred. 'The same day several others sent word to Gov. Lundy, that if he did not march the men that day, the enemy would certainly prevent their getting together in an orderly body, and therefore entreated him to be with the men that night at Cladyford and Lifford.' Lundy, having issued his orders, was not minded to change them. Furthermore, he argued that he already had troops at the fords. Technically, this was true: vedettes – mounted sentries – and some dragoons from Coleraine were in position. But these forces were nothing more than a token presence.

The fords to be defended could be viewed as an inverted 'Y'. The bottom right arm of the 'Y' was the Mourne River, with Strabane on its right bank; the bottom left arm was the Finn River, with Lifford on its left bank. These two arms joined to form the Foyle. On Sunday 14 April, the day Cairnes and others felt Lundy should be getting his troops into position, the Jacobites made an almost unopposed crossing of the Mourne. They were now on the triangle of land between the Mourne and the Finn. The Finn was a more substantial obstacle. There were two places where they could attempt to cross: Lifford and Cladyford. Once over the Finn, they would have to cross the great marsh about four miles north of Lifford. The pass through the marsh was known as the Long Causey. Then it was straight up the left bank of the Foyle to Derry. These place names would shortly be associated with Lundy's greatest error to date.

Meanwhile, King James was nearing Derry. He arrived in Omagh on 14 April. That day's march had been tough: the wind was so strong that it frequently and literally stopped the horses in their tracks; rain eased only to be replaced by hail; the road was 'frequently intersected by torrents that might almost be called

rivers'; and there were 'several fords where the water was breast
high'. The countryside was even more despoiled than that around
Dublin. Avaux counted only three miserable cabins during his
journey; 'Everything else was rock, bog and moor.' He found
Omagh in a woeful state. Its Protestant majority had fled twenty-
four hours earlier and 'They had taken everything away, even the
locks of the doors, and broken all the windows and chimneys,
and as no precaution had been taken to carry anything with us
we found nothing for ourselves or our horses.' Avaux presented
himself to the billeting officer, who first told him there was a room
for him in the king's house and then that Melfort had taken it.
Avaux was sent instead to a wretched house without doors,
windows or shutters. It offered no shelter or protection against
crime, 'for the soldiers are great thieves . . . Rosen, Maumont,
and Léry all had sentries. I never had a sentry before or since that
day except when I arrived in Dublin'. This observation speaks
tellingly of the lack of discipline and the disorderliness on the
Jacobite side.

That night, Avaux had an interview with James, who revealed
that he intended to sleep in Strabane in two days' time. Avaux
had bluntly restated his opinion of the folly of James venturing
north in a letter to Louis XIV, written a couple of days earlier:
'I shall do my utmost, Sire, to hinder the King of England from
going to Londonderry, for I am persuaded that if these people
are seized by terror, the presence of his Britannic Majesty will be
unnecessary, and if they defend themselves, the King of England
will not be in a position to subdue them and must retire shame-
fully.' Now he tried to dissuade James from going to Strabane.
But it was a Jacobite article of faith that Derry would be overwhelmed in a few days. After all,

> to a military eye, the defences of Londonderry appeared
> contemptible. The fortifications consisted of a simple wall
> overgrown with grass and weeds. There was no ditch even
> between the gates. The drawbridges had long been

neglected. The chains were rusty and could scarcely be used. The parapets and towers were built after a fashion that might well move disciples of Vauban to laughter. And these feeble defences were on almost every side commanded by heights. Indeed, those who laid out the city had never meant that it should be able to withstand a regular siege, and had contented themselves with throwing up works sufficient to protect the inhabitants against a tumultuary attack of the Celtic peasantry.

Avaux suggested that it would be no triumph for James to be present at such a feeble opponent's capitulation. It would be undignified. However, if the unthinkable happened and Derry resisted successfully, James would be humiliated. In other words, irrespective of which way the campaign went, James would be harmed by leading it.

Avaux retired to his dismal quarters with his argument having gone unheeded. Then he was recalled to the king's presence and told the ominous news that had just arrived: the rebels intended to mass at the fords to block his army, and there was an enemy fleet in the Foyle. This information precipitated a royal crisis. James announced he would retreat to Charlemont the next day. Avaux, naturally, was delighted. He suggested James should send Rosen and all his other generals to the fords. The agitated king gave the order.

Around this time, the Jacobite vanguard was making its first attempt to push across the Finn at Lifford. The fighting contin-ued through the night. The defenders, one of whom was George Walker, fought 'with great resolution and success, killing . . . several of them, with their cannon and small shot'. The defenders had made the most of their considerable strategic advantage to repel the attack.

As dawn came on 15 April, the vedettes and dragoons on the Finn's western banks must have felt reasonably confident. Shortly after ten o'clock the levies from Derry would be joining them.

With these extra troops the Jacobites could surely be kept on the other side of the river until they ran out of supplies. Then they would have to retreat and Derry would be safe. However, Lundy's orders were rather vague about where the reinforcements should converge. Several thousand men in unfamiliar terrain searching for rendezvous points stretched over a distance of about eight miles was likely to end in disaster.

Back in Omagh, Avaux was with James when a dragoon officer approached with more bad news. He had met some enemy soldiers on the road from the west. They had fired on him and were marching on Omagh even as he spoke. Avaux suggested positioning soldiers on the bridge, which was the only entry point into Omagh, and sending a detachment up the road to see if anyone was indeed coming. While this was being done, James had his boots fetched. Avaux counselled waiting until the patrol reported back but James would not hear of it. With Avaux and a small escort, he galloped out of town, heading away from the enemy. The party had gone hardly a quarter of a mile down the road before they learned there had been a mistake. The alarm had been false. The soldiers who had fired on the dragoon officer were Jacobites, and they were marching towards James. They had fired in greeting. James returned to Omagh and received further good news: there was no English fleet in the Lough and the Finn had been crossed.

Richard Hamilton and his troops had been first in the area. Leaving most of his little army at Strabane, Hamilton, with about 350 foot and 600 cavalry, probed the eastern bank of the Finn. Following the river's course, he came on Cladyford bridge, which had been partially smashed by some of Lundy's forces. To the side of the bridge there were trenches with a number of foot soldiers and 'about thirty dragoons of Col. Stewart's regiment, commanded by Capt. Murray', hunkered down inside. The Jacobites fired volley after volley at the enemy. The foot soldiers 'were beat off', but the dragoons 'opposed the enemy's coming over . . . until all their ammunition was spent'. As Lundy had issued only three rounds to each man, this didn't take long. Now was the time to resupply, 'But there was no more ammunition sent them; nay, so strangely had the Governor managed things, the most part of the ammunition was coming from Derry.' The dragoons withdrew. Major Stroud was in the vicinity with a party of horse but he 'was so ill placed, that he could not bring them on, so that they were forced to retire from the bridge'. Then, 'The enemy [that is, the Jacobites] perceiving this, and observing the scattered condition of our men, several troops of their horse rushed into the river'. Hamilton himself, plus Maumont and Pusignan, swam over as well. And with the cavalry went the infantrymen, each man clinging to a tail or mane. As the fighting on the other side would be at close quarters, foot soldiers might turn out to be more useful than men on horseback.

The Jacobites were clearly expecting a fight. Though they had vanquished the first line of rebels from the trenches, they could see a whole Protestant army ahead of them. The exact number of Protestants is uncertain, but it was at least five thousand and possibly as many as ten thousand. Either way, Hamilton's men were hugely outnumbered.

Some of the Protestants 'fired briskly on the passengers [the Jacobites], though to no purpose'. Emerging sodden from the river, water pouring out of their boots, pockets and scabbards, the attackers faced their greatest danger – counter-attack when they were at their weakest and when their powder was far from dry. It was a golden opportunity for the defenders: they could have hacked down the Jacobites with pike and sword, or pushed them back into the Finn. 'But Gov. Lundy was so far from putting the Protestant forces into any posture to oppose' Hamilton's men that the Williamites could not charge the enemy.

Now the Jacobites capitalized on the risk they had taken by swimming over. The rest of their infantry patched the bridge with some pieces of timber and surged across. Some small detachments of Protestants close to the river now fell back, and the thousands of Protestants in the distance saw their vanguard fleeing. They panicked and began to retreat, too. In no time at all, the entire leaderless force was in headlong and ignominious flight from a few hundred Jacobites.

The men at the forefront of the retreating troops met Lundy coming the other way along the road from Derry. The Governor did not mince his words: 'Gentlemen, I see you will not fight!'; 'You are all cut off, shift for yourselves'. He was also reported as stating that 'Derry was his post', as if to say he should never have been at Cladyford in the first place. These remarks were all quoted by Lundy's enemies, and may well be fictitious. More certain is that he made no attempt to rally his troops. Instead, he 'gave order to all thereabouts to flee to Derry, himself leading the way'.

In the midst of this calamity, the unlikely figure of Lord Kingston appeared. He and a garrison of about a thousand men had been occupying Sligo town. Their appeals to Lundy for aid had been ignored: they had simply been ordered to quit Sligo and come to Derry. The forces had fallen back to Ballyshannon and the previous night Kingston had learned about the Williamite rendezvous at the fords. Being thirty miles away, his infantry would never make it in time, but Kingston decided to ride over himself with a couple of officers to see what was happening. Outside Stranorlar, due west of Cladyford, he met some retreating Protestants, who told him the Jacobites were across the river. Kingston returned to Ballyshannon, dispersed his troops and sailed immediately to England. He had neither held Sligo town (which was now in Jacobite hands) nor been given the opportunity to get his considerable force to the fords. These joined the ever-expanding list of Lundy's errors.

Another example soon came to light. Those at the forefront of the retreating troops met the ammunition train three or four miles out of Derry, coming the other way. If they had tried to hold the line, they would have had no ammunition with which to do so for at least three hours. Lundy's mistakes were so numerous and so glaring that the defeated soldiers and anxious citizens began to search for an explanation. The one they finally came up with has stuck to Lundy ever since: he was in league with the Jacobites.

While Richard Hamilton was surveying the river at Cladyford, the sixty-two-year-old Lieutenant General Conrad, Count de Rosen, arrived at Lifford. Rosen, originally from Livonia in modern-day Estonia and Latvia, was renowned as intrepid, ruthless and fearless. He had with him a small unit of two troops of horse and one of dragoons. At first he thought it would be impossible to force his way across: the river was in flood and there were numerous Protestants on the other bank. He was outnumbered by as many as ten to one. The defenders also had a small fort and artillery.

Then, in the distance, Rosen saw the enemy retreating from Cladyford before Hamilton and his men. He seized his chance and led his forces into the river. The appalled Protestant defenders fired once, then retreated. To their credit, rather than join the stampede to Derry, they went to Long Causey, 'expecting the Irish would take that way and Lundy would come thither from Raphoe'. But there was to be no last stand at Long Causey, even though it was on the most direct path to Derry. The defenders 'stayed there until towards evening. But fearing the enemy might come from Raphoe, to intercept their passage to Derry, they retired thither.'

The Jacobites never came because, as the bulk of the Protestants fell back towards Raphoe, the Jacobites chased them, harrying the rearguard. Among others, they caught Colonel Montgomery's regiment of foot and killed some four hundred Protestant infantrymen. It might have been even worse if the remaining troops 'had not got into bogs and marshy places'. The Jacobite cavalry could not follow them in this terrain and they were able to wend their way back to Derry.

The chase from Cladyford towards Raphoe went on for four or five miles until Hamilton stopped it. 'This halt gave opportunity to the rebels to get safe into Londonderry . . . which is looked upon to be the first imprudent management of the northern enterprise.' The Jacobites should indeed have harried their enemy all the way to the gates of the city. Had they known what Lundy was about to do next, they might well have done.

The Governor returned to Derry before the main body of his army. The balance of his forces, still streaming up from the south, numbered between four and eight thousand men. He would need all of them when the Jacobites arrived, as they now inevitably would. Yet at this point 'Gov. Lundy being come into the town, ordered the sentinels to shut the gates.' His spurious reason for this action was to protect the city's meagre supplies from tired and hungry soldiery. He seemed to have forgotten the bad feelings roused just a few weeks before by the rumour that the Coleraine garrison was going to be locked out. He also failed to consider the effect on morale. His troops were scurrying towards home. If they were excluded they would surely think that Lundy was sacrificing them to the Jacobites. And there was one more reason why Lundy's decision was ill judged. Derry's resources were not as meagre as he imagined. William's promised assistance had arrived, in the form of a fleet in the lough.

The relieving force consisted of nine ships bearing two regiments, or about sixteen hundred men, and an accompanying man-of-war. At about ten o'clock in the morning, roughly the same time as Lundy's forces were supposed to muster at the fords, Colonel Cunningham, aboard the frigate the *Swallow*, had put a man ashore at Greencastle, at the mouth of the lough on the northern side. He had instructions to report to Lundy that the flotilla was sailing towards Derry. By the time the messenger reached Derry, Lundy had left. Word of this went back to Colonel Cunningham, who was now at Redcastle, further down the lough. He wrote a letter to Lundy:

Hearing you have taken the field, in order to fight the enemy, I have thought it fit for their Majesties' service, to let you know there are two well-disciplined regiments here on board, that may join you in two days at farthest. I am sure they will be of great use on any occasion but especially for the encouragement of raw men, as I judge most of yours are. Therefore, it is my opinion, that you only stop the passes at the fords of Finn till I can join you, and afterwards, if giving battle be necessary, you will be in a much better posture for it than before. I must ask your pardon if I am too free in my advice. According to the remote prospect I have of things, this seems reasonable to me. But as their Majesties have left the whole direction of matters to you, so you shall find that no man living shall more cheerfully obey you than your humble servant, John Cunningham.

A messenger was sent with this letter, and while he rushed overland the flotilla sailed on towards Derry. Come evening, when the fleet had reached Culmore Castle, just a few miles north of the city, the tide turned and the ships could go no further. Cunningham had still heard nothing back from Lundy, and he was anxious for 'orders and directions, for the best and securest way of putting into the town the two regiments then on board the fleet at anchor near the castle'. He wrote a third letter and selected Major Zachariah Tiffin, Captain John Lyndon, and Captain Wolfranc Cornwall, the commander of the *Swallow*, to carry it. The little party set off.

Meanwhile, back in Derry, Lundy had received the first two letters from Cunningham. He replied:

I am come back much sooner than I expected, when I went forth. For having numbers placed on Finn-water, as I went to a pass, where a few might oppose a greater number than came to the place, I found them on the run before the enemy, who pursued with great vigour, and I fear march on with their forces. So that I wish your men would march all night in good order, lest they be surprised. Here they shall have all the accommodation the place will afford. In this hurry pardon me for this brevity. The rest the bearer will inform you.

Then he added a postscript – 'If the men be not landed, let them land and march immediately' – and sent the messanger on his way. At some point on the road Lundy's man and Tiffin's party met. Lundy's man, for whatever reason, decided to lead the Englishmen back into Derry, rather than deliver the letter with its stirring postscript to Cunningham.

By the time the party returned Lundy had fallen into despair. The awful truth of what had happened earlier had finally sunk in. His forces had been weak and disorganized at Cladyford because he hadn't been there to lead them. This, the nadir in a series of gaffes, highlighted, as never before, his inability to command effectively and his tendency to make mistakes. When Tiffin arrived, Lundy told him 'affairs were in great confusion, and a much worse posture than could be imagined'. He then took the opportunity to amend his request to Cunningham. Now, he told his visitors, he desired the soldiers be kept on board and that Cunningham 'come next morning to town with Colonel Richards, and other officers they thought fit; where he intended to call a Council of War and give a further account of the condition of the garrison'. Then he added a second postscript to the original letter:

Since the writing of this, Major Zachariah Tiffin is come here, and I have given him my opinion fully, which I believe when you hear and see the place, you will both join with me. That without an immediate supply of money and provisions, this place must fall very soon into the enemy's hands. If you do not send your men here some time tomorrow, it will not be in your power to bring them at all. Till we discuss the matter, I remain, dear sir, your most faithful servant.

Tiffin and his party returned to the *Swallow* and handed over the messages. Colonel Cunningham issued his orders: the troops would remain on board while he went to Derry.

Over the course of the same evening, as messengers shuttled between Culmore and Derry, and as Lundy's mood plummeted, many of those who had fought (or not) that morning were making their way home. On reaching Derry, they found the gates locked. By the next morning, 16 April, the soldiers' tempers were fraying. 'They called to the sentries to open . . . [the gates], which they refused. But when one of the Captains of Col. Skeffington's regiment fired at the sentry, and called for fire to burn the gate' the sentries calculated that the wrath of those outside would be worse than that of Lundy and their superiors inside. They opened the gates and the troops flooded in, expressly against Lundy's orders.

One of their number, the tireless George Walker, immediately sought out the Governor. He pressed Lundy to assemble his troops and return them to the field. Lundy demurred, citing the poor performance of the forces the day before. Perhaps to emphasize just how inadequate he thought his troops, he suggested Walker might dismiss his men. This 'did not agree with Mr Walker's sentiments' and he decided he would 'stand by his men that he had brought from their own homes, and not to expose them again to the enemy, by dismissing them'. Once Walker made this decision (for him, the equivalent of the moment when the apprentices had slammed the gates) Lundy could no longer count on his support or loyalty.

Sometime that same morning, Colonels Cunningham and Richards arrived in Derry with three or four officers from each of their regiments, and Captain Cornwall of the Royal Navy. What they found must have appalled them. Derry had been built for a population of about a thousand; there were now about thirty thousand civilian refugees and seven or eight thousand soldiers behind the walls. The crowds were sleeping in shifts not only in the houses but in the streets.

The military party went to Lundy's house, where he pro-
posed a council of war in the Council Chamber. However,
'none were admitted to it but the Colonel's own creatures', as
George Walker observed tartly: James Hamilton, Lord Blayney,
Captain Chidley Coote (one of Kingston's commanders in Sligo,
he had come to Derry rather than sail to England), along with
John Mogridge, a city burgess, who was to record the minutes.
Behind closed doors, Cunningham handed Lundy the orders he
had received in March. From these, the Governor learned that
Cunningham's two regiments were only the start. There were
'further succours of money, men, arms, and provisions of war'
on their way. Of course, there was then the quid pro quo: 'we do
expect from your courage, prudence, and conduct, that in the
meantime you make the best defence you can against all persons
that shall attempt to besiege the said city, or to annoy our
Protestant subjects within the same'. The letter concluded: 'not
doubting . . . your own courage as well as your affection to the
Protestant religion, . . . we shall not fail to reward [you] with our
royal favour and bounty'. So all Lundy had to do was hold Derry
'until, upon the arrival of an army, which we are sending from
England . . . we may . . . restore in a short time our kingdom of
Ireland to its former peace and tranquillity'.

The Governor and his visitors then addressed themselves to
achieving this. Lundy's summation was blunt and dark: the
'enemy was near their gates with 25,000 men' while William's
promised army would not be coming immediately. As for the
1,600 troops aboard the vessels lying at anchor at Culmore, there
simply were not the resources within Derry to victual a force of
that size as well as the existing garrison for more than a short
time.

Lundy, of course, was bending the truth here; or stretching it
to breaking point. The Jacobite army numbered about 7,000, not
25,000. And the town had provisions, perhaps sufficient for 3,000
men for six months – or so Sir Arthur Rawdon would testify later
before the parliamentary committee of inquiry, and he had been

given that figure by Lundy himself. However, Lundy's guests were hardly in a position to challenge him. As a result, 'Those of the Council . . . from England, thinking it impossible the Governor should be ignorant of the condition of the town, and observing the account to pass without any contradiction from those there who had been for some time in it . . . soon agreed in the opinion of returning for England'. The only dissenting voice belonged to Colonel Richards, 'who looked on deserting that garrison not only as quitting the city, but the whole kingdom'.

Despite Richards' scruples, the following resolution was then unanimously adopted by the council:

> Upon inquiry, it appears that there is not provision in the garrison of Londonderry for the present garrison, and the two regiments on board, for above a week, or ten days at most. And it appearing that the place is not tenable against a well-appointed army, therefore it is concluded upon and resolved . . . not . . . to land the two regiments under Colonel Cunningham and Colonel Richards . . . [C]onsidering the . . . likelihood that the enemy will soon possess themselves of this place, it is thought most convenient that the principal officers shall privately withdraw themselves . . . as well as for their own preservation as in hopes that the inhabitants, by a timely capitulation, may make terms the better with the enemy.

The citizens, it goes without saying, were not going to like this. The mob could be ugly, as Governor Lundy knew from his dismal experience on the bridge at Coleraine. So the participants in the council agreed to keep their decision secret. However, as the people 'were earnestly begging that the English forces might land', as they made their way back through the streets, Cunningham and his party, let everyone believe that the Red-coats would shortly be returning. Those left behind also took part in the deception:

Col. Lundy, to delude both the officers and the soldiers in the town . . . told them publicly, 'It is resolved the English forces should immediately land, and when they are in their quarters the gates shall be opened, and all join in defence of the town.' And to cloak the intrigue the better, the Sheriffs were ordered to go through the City to provide quarters for them, who accordingly did so. But this was all mere sham to amuse the town, while they might get away with the greater ease and safety.

The duplicity was exposed, though, because 'one of the Officers of this Council' decided to warn a few select officers, so they could escape too. He 'acquainted Col. Francis Hamilton and Capt. Hugh McGill with it, and advised them to go off . . . Capt. McGill discovered it to several friends, and particularly Sir Arthur Rawdon (who then lay extremely weak)'. Now that Rawdon knew of Lundy's perfidy, news of it would spread through the city in a matter of hours.

CHAPTER TWELVE

Murray's Coup

The resolution drawn up on 16 April was merely an aspiration of surrender. In order to advance the process, terms would have to be agreed with the Jacobites. The members of the council therefore set to drafting an instrument of surrender. George Walker, who may have been present by this time, notes that 'it was recommended with this encouragement. "There was no doubt that upon surrender of the town, King James would grant a general pardon, and order restitution of all that had been plundered from them."'

This statement provoked a variety of reactions. Some, says Walker, motivated by financial self-interest, 'were influenced by these considerations to subscribe'. Others 'did not only refuse, but began to conceive some jealousies of their Governor'.* A third group 'expressed themselves after a rude manner, threatening to hang both the Governor and his Council'.

Until now, the Governor had generally been viewed simply as incompetent, a man who had no common touch and was shifty; he had never openly favoured capitulation. Doing so now, he put

---

*'Jealousies' here means enmity.

himself on a collision course with the citizens who wanted to resist, but at this moment he still retained sufficient authority to get his way. So the council agreed to send Captain White 'out to the King to receive proposals from him'. White went to St Johnston, about five miles from Derry, where it was thought the king was based. He wasn't there, but Richard Hamilton was. He passed White on to Rosen, who was the senior officer. Rosen referred his visitor to James's proclamation of 1 April: if the city surrendered, those terms stood, he said. White undertook to take this message back to Derry. In the meantime, Hamilton agreed 'that he should not march the army within four miles of the town'. This was cunning: it made the Jacobites look conciliatory whereas, in fact, Hamilton was simply keeping his poorly armed troops out of sight of the defenders. It was especially important not to let them see that he lacked substantial artillery, the essential tool of an aggressive siege.

Hamilton must have been encouraged by the captain's visit, but he would also have known that nothing was settled until his soldiers manned Derry's walls. The city's authorities might have been wobbling, but they had not capitulated. In this situation a wise man would now apply further gentle pressure to nudge events in the desired direction. Hamilton was a wise man. He dispatched an Anglican minister, the Reverend Whitloe, from Raphoe. The latter's task was to discover if 'they in the city would surrender on honourable terms . . . to prevent the effusion of Christian blood'. Derry had a choice to make: sweet peace or bloody war; there was no third way.

Whitloe was admitted to the city. In the streets he bumped into an old acquaintance, Cornet Nicolson. The young man asked the reverend if he knew what Lundy intended. Surrender by Saturday, replied the minister. He added, helpfully, that Nicolson should make himself scarce: once the Jacobites got in, things might turn nasty. As Nicolson spread the news, more of Lundy's authority evaporated.

*

With events rushing forward in Derry, it was essential that James II, who viewed the city's capitulation as the first step in his long-term goal of retrieving England and Scotland, was briefed. In his quarters in St Johnston, the Duke of Berwick, James's dutiful illegitimate son, wrote an account of what had happened with Captain White and the military operation against Derry to date. The generals were confident that Derry was going to surrender but his father's presence was still necessary. He sent this express to James, who was still at Charlemont with Avaux.

James read it the following morning, then summoned Avaux, and told him he intended to ride north at once. The Frenchman was, as usual, appalled, but James just as predictably ignored his remonstrations. He was determined to show his generals how high a regard he had for their opinion (this was, after all, their idea). And he reckoned he would shorten the conflict by parading in front of the obstinate citizens. (A rumour was doing the rounds that he had died in France, so there was some logic in his thinking.) James left the greater part of his train at Charlemont and set off on the first leg of his journey to Derry. His immediate destination was Newtownstewart, thirty-six miles away.

While James rode hard, Lundy summoned yet another council of war. He told the assembled officers and gentlemen that it was impossible to hold the city; they must surrender. Given this bleak prognosis, the council decided 'to send to King James, to know what his Majesty's demands were, and what terms he would grant to the city'. Three emissaries were selected: Archibald Hamilton, Captain Charles Kinaston and Captain Francis Nevill. They trooped off to St Johnston.

Later that day Richard Hamilton received them. He said if Derry surrendered, and handed over all serviceable arms and horses, the citizens could live in peace. He asked for the reply by noon of the next day, Thursday 18 April. The three emissaries started back to Derry.

While they did so, tension in the streets of the city was rising. Two Jacobite agitators – William Blacker and Ensign Twinyo –

had sneaked in. Their job was to 'amuse the garrison with such accounts of the clemency of the King on one hand, and the formidable strength of his army on the other, as might incline them to a further surrender'. However, with the enemy closing in and increasing anti-Lundy feeling, their talk 'soon exposed them to the suspicion of the garrison'. They were seized and imprisoned. Blacker immediately wrote a letter to the Jacobite camp, naming some of the few contacts he and Twinyo had made in Derry – including a captain and a revenue collector. The letter was intercepted; the named men were brought before the council and dismissed.

Although this showed capitulation had not yet occurred, many officers now looked 'on the town as betrayed' and, thinking it 'madness . . . to stay behind, merely to be exposed as a sacrifice to the fury of the Irish', they were flitting away to Redcastle and boarding one of Cunningham's ships. This, in turn, undermined the deference normally shown by the ranks to their superiors. 'The common soldiers . . . were so enraged at their Officers, several of whom . . . left them and fled for England, that they could not forbear expressing it with some violence upon them. One Captain Bell was shot dead and another Officer hurt that had (as was supposed with that design) got into a boat with several other officers' to escape Derry.

Lawlessness was not only the only sign of social collapse:

This day some in the town sent one Capt. Cole to Col. Cunningham, to offer him the government of it, because they suspected Col. Lundy's integrity. Col. Cunningham's answer was, 'That he being ordered to apply himself to Col. Lundy for direction in all things relating to their Majesties' service, [he] could receive no application from any that opposed that authority.'

When night fell the anxiety of those behind the walls had increased further and behaviour was consequently even less

rational. When the three emissaries returned from their interview with Richard Hamilton, they 'were refused entrance by the
multitude'. Even without knowing their mission, their association with a discredited regime and the very fact of their having
been in the enemy's company were sufficient reasons to keep
them out. Eventually, Archibald Hamilton and Captain Kinaston
persuaded Colonel Thomas Whitney, in charge of the night
guard, to allow them in. Captain Nevill was not so lucky:
Whitney pretended not to recognize him and kept him out,
even though the captain 'had before been very active' in the
defence of the city. Nevill went off to spend the night in a hut
near the walls, hoping he would gain entry the next day. It was
not to be.*

Later that same night there were more mysterious ill omens.
'Major Crofton finding the gates open, and two keys missing,
doubled the guards and changed the word.' The Governor questioned Crofton regarding this security lapse but the major
'thought fit not to insist upon it, and so there was no more
made of it'. The assumption was made that Lundy himself had
arranged for the gates to be left unlocked.

James arrived at Newtownstewart late on the evening of
17 April. By daybreak he was back in the saddle, and reached
Strabane at 8 a.m. There he found a letter waiting for him from
Rosen, who wrote that the Protestants had sent men out to sue
for surrender. He urged James to show himself to the city to
speed the process. This seemed like sound advice. James crossed
the rivers Mourne and Finn and headed for his troops. He overtook the infantry, commanded by Pusignan, two miles north of

---

*He was taken prisoner and shipped to Dublin, where he experienced considerable hard-
ship before escaping and returning to Derry after the siege was lifted. He then made
a map showing the city and the disposition of the surrounding Jacobite forces during
the siege that was of immeasurable value to historians in the centuries to come. A
version of this map is reproduced on the endpapers.

Lifford. The French general told him Rosen was up front with the dragoons and the cavalry. The plan was that these forces, Hamilton's and Berwick's would unite in sight of Derry and together make a threatening whole. James overtook Rosen two miles from Derry. He put himself at the head of his forces and proceeded as far as a hill to the south of the city, and within cannon shot of the walls.

Men on the ramparts spotted him. Word that the enemy had arrived went back to the council – then in session again under Lundy. They decided 'that none should dare to fire till the King's demands were first known, by another messenger to be sent to his Majesty for that purpose'.

When the Jacobite infantry arrived, Rosen posted them from the river on the south side of the city right round to the river on the north. Derry was encircled by water and by hostile Jacobite forces. To those watching from the ramparts, it must have been obvious what was happening, but not a shot was fired. When the encirclement was completed, James became anxious to summon the city in order that it might learn of his presence. Rosen counselled him to hold back until his troops could be brought closer to the walls, and James agreed. Rosen moved some cavalry and dragoons from Derry Hill forward. Then he did the same with the infantry, believing the sight 'of so considerable an army would fright them into a compliance' . . . and 'dare the rebels to a conclusion without more ado'. Many of Rosen's troops were now well within range of the Derry cannons.

Back in their meeting-place the council deliberated. The men on the walls were jittery – it would be hard to control them. To surrender a city was invariably tricky, but this time it could be disastrous as it went against the wishes of the majority. Over the previous twenty-four hours members of the council had had to lie low because of the mob's antagonism.

One unexpected consequence of all this pressure was the effect it had on John Mogridge. So far he had stayed silent about the resolution agreed with Cunningham, but now he would conceal no longer the result of that Council, viz. 'That Col. Cunningham should return with the two regiments, and all Gentlemen and Officers quit the garrison, and go with him.' He desired Governor Lundy to produce the order, which was a great surprise to this present Council, who (though they generally agreed too well with Col. Lundy about surrendering), yet deeply resented the concealing so material a thing from them.

Considering they had been kept in the dark, the council members were generous. Lundy's decision, made without their approval, had made surrender inevitable, yet they remained committed to him. But when Mogridge's revelations leaked into the city, 'This discovery occasioned great uneasiness and disorder in the town, which had like to have had very ill effects upon the Governor and some of his Council . . . [T]he wrong . . . done my Lord Kingston and his party did also add much to the rage and violence of the garrison'.

In spite of this, Lundy still expected to surrender. However, a new character was about to enter the drama. He was Adam Murray, an Ulster-Scot in his twenties or early thirties. His father Gabriel, a sprightly octogenarian (Adam was presumably the offspring of a late marriage), had a farm at Ling in the valley of the River Faughan, a few miles south-east of Derry. Murray had enlisted in Colonel Stewart's regiment and was in the trenches at Cladyford. A unit of dragoons under his command had 'opposed the enemy's coming over . . . until all their ammunition was spent'. He had then been among those locked out of Derry on Lundy's orders. Needing forage for his animals and knowing there was none in the city, he took his horse up to the fort at Culmore. Thousands of other soldiers also congregated here. Some of these, 'having observed Col. Lundy's ill conduct and the confused posture affairs were in', boarded one of the ships that would go to England, but others stayed, and these men, aggrieved by everything that had happened, formed a community of intransigents with Murray as their leader. They 'resolved to sell their lives dear, rather than fall into the hands of an enemy from whom they expected no mercy'.

On the morning of 18 April, Murray left Culmore and moved towards Derry four miles to the south. He had with him a considerable party of horse and fifteen hundred infantrymen. Leaving the latter at Brookhall, he rode on to Pennyburn Mill, about a mile from the city, and paused. He could see the walls and the Cathedral tower. It was then without its steeple, and two guns had been mounted up there. As the Cathedral stood on the highest ground inside the walls, the top of the tower commanded a view of all places outside the city within cannon range. Thus, those manning the guns could see both Murray to the north, as well as the Jacobite troops who were intent on fanning across the ground between Derry and Pennyburn, and James to the south. This would be crucial to what happened next.

At this moment James decided the time had come to summon the city. He sent a trumpeter forward. Rosen, meanwhile, was continuing to move troops, posting soldiers at the Windmill, close to the Bishop's Gate, and near the Butchers' Gate on the western, weakest, side of the city. As these troops took up their positions the trumpeter returned to James and told him he would have an answer in an hour, but for the moment the Jacobite troops were to stay back. Rosen continued to edge his troops closer. It was too much. Suddenly, those in the Cathedral tower and on the walls at the southern end of the city shouted, 'No surrender,' and loosed fusillade after fusillade at the Jacobites. They did this partly because of 'how little the Council or their orders were valued' and partly because the appearance of Murray and his little army at Pennyburn Mill, which the lookouts in the cathedral tower had seen and communicated to others, 'encouraged the men on the walls to accost the Irish army so rudely'. The firing from the city on an unprepared enemy had an immediate effect. The Jacobites 'could not be kept in any order by their officers . . . some took to their heels, others with less labour . . . [hid] . . . themselves, and a great many were killed'. Several of James's escorts were hit, and he himself had to retire out of range 'in much disorder and some surprise'.

In their chamber the council heard the firing. They were appalled: their troops had shot at the monarch to whom they had hoped to surrender. Also, the presence of Adam Murray and his cavalry outside the walls might make the Jacobites think the surrender negotiations had been a subterfuge. The firing had to be stopped. Lundy chose Colonel Whitney, who had protected him on the bridge at Coleraine, for the task. Whitney scaled the ramparts, where some of the soldiers wanted to throw him over the top, but the order to cease firing was eventually obeyed.

Back in the council, some doubted that James was actually outside the walls. Derry was rather a long way to come, they suggested. But others had no doubt he was there. Moreover, he must be offended, and they would have to placate him after firing on him. To speak on their behalf, they sent two men whom the Jacobites would recognize as reliable intermediaries and whom their own side would trust, too: Captain White and Archibald Hamilton. They were to apologize 'for what had passed, and lay all blame for it on the ungovernable-ness of the people', then explain that the council would not be able to restrain the 'violent humour' of the rabble while James's army remained so close.

The council then turned its attention to Murray, who was still lurking up at Pennyburn Mill with his little force. A relative of Murray was located and sent with a message for him: 'That he should immediately on sight thereof, withdraw his men to the back of the hill, out of the sight of the city.' Murray received this message, read it and didn't understand it, but 'the messenger being his relation explained the mystery to him': the Governor and the council were about to surrender, and the sight of Murray and his troops might disturb the negotiations. The relative added some thoughts of his own: he said several of Murray's friends wanted him back, believing he alone could oppose the enemy effectively. If he didn't return, Derry would certainly pass to the hands of the Jacobites.

Murray decided to march his horse straight to the city. Along the way he met a party of Jacobite dragoons, part of the cordon Rosen had thrown around Derry, who fired on him. He evaded them 'with some difficulty . . . and came to Ship Quay Gate'. It was closed. He demanded admittance but was refused.

Meanwhile, at the opposite side of the city, White and Hamilton met James. White returned alone to the city because Hamilton accepted the king's protection and stayed behind. A little later, the Earl of Abercorn, from the Jacobite side, appeared at the walls with terms. In return for surrender, James offered the citizens their lives, their estates, their religion and a free pardon for all past offences. He asked for twenty commissioners to come to St Johnston and parley.

However, 'the people took an occasion from the sight of the army to tell their fellow-citizens and the soldiery that there was no depending on the King's word'. Those on the ramparts shouted down to Abercorn that the people would not surrender on any terms. Extraordinarily, though, the lines of communication to the council were still functioning. James's offer and his request for twenty commissioners reached Lundy, so surrender was still a live prospect if only Murray could be got rid of.

Since Murray refused to withdraw, the council now sent Walker down to Ship Quay Gate to talk to him. Walker offered to bring Murray in alone, by means of a rope lowered over the ramparts. Murray disdainfully refused: he was a citizen and would enter through the gate.

At this point, James Morrison re-enters the story. That morning he was the captain of the guard at Ship Quay Gate, and, without any orders to do so, he let in Murray and his troops. Then the gate was closed behind them. 'The multitude having eagerly desired and expected his [Murray's] coming followed him through the streets with great expressions of their respect and affection.' There was probably a great deal of anger, too – directed at the council. Mogridge's revelation had confirmed the Governor's treachery for the mob.

Safe, for the moment, in their chamber, the council drafted the city's surrender. Then they turned their attention to a new letter from Richard Hamilton which had just arrived. Again it offered the defenders in Derry two stark alternatives. The first was capitulation. If Derry sent twenty witnesses to St Johnston to verify what was offered and delivered the keys of the city into James's royal hands, thereafter they would be 'treated as favourites and finishers of this difficult siege'. As their reward they might expect 'all the lands of the absentees and other such forfeiting persons . . . and besides, your own estates (which are now forfeited) shall be confirmed to you by an Act of Parliament now sitting'. The royal largesse didn't stop there: for 'such of you as are strong and stout shall serve with us in Scotland and in England, where thousands of both nations are ready to receive and join us.' And, besides enjoying the pleasures of war, 'when it shall please God to give us victory in England, which in a few months we hope to accomplish, we assure you that even there you shall come in as sharers of the forfeited lands'.

If, on the other hand, they chose to resist, they would be ruined. The Jacobite army was well disciplined and powerful. Once the siege started, cannons and mortars would smash the walls to pieces. Then the city would be stormed. The women and children of Derry might fall to their knees when the Jacobites entered but their piteous cries would be drowned by 'the loud acclamations of our victorious army, which will then be deaf and merciless'. Not even James himself could save the population 'from the rage and slaughter of an enraged army'.

While Lundy and his colleagues were digesting this apocalyptic document, the city was spiralling into pandemonium. Murray was moving through the streets and a huge crowd surged around

him. 'He assured them he would stand by them in defence of
their lives and the Protestant interest, and assist them immediately to suppress Lundy and his Council, to prevent their design
of surrendering the City.' This was insurrectionary talk, the prel-
ude to a coup. He next asked everybody to tie a white cloth
around his or her left arm as an emblem of their willingness to
fight. It was a brilliant *coup de théâtre* that created a feeling of unity
among the citizenry.

These events 'greatly alarmed and perplexed the Governor
and his Council'. They agreed to send for Murray. The upstart
arrived at the Council Chamber, striking, as he entered, 'a cold
damp on the Governor and his Council'. The Governor 'desired
to know the occasion of his [Murray's] jealousies of him,' and
Murray replied brutally: he told Lundy that he was either a fool
or a knave. The Governor, he said, was guilty of 'gross neglect':
he had failed to secure the fords; he had refused ammunition to
the soldiers at the front; he had ridden 'away from an army of
10,000 or 12,000 men, able and willing to . . . encounter the
enemy'; and he had neglected 'the advantageous passes of Long
Causey'. In conclusion, he urged Lundy 'to take the field and
fight the enemy' immediately, assuring the man who was still
technically his superior of 'the readiness of the soldiers' to fight.
This was cunning because no one could accuse him of being a
usurper or disrespectful of authority.

Lundy declined the last opportunity he would have to change
his reputation from traitor to hero. He attempted to persuade
Murray 'to join with the gentlemen there present, who had
signed a paper for surrendering the Town, and offered several
arguments to that purpose, drawn from their danger'. Murray
'absolutely refused it, unless it were agreed on in a General
Council of the Officers, which he alleged this could not be,
since there was as many absent as present'.

Nothing having been achieved by the exchange, Lundy and
the others went back to the job of preparing for surrender while
Murray returned to the waiting crowd and delivered the news:

'the Council were resolved to give up the City' but Murray was resolved to stay 'and do his utmost to prevent what he saw the Council intended'. He could say this with some certainty, he said, because he enjoyed the 'affections of the common soldiers, whom he knew to be generally as adverse to surrender, and as resolute for defending the city, as himself'. He was convinced by their reaction that the people were with him.

Back in their chamber the council now began to discuss who should go to the king to surrender. Nobody was nominated. With Murray and his multitude outside, it was unlikely one man could be found who would agree to go, let alone the required twenty. The whole council, and especially Lundy, were well aware that authority had passed to Murray. He was now the only man in Derry who could bring about the surrender.

Desperate times called for desperate measures. The mob in the streets with white strips of cloth tied on their left arms were mostly non-conformists, so Lundy summoned some of their ministers. He hoped that the sight of them going in to talk to the council might quell the multitude, and that the ministers might be persuaded to try to change Murray's mind. The ministers refused to go. In the streets Murray and the crowds were exultant.

Lundy ended the last session of the council he would chair. Everyone slipped away and thereafter few of this council dared 'for a while appear in the streets, for fear of the armed multitude [while] Col. Lundy kept his chamber', having first posted a party of his own Redcoats outside the door to protect himself.

Meanwhile, attempts were under way to establish a new regime. Three messengers were sent to Colonel Cunningham to see if he would take charge, but they never returned. Murray was appointed Governor until a permanent appointment could be made.

Outside the city, on top of a hill and just out of cannon range, James was sitting on his horse in the rain that was now pouring down, watching the intermittent firing. He had arrived that morning expecting capitulation, but instead had been shot at. As the day ended it became clear to him that Derry would not admit him, so he drew off his troops – on account of the bad weather – to quarters close to Derry, 'there to expect the arrival of the cannon and other things necessary for the forming of a siege or a blockade'. Then he retired to St Johnston to rest and ponder what to do next. He had not yet given up all hope that Derry would yield through diplomacy.

In the city James left behind, Murray's triumph had not created harmony. On the contrary, there was still a small but important knot of sceptics who believed the Jacobites would win and then punish the citizens for their insolence in firing on James and refusing his offers.

All that night, Walker reports, 'gentlemen left us . . . and made their escape to the ships'. Cunningham's flotilla, now at Greencastle at the mouth of the lough, was about to sail back to England. One or two, like Sir Arthur Rawdon, 'who was dangerously sick and forced from us by the advice of his physician and his friends', left with the approval of the more implacable citizens. But, for most of those who left, it was extremely dangerous, 'for the soldiers were under great discontent, to find themselves deserted by those that engaged them in the difficulties they were then under and were not easily kept from expressing it with violence upon some persons'. It seems, though, that no one was set upon by the mob this time.

Then, in a repeat of the mysterious events of the previous night, the key to the Ferry Quay Gate was found missing and the gun on the rampart above was discovered uncharged, the gunner vanished. Most likely the man had simply deserted, but Murray thought it was the work of the recently discredited council and its leader, Lundy. He reacted as if an enemy strike was imminent, and had all soldiers mustered to the ramparts. Once it was clear the Jacobites were not launching a sneaky night attack and the soldiers were stood down, Murray seized the keys from Captain Wigston, who was in command, and posted his own men on the walls and gates. Those who had carried out the coup were deepening and extending their control, but surrender could not be completely ruled out – not yet.

CHAPTER THIRTEEN

The Siege Begins

In Derry the first task on the morning of Friday 19 April was to establish a new leadership. Adam Murray was the popular choice for both General and Governor, 'but he modestly refused it, because he judged himself fitter for action and service in the field, than for the conduct or government of the town'. Next, a council of officers – fifteen, including Murray – was convened. This selected nominees for Governor from among themselves and voted: Henry Baker and George Walker were jointly elected. Both were not only popular but, crucially, untainted by association with the worst of the previous regime. They had been barred from the meeting with Cunningham when Lundy had persuaded the colonel to return to England. They could therefore be counted on to prosecute the good fight.

Except that the very first action of Walker and Baker on election was not to accept their posts but to visit Lundy, who was lurking in his chamber. They asked him to return to his post, but he turned them down flat. He knew he was hated by the multitude, and his sincerest wish was to exit Derry immediately. Walker and Baker promised to do everything they could to ensure his safety.

Next, they wrote to Colonel Cunningham, who was readying the *Swallow* for its return home, and asked him to take charge. As before, he declined the offer, saying his instructions had been to obey Lundy, who, of course, favoured his returning to England. Cunningham having refused, Baker and Walker finally accepted the government of the garrison. There was much to do.

First, guessing James would not have been best pleased with his treatment the previous day, Baker and Walker ordered Captain Kinaston to go to him 'to make an excuse to him for the garrison firing upon him'. When Lundy – who still had allies to tip him off – heard of this mission, he sent Captain Vernon Parker to Kinaston with the request that the latter pay him a visit. Kinaston wisely went to Baker for advice. The new governor told Kinaston to do as he was asked: he might learn something.

Kinaston later alleged that Lundy gave him several extraordinary messages to pass on to James: he (Lundy) had done his utmost to serve the king; he had arranged matters at Cladyford so that Richard Hamilton was able to cross; and he had prevented Colonel Cunningham from bringing his regiments into the city. Most amazingly, Kinaston also claimed that Lundy produced a letter purportedly from Cunningham and read it aloud. In it Cunningham advised Lundy to make the best terms he could with the Jacobites, as he couldn't hope to hold out until supplies and relief arrived from England. Furthermore, Cunningham assured Lundy, he would emphasize to King William that Lundy had had no option but to surrender. Then Lundy allegedly said he had forged the letter, and had read it to the council two days before. This was the council meeting that had agreed it was impossible to hold the city and had decided to surrender. The fake letter, it seemed, had tipped the balance to surrender. It was more proof that Lundy had always served King James. Kinaston claimed to have asked for the letter to show James, but Lundy wouldn't give it to him.

Kinaston then went to St Johnston. He communicated the apology for firing on James and blamed 'the rabble [that,] being drunk, seized upon the cannon and fired without order from any people of authority in the town'. James accepted the apology. Kinaston then related Lundy's messages. James, according to Kinaston, exclaimed, 'Alas, poor man,' and indicated that he believed Lundy had done everything he could to help him.

Fortunately for Lundy, the details of Kinaston's conversations remained secret at the time. If the mob had learned of them, he might not have survived until the new Governors smuggled him out. This task, though, would have to wait: first, the Governors attended to the appalling state of their forces. Most officers had fled to Cunningham's ships. The soldiers who remained were therefore disorganized and leaderless. Baker and Walker concentrated the remaining troops, a total of 7,020 men, into 117 companies, each with 60 men. They determined that these would be organized into eight regiments, seven of foot and one of horse.

While this reorganization was being undertaken, the Jacobites in St Johnston were waiting for the twenty commissioners whom they believed were on their way. Come 4 p.m., and with still no sign of them, Melfort composed a short and pleasant letter promising their safe conduct. He then sent Lord Abercorn off to Derry with the letter, and a request that the commissioners return with Abercorn. When Abercorn delivered it, he could not resist intimating that non-compliance with James's request would be met with savage violence, including the use of bombs. Gratuitous threats were part of war, but as fear of Catholics had largely contributed to the current impasse, these remarks were only going to exacerbate matters. In other words, Abercorn had failed to understand both the nature of the enemy and the policy of which he was the agent: the securing of the city's peaceful surrender. He should have stayed silent.

The Governors and council set to work drawing up the list of commissioners. Once again, the new regime seemed to be on the same tracks as the previous one. Adam Murray was proposed as one of the twenty but he refused, left the chamber and went up on the walls. Nevertheless, the twenty were subsequently chosen. However, the new council (eager to repeat Lundy's mistakes, it seems) had forgotten that Murray was on the ramparts. When the commissioners appeared in the street, the men on the walls were 'so enraged, that they threatened, "That if a man of them offered to go out on that errand, they would treat them as betrayers of the Town, the Protestant Religion, and King William's interest."' The commissioners, terrified, stayed where they were. From that moment on, surrender, at least in public, was no longer an option. Reflecting this new order, and in lieu of the commissioners, a Captain Maltis drafted a pugilistic communiqué:

> Sir, The cause we have undertaken we design for ever to
> maintain; and question not but that powerful Providence
> which has hitherto been our Guardian will finish the
> Protection of us against all your attempts and give a happy
> issue to our arms. We must let you know that King William
> is as capable of rewarding our loyalty as King James; and an
> English Parliament can be just as bountiful to our courage
> and sufferings as an Irish one; and that in time we question
> not but your lands will be forfeited rather than ours and
> confiscated into our possession as a recompense for this
> signal service to the Crown of England and for this
> inexpressible toil and labour, expense of blood and treasure,
> pursuant to their Sacred Majesties' declaration to that
> purpose, a true copy whereof we send you to convince you
> how little we fear your menaces. We remain, &c.

Interestingly, this letter conflates religious conviction with the acquisition of property. Though this was a religious conflict and part of a greater European conflict, with the forces in Ireland acting as proxies of distant powers, it was also a conflict about land and who owned it. Some of those who had once owned the land were outside Derry, and some of those who now owned it were inside. To the victor would go the spoils – that is, the land – and in Irish society this was the basis of wealth and status. Both sides knew that. The letter was sent to Melfort.

By 'persuading' the commissioners not to leave, the multitude had assumed real authority, notwithstanding the fact that Baker, Walker and the council were nominally in power in Derry. As if to emphasize this, it was now that the soldiers – instead of having them imposed from above – selected their own captains (341 amateur officers were elected, bringing the fighting total to 7,361); they, in turn, picked their colonels and, by association, their regiments. The effect of this realignment was that the regiments varied enormously in strength: Baker's had 25 companies; Mitchelburne's 17; Walker's 15; Hamill's 14; Parker's and Whitney's 13 each; Crofton's 12; and Murray's (the single cavalry regiment) 8. The majority wanted to attach themselves to Baker, the more popular Governor. Murray's regiment would have been just as popular, but was limited by a lack of horses.* The colonels chose only their regimental chaplains, who were clearly important figures for an army that believed God was on its side. Some named Episcopalians and others nonconformists. Now that they faced a common enemy in the Catholics, the quarrelsome Protestant sects forgot their differences and worked together.

The new Governors' next step was to initiate a simple but effective defence plan. The city was divided into eight sectors, with one regiment assigned to each sector. This was done so that the men would all have an intimate knowledge of their particular zone. The regimental drummers were quartered together 'so that on the least notice they repaired to the respective post of the company they belonged to'. They could then muster the troops who would rush straight to their designated places. Adjutants

---

*David Cairnes was one of the lucky ones who did manage to squeeze into Murray's regiment. He was made Lieutenant Colonel and served throughout the siege. He later represented the city in the Irish Parliament for some years.

were also gathered together so they could be found on all occasions. During the hours of darkness, two regiments would be stood to (with the adjutants staying in the Main Guard until their regiments were relieved.) This would ensure that the adjutants (who would relay any message to their regiment) could always be found. After 8 p.m., besides there being no drinking, no 'candles were to be lighted, which might direct the enemy to fire their cannon against the town in the night-time'. As a precaution, ammunition was removed from the main magazine 'and lodged in four . . . places, in case of accidental fire or treachery, so that all might not be lost at one time'. Whatever the future held, it wasn't going to be a repeat of the debacle at Cladyford.

The Governors also viewed the stores and decided that the weekly ration for a private soldier should be 'a salmon and a half, two pounds of salt beef and four quarts of oatmeal'; innkeepers were forbidden to charge more than a penny for a quart of beer. Many merchants had abandoned their stocks and fled, so, to prevent looting, instructions were issued to have these goods moved to a common store and itemized.

Walker, looking back on that day, recalled the mood of apprehension:

> we had no persons of any experience in war among us, and
> those very persons that were sent to assist us had so little
> confidence in the place that they no sooner saw it but they
> thought fit to leave it . . . we had few horse to sally out
> with, and no forage; no engineers to instruct us in our
> works, no fire-works, not so much as a hand-grenado to
> annoy the enemy, not a gun well mounted in the whole
> town . . . [The enemy] were so numerous, so powerful and
> well appointed . . . that . . . we could not think of ourselves
> in less danger than the Israelites at the Red Sea.

However, he seems to have thought at that time that Derry's story, like that of the Israelites, would have a happy ending. But many of the thirty thousand refugees huddled behind the walls did not share his belief. A siege was never pleasant, and if the Jacobites gained entry there could be carnage. So it was hardly surprising that, once the message arrived from James that he was prepared 'to receive and protect all that would desert . . . and return to their dwellings', there was a huge exodus of refugees. As many as a third, ten thousand, of the civilians in Derry decided to take advantage of the offer. Over the next few hours and days they crossed to the Jacobites and accepted protections. However, two-thirds, twenty thousand, did not. The majority of them were Presbyterians.

For the Jacobites to encourage this mass departure was a terrible mistake. They had hoped to gain intelligence, but nothing they learned was worth the advantage they had given their enemy. By their generous offer they had not only taken out of circulation those who were most equivocal about resistance, thereby consolidating the grip of the hardliners, but had also caused Derry to have fewer mouths to feed. At a stroke, starving out the defenders became much less likely.

As evening fell, a trumpeter from St Johnston appeared. Maltis's letter had apparently not reached the Jacobites, so they were still awaiting the twenty commissioners. The defenders, longing to be taken seriously, thought the trumpeter was being insolent. On their behalf, Colonel Whitney scribbled out a few lines for the trumpeter to take back to James. Shorter and sharper than Maltis's original, the Whitney letter said 'that no such terms and determination as those proposed by Governor Lundy and his Council would be acceded to; and that the garrison and citizens were determined to abide the consequences'.

The trumpeter was soon back with St Johnston's reply. This was a carte blanche – a document signed at the bottom but with the middle left empty for the garrison to insert its own terms of surrender. The hapless trumpeter was turned away with a verbal message even starker than Whitney's note: the people behind the walls were for William and Mary and if any more messengers 'came thither to frighten and terrify their people from their allegiance they would hang and shoot them'.

Throughout Friday, Cunningham's flotilla remained moored just off Greencastle, on Lough Foyle but not far from the open sea. As well as the sixteen hundred Redcoats and the crews, the ships were now crowded with refugees from Derry. Some, such as Sir Arthur Rawdon, had been compelled to go aboard by illness, but others were officers who had deserted their troops. Captain Wolfranc Cornwall, knowing these were desperate times, was charging £4 a passage, a considerable sum. The sailors happily stripped passengers of their swords, watches, clothes and other personal effects if they didn't have the cash to pay.

Lundy was still in touch with the flotilla. At some point he had sent Cunningham a message, requesting that the colonel wait for him. Unfortunately Lundy had still not made it to the *Swallow* by the evening, and Cunningham set sail for England without him.

At about the same time, James, having recognized Derry had spurned him, made preparations to return to Dublin. He left St Johnston on the morning of Saturday 20 April with Rosen and Léry, leaving Maumont in charge, supported by the Duke of Berwick, Pusignan and Richard Hamilton.

Adopting the dispositions Rosen made during his brief visit, Maumont ringed Derry with sixteen infantry regiments. On the left bank these were arranged in a semicircle running north–south, so the city was completely surrounded. On the opposite bank of the Foyle, Maumont established a strong point under the command of Lords Bellew and Louth in the orchard of a Protestant colonist called Stronge. This was on slightly raised ground just north of the Waterside with a direct view across the Foyle of the Ship Quay Gate and that end of the city. In this place the Jacobites would soon have a mortar battery established.

This army, on paper at least, was formidable. It supposedly numbered around twenty-one thousand, all told. However, not all the regiments were up to strength. Over the coming months, some would have to be temporarily amalgamated, producing new hybrid units with just two battalions. Nor was there ever a time when all thirty-five regiments were present: some were always needed out in the field, guarding the army's lines of communication against the resisters in Enniskillen. And, because the Jacobite soldiers were poorly and infrequently paid, hundreds of them were often absent as they scoured the surrounding countryside for food. Though reinforcements arrived from time to time, a high casualty rate, plus sickness and desertion, also thinned the ranks.

Perhaps the Duke of Berwick was taking all this into account when he put the size of the besieging army at ten thousand: seven thousand on the west bank and the balance on the Waterside. If this is accepted as a more accurate indication of the Jacobite force, the two armies were on a roughly equal footing with the balance just tipped to the Jacobites because of their cavalry and dragoons, who were better equipped and had more experienced commanders than the Williamites. However, cavalry rarely played a leading role in the siege of a walled town. The troops that counted were the infantry, and here the Jacobites were at a disadvantage. They weren't well trained or disciplined and they were generally armed with pikes rather than muskets. They also suffered from a shortage of artillery. The chief requirement for a successful siege of a walled town was heavy weaponry. Half a dozen cannons, firing continuously at a chosen spot, would eventually make a breach in the wall through which the infantry could pour in. A body of experienced French artillerymen supported the Jacobites at Derry, but without ordnance they couldn't do their job. The author of *A Jacobite Narrative* estimates 'there was not in the camp above eight cannon, two of which were eighteen pounders, and the rest were petty guns'. Even allowing for the two cannons, a great mortar and some petty guns that James subsequently sent north, the Jacobites never had the necessary firepower to demolish a section of wall.

The Jacobites were at a further disadvantage because of another factor: the weather. During the spring and summer of 1689, it was execrable – wet, cold and miserable. Those inside the walls, living in crowded, unhygienic houses, short of food and sometimes water, and subject to incessant mortar bombing, were hardly commodiously accommodated, but at least they had shelter. The Jacobites didn't have sufficient tents and the soldiers were forced to live in structures constructed from turf sods with improvised roofs, or in dugouts. These structures offered some shelter from the weather and enemy shot, but they were prone to flooding. Disease inevitably spread through the ranks.

Finally, critically, the Jacobites were handicapped by their commanders' attitudes to their own men. Neither James nor Rosen ever gave any indication that they grasped, let alone had a strategy for improving, the poor quality of the troops or their woeful conditions. Their understanding stretched only as far as belittlement. Hence James's remark that if he'd had an army of Englishmen, they would have brought him Derry 'stone by stone', and Rosen's observation that 'the greater part of the officers of the Irish army are wretches without heart or honour. A cannon ball passing as high as a church steeple will send a battalion to the earth, and one cannot induce them to rise [again] unless by riding over them'.

Culmore, a poorly built fort on a meander in the Foyle, lay four miles downriver from the city. It had a turbulent recent history: its Protestant defenders had been withdrawn earlier by Lundy and it had then been reoccupied by a larger garrison, including three hundred men from the city, under the command of William Adair of Ballymena. Most of its ordnance, eighteen guns, had been transferred to Derry during the last days of Lundy's rule. This had left the garrison with one iron gun and four small pieces of artillery.

In the cordon that he threw around Derry, Maumont placed himself at the northern end, along with his staff officers, Pusignan, Berwick and Hamilton, and about eleven hundred troops. By being here, he occupied the road between Derry and Culmore. There was another route to Culmore, up the opposite bank and across the Foyle lower down; Maumont blocked this with a detachment from Sir Michael Creagh's regiment.

Culmore was crucial. If Maumont were going to lay siege zealously to Derry, he didn't want a garrison three hundred strong in his rear. There was also the matter of the fort's strategic significance: if it eventually became necessary to starve Derry into submission, Culmore would be the key. In Jacobite hands no ship could pass it and Derry would be sealed as tight as a bottle.

The Culmore garrison knew this as well and, fearing attack, sent an emissary called Johnson to Maumont. The fort would surrender, Johnson explained, only if it had proof that James was in Ireland. Maumont realized there was only one answer to this: James had gone, so Maumont would have to send Johnson after him.

Johnson left the Jacobite lines and hurried after James. He caught up with him that evening in Strabane and had his audience. He left promising that he would persuade Culmore to surrender. He was as good as his word.

Meanwhile, within Derry, a council of war was held with Walker and Baker taking the chair together. Everyone agreed the city was in trouble. Not only were they surrounded, but the relief – Cunningham's flotilla – had been sent away. When the ships got back to Liverpool and Cunningham told his story, the authorities would assume the city must have fallen and they would not send a second relief. It was vital to get word to London that they were holding firm. But a soldier could not be sent out with a letter: the Jacobite lines would cut him down. If he went disguised as a civilian and was caught, the enemy would be perfectly entitled to shoot him as a spy. The messenger had to be got out in uniform but in such a way that his life was guaranteed.

The man selected for the job was Captain Joseph Bennett. He slipped from the city and began running pell-mell towards the Jacobite lines. As he did so, a detachment of guards posted at the Windmill in front of Bishop's Gate fired towards him, taking particular care not to hit him. On reaching the Jacobite lines, he presented himself, quite credibly, as a deserter. The Jacobites weren't immediately convinced and took him prisoner. Eventually he escaped, reached Scotland, then went to England to communicate his message. Later he wrote *A True and Impartial Account*, in which he described his experiences in Derry.

Despite James's departure, the besiegers hadn't entirely given up hope of a deal. To this end, Lord Strabane appeared outside the Bishop's Gate with a trumpeter. His offer was a full pardon, as well as James's protection and favour, in return for surrender.

Adam (now Colonel) Murray sallied out to meet him. Strabane urged Murray to switch sides, promising a colonelcy in the Jacobite army and £1,000 from the Crown. Predictably, Murray refused. Then it was noticed that the Jacobites had been manoeuvring their ordnance into Stronge's orchard. Strabane was told that if he didn't withdraw the garrison would fire on him. He declined to go and continued to reiterate James's generous offer 'till we plainly told him, we would never deliver the town to any but King William and Queen Mary'. Strabane finally retired, escorted by Murray past the city's outlying guards. There were several more approaches by trumpeters bringing offers from the Jacobites over the course of the day, but these were similarly rebuffed.

The night of Saturday 20 April finally saw the evacuation of Lundy, courtesy of Derry's two new Governors. They were anxious to help their former superior to escape the wrath of the mob, so they had to smuggle him out without anyone noticing. Here they had a stroke of luck. The previous day, Benjamin Adair, an officer from the fort at Culmore, had come to Derry for powder. Now he needed to return to his post. He couldn't

Oliver Cromwell, Lord Protector

James Butler, Earl of Ormond and Ossory, later Duke of Ormond

James, Duke of York, as a young man

Anne, Duchess of York, daughter of Edward Hyde, 1st Earl of Clarendon, and first wife of James

Charles II

Titus Oates

James II's arrival at Kinsale, with Derry under siege in the background

Richard Talbot, Duke of Tyrconnell

Frances Talbot, Duchess of Tyrconnell and sister of Sarah, Duchess of Marlborough

Queen Mary, older daughter of James II and wife of William III

Queen Anne, younger daughter of James II

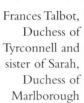

James II, Duke of York

Mary of Modena, second wife of James II

William III,
Prince of Orange

William and Mary at the time of their coronation, February 1690

John Churchill, 1st Duke of Marlborough

Sarah Churchill, Duchess of Marlborough, and sister of Frances, Duchess of Tyrconnell

A Jacobite gun battery with Derry in the background

George Walker, Rector of Donoughmore,
Co. Tyrone, and joint Governor of Derry

Colonel Henry Baker, joint Governor of
Derry, until his death on 30 June 1689

Colonel John Mitchelburne, who became
joint Governor of Derry after Baker's death

Counsellor David Cairnes

Jean-Antoine de Mesmes, Count of Avaux,
French Ambassador to James

General Godert de Ginkel

Contemporary illustration of Derry under siege

A panoramic view of the siege of Derry, showing the walls, the defenders' entrenchments and the besiegers

The Governor Walker Memorial Pillar, Derry

go by road because the Jacobite troops were blocking the way, so a boat was prepared for him. The plan was to send Lundy with Adair when he went. The old Governor was disguised as a private soldier and made it to the quayside unchallenged. He reached Culmore, from where he boarded a ship for Scotland, but it was not the end of his story.

In January 1689, when Richard Hamilton joined the Jacobites, John Temple had been accused of recklessness. Why, it had been asked, had he proffered himself as Hamilton's guarantor when the Irishman clearly wasn't to be trusted? He must be a poor judge of character. Then, in March, Hamilton had led an army into Ulster, laid waste to several towns and threatened Derry. In London there was apocalyptic talk: in Ireland much more blood would shortly flow and the fault would be Temple's.

However, in April the recently crowned William III did not see the situation like this. He made Temple his Secretary of War. A few days after his appointment, Temple hired a Thames boat to take him to Greenwich. As the boat passed under London Bridge, he threw himself into the filthy water and drowned. He left a note written in pencil: 'My folly in undertaking what I could not execute hath done the King great prejudice, which can be stopped no easier way for me than this. May his undertakings prosper, and may he have an abler servant than I!'

Clarendon described Temple's death in his diary on 20 April: 'People discoursed today very variously of Mr Temple's having made himself away. Some said it was trouble of mind, for having made a correspondence in Ireland with Mr Ellis for the obtaining of that kingdom . . . But others said it was a perfect frenzy, he having had a feverish indisposition for some days, which was true.' Macaulay, writing much later, reckoned 'the cold magnanimity of the master was the very thing that made the remorse of the servant insupportable'.

Temple's suicide was not forgotten, and would later become a much-spun thread in Williamite accounts of the wars in Ireland.

CHAPTER FOURTEEN

The Fighting Begins

About a mile north of the walls, the Pennyburn River fed into the Foyle. This small village where Murray had briefly paused on his way to Derry was occupied by neither side. But, looking south from his camp towards the city, and spotting the village in his line of sight, Maumont saw that if the rebels took Pennyburn, they would acquire a forward observation point, or even a base from which to attack his troops. He therefore sent orders to Brigadier Ramsey, who commanded the Jacobite infantry and was currently camped with them on the St Johnston side of the city, to take possession of Pennyburn.

Ramsey thought two hundred men should be enough. He gave the command to yet another member of the Hamilton clan, Colonel John Hamilton. The Jacobite infantry moved around the city clockwise and pitched their tents on Pennyburn Hill in the evening. The lookouts on the walls saw everything, and it was obvious what the next Jacobite move would be. But before they did the expected, the Jacobites surprised the garrison the following morning, Sunday 21 April, by firing their heavy ordnance at the city for the first time. The cannon balls smashed roofs and crashed through walls. One man was killed. While the bombardment continued, John Hamilton's soldiers began marching towards Pennyburn village.

This news was relayed to Adam Murray, who decided to challenge the Jacobites. This would give his men combat experience, which they needed, and might keep the Jacobites out of Pennyburn. The muster call was sounded and five hundred musketeers answered. They were ordered to go out in small groups and hide behind the hedges that lined the road to Pennyburn. A hundred or so troopers and their mounts went too. Because there was a shortage of forage in the city, most of the horse and their riders were grazing in fields beyond the walls, which was why so few mounted men answered the call.

John Hamilton and his forces entered Pennyburn village, unrolled their tents and set about pitching them. Murray meanwhile called up another five hundred musketeers. At noon the troops sallied out, 'as many as pleased, and what officers were at leisure'. If their progress sounds insouciant, it probably was: Murray didn't want them to draw attention to themselves. The infantry was ordered to the high ground that overlooked Pennyburn; the horse, meanwhile, were ordered to go forward along the road.

John Hamilton, amid his tents, noted these developments with alarm. Given the size of the force on the way, he could not withstand an attack: he would either be driven from Pennyburn or perish. He sent a message back to headquarters asking for reinforcements, and Maumont responded immediately in person, despite strenuous attempts by Brigadier Sheldon to dissuade him from this action. Like Murray, however, he too was short of cavalry, most of whom were similarly out foraging. Only about forty men were immediately available, but Maumont set off at full gallop for Pennyburn, three miles away, and mustered another forty or so dragoons on the way. A hard ride is not the best preparation for a cavalry encounter.

Arriving at Pennyburn, the Jacobites collided with Murray

and his troopers. There was a short, sharp clash. Among those slain on the Jacobite side was General Maumont himself, but the superior skill of the Jacobites still told: Murray and his men were pressed back towards Derry. The Jacobites followed, not knowing that the musketeers were hidden in the hedges. Although these troops fired on the Jacobites as they passed, the latter galloped on, probably under the command of the young, brave Duke of Berwick. However, if he was courageous, Berwick was also foolish. With Murray's troopers pushed back to the city walls, the garrison members on the ramparts could now fire down on the Jacobites or rush out to join the fray. Among those who did so was Governor Walker. According to his own account, he rode out 'to relieve Colonel Murray, whom he saw surrounded by the enemy, and with great courage laying about him'. The Jacobites were in serious trouble. They were faced by the troops emerging from the city, while at their rear were the musketeers, who by now had reloaded. As they rode past, the Jacobites were decimated.

Meanwhile, two regiments of Jacobite horse – a force of more than a thousand – were working their way around the flank of the rebel musketeers on the hill overlooking Pennyburn with the intention of cutting them off. This party on the hill had no pikemen to defend them, and musketeers on their own had little chance against cavalry.

In order to avoid an inevitable slaughter, the party of musketeers marched down the hill and moved smartly back towards the city. This manoeuvre took them right past the Jacobite heavy gun that had been firing since morning, just across the river. For the gunner here was a splendid opportunity – the enemy in range and unprotected – and he immediately commenced firing. The musketeers hurried to the shadow of the walls, then the Derry gunners on the east wall returned fire, disabled the Jacobite gun and killed its gunner.

For the moment, this was the end of the fighting. Now came the unvarying ritual that followed action – the gleaning from the dead of their weapons and other booty, and the reclaiming of lost comrades. The men from Derry were first out. Strewn across the countryside were perhaps a hundred dead men. These included just ten or twelve of their own. From the Jacobite dead, the Derry search parties took not just the talismans of military triumph – the colours the enemy had dropped, their personal effects, swords and firearms – but also their clothes, including hats, belts and especially boots. Soldiers have always plundered, but the motive here was less greed than need: only about one in twenty behind the walls had shoes.

It had been a good day for the defenders. Their losses had been relatively small, considerable arms and booty had been captured (an important measure of success), and, after a long series of reverses, they had finally scored a victory. It was a boost to morale. The Jacobites, on the contrary, had lost nearly two troops of horse, several officers and, of course, their commander-in-chief.

A dispatch with the news was sent south after James. He was obviously displeased, and ordered that Maumont's body be embalmed. It was then to be sent to Dublin under guard or kept at Derry until the siege was over. James still clearly believed his forces (now under the command of Pusignan) would shortly subdue the city.

After the excitements of Sunday, both sides needed to consolidate on the Monday. In Derry, stores were inspected and military responsibilities delegated. Outside, the Jacobites moved several more cannons to Stronge's orchard. Their first position had been about five hundred yards from the walls; the new position was half that distance from the city. They also continued negotiations with the garrison at Culmore. The next day, St George's Day, their efforts were rewarded: the garrison agreed to surrender. The signatories for the Jacobites were Richard Hamilton and Berwick, and for the garrison William Adair, Benjamin Adair (who'd spirited out Lundy) and Richard

Johnston.* The instrument of surrender guaranteed a free pardon and the right of all garrison members to return to their homes with all their possessions, including their swords. The officers were allowed to keep their horses and pistols, and a gun each for sporting purposes. However, on arrival in Coleraine (where they'd asked to go) the garrison members were disarmed, stripped of everything other than the clothes they stood in and relieved of all their money. They were then told to beg, if they wanted anything, and sent away. All this was done by order of Colonel Charles Moor, the Governor of Coleraine.

St George's Day also saw the newly positioned cannons in the orchard starting the work of bombardment. All day ten-pound balls were fired incessantly at the houses along Ship Quay Street, battering the garrets and rendering it unsafe for the occupants to remain upstairs. The defenders had gunners on the ramparts, but they had to protect themselves from shards of stone flying up from the cracked pavements. Screens had to be erected at the back of the ramparts before they could return fire. 'The besieged, having made a blind in the street to preserve the people, repay them [the Jacobites] in the same coin and killed Lieutenant Fitzpatrick, Lieutenant Con O'Neill, two sergeants, some soldiers, and two lusty friars.' Walker adds nastily that it was a 'great grief to the enemy, that the blood of those holy men [the friars] should be spilt by such heretical rabble, as they called the besieged'. Hatred would be a great nourisher, and contempt such as this would sustain the defenders in the months to come.

Since the skirmish at Pennyburn four days before, the Jacobites had reinforced the original two hundred infantry camped there. On Thursday 25 April Murray attempted to dislodge them.

---

*The emissary sent from Culmore to see the king was Johnson. The signatory might be the same man with his name misspelled or it might be a different man. The records aren't clear.

Forage was in short supply, and his horses soon wouldn't be any use at all; he had to make the best of them while they had some strength left.

At nine o'clock Murray sallied out with horse and foot and headed for Pennyburn. He found the Jacobites crouched down in defensive ditches in front of the village, waiting to repel precisely such an attack. But the Derry infantry was eager to succeed, to claim some booty, and the Jacobites were pushed out of their ditches and retreated. The garrison gave chase, but just then a party of Jacobite horse appeared. The infantrymen now had to fall back towards their main body of troops, chased by the Jacobite cavalry. Some Derry soldiers, observing this, got into a ditch and, as the Jacobites passed, fired at them from the side. The Jacobite horse discovered that they had ventured too far, so they retreated to the safety of Pennyburn Mill. Murray's soldiers ran forward again. They had the Jacobites trapped. The latter had to be reinforced, so some dragoons were mustered from about a mile upriver. These hurried down, on foot, to assist their beleaguered colleagues.

Back at the Jacobite camp, another story was unfolding. In the morning a local woman had entered the camp. She was old, hungry and had heard the Jacobites had provisions. She had come to beg. As she made her way along the lanes between the tents, she came upon some oatmeal that had got mixed up with dung on the ground and began to pick it out. This could not be done discreetly. A soldier spotted her and called her a witch. This was more than a simple insult. It was believed that if the dung of an animal were burned by a sorceress, that animal would fall ill. Failing to recognize her hunger, the soldier was accusing the old woman of wanting to sabotage the Jacobite cavalry. A crowd gathered and the 'witch' was hauled away.

The Reverend Andrew Hamilton and Mr Anthony Dobbin, a justice of the peace resident in the neighbourhood of Derry, had meanwhile entered the Jacobite camp. They had business with Richard Hamilton, but he was still at Pennyburn. As they waited, the two visitors heard gunfire close by and were told about the 'witch'. Hamilton, fearing the worst, pleaded for the woman's life. He and Dobbin went towards the sound of the shooting and spotted the woman with one breast exposed. A group of soldiers had been firing at her and had wounded her in several places. Then, before Hamilton and Dobbin could stop him, one of the soldiers placed his musket close to the woman's breast, fired and killed her.

Back at Pennyburn, the two sides sniped at each other for the rest of the day. As evening fell, they were locked in a stalemate – neither side having the resources to overpower the other. Nevertheless for Murray and his men this was another relative success. They had pinned down the Jacobites for the whole day at Pennyburn Mill for the loss of only two men (with eight or ten wounded, all of whom recovered).

Now, just when things were going well, there was an incidence of extreme negligence. Colonel Parker, the commanding officer of the Coleraine regiment, had been sent out with a rearguard to protect the Derry fighters at Pennyburn. At about 7 p.m. a considerable force of perhaps a thousand men commanded by Ramsey appeared from the Jacobite camp. They bore down on the Williamites, and Murray's troops retired at the double. Parker, though, was casual, and thereby exposed the soldiers he was there to protect to great danger. From the ramparts, the troops saw what was happening, and were appalled by his performance.

Once the troops were back in Derry and the gates closed, the carping started. Parker was threatened with a court martial. Knowing his position was hopeless, he slipped over to the Jacobite lines later that night and served with the Jacobites for the rest of the siege.

Colonel Parker's defection, besides boosting Jacobite morale, was a welcome addition to their forces. The Marquis de Pointis, the crucially important commander of the French artillery, had been wounded, though not mortally, while the Duke of Berwick was also hurt. Most seriously of all, General Pusignan had been fatally wounded in the fighting around Pennyburn. Two commanders had therefore been lost in less than a week. The Jacobites had good reason to think their luck had changed for the worse. Furthermore, Richard Hamilton was next in seniority. He was neither a great general nor a skilled siege commander, but with no alternative officer to hand he now assumed command.

Over the preceding days the Jacobites had added mortars to the artillery in Stronge's orchard, and, as the fighting raged at Pennyburn, they now began to lob exploding bombs rather than cannon balls. The defenders reacted to this new threat with insouciance. Walker speaks of the shells from the lighter sort of mortar falling harmlessly in the streets, hurting none except an old woman in a garret. One of the larger bombs also fell on her house: it entered, through the ceiling, a room where several officers were eating, passed straight through the bed and the floor beneath it, and exploded in a lower room, killing the landlord. It also blew out the side of the house, which, says Walker, was fortunate: it gave the officers a means to exit because the doorways were clogged with debris.

But it should not be forgotten that behind the nonchalance there were simmering tensions. For instance, although a rota had been agreed which specified set times for groups to worship in the Cathedral, nonconforming and conforming ministers were in dispute over rations, with the first alleging they had received no allocation from the stores – though many had contributed provisions – while the latter 'were maintained by the store for some time, and after that had 2s. 6d. paid to them while the others had no such allowance'. Once again the established Church had organized matters for the benefit of its own and to the disadvantage of the dissenter. Blame for this was laid squarely at the door of Governor Walker.

On the evening of Friday 26 April, just after James arrived back in Dublin, Avaux wrote to Louis XIV to tell him that his predictions had come to pass: James had gone to Derry, had summoned the city to surrender four times and had been refused each time. Furthermore, France had lost some fine generals. James was as exercised as Avaux by these fatalities, and he wrote to Richard Hamilton to remind him that generals were to practise discretion in revealing themselves to the enemy. The new commander was hardly going to argue. He had much more pressing problems, which he enumerated in letters of complaint that he sent south. Many of his battalions, he said, were not up to their full strength of six hundred men. Worse, only a tenth of his men were armed with muskets, and those weapons he had mostly weren't fit to shoot. If he were to conduct a successful siege, he needed reinforcements, artillery and working firearms.

Yet, despite the shortages, the Jacobite artillery was still inflicting pain. On the night of 26 April,

> the bombs played hotly on the city, with little intermission
> from the setting of sun until morning. This night was one of
> intense suffering; terror prevailed in all directions, except in
> the hearts of the intrepid heroes under arms. The shrieks of
> women and children formed a terrific contrast with the
> thunder of the artillery and the crash of walls and houses
> thrown down by the shells.

And these were only the small bombs.

The new day dawned and witnessed a strange episode that illuminated both the porous nature of the walls at this early stage and the conflicts that still bedevilled the Derry garrison. When James Hamilton had arrived in the *Deliverance*, he had brought not only money and ordnance but a Captain Nicholas Darcy. When it was discovered that the captain was a deserter from King William's service he was put in Derry's jail. He had been there a month and was just one more mouth to feed, so Governor Baker issued him with a pass, to go with his arms and one or more horses to the Jacobites. Darcy left with several horses and a quantity of flour. Questions were asked and it transpired that the vendor was Colonel Whitney, the officer who had defended Lundy on the bridge at Coleraine. Later, of course, he had also stopped the unfortunate Captain Neville from returning to the city, and had ordered the gunners on the walls to cease firing on James. He now commanded one of Derry's eight regiments. Whitney was arrested, charged with selling items that were not his (the horses rather than the flour) and tried at a council of war. He was found guilty and imprisoned in the jail on the rampart over Ferry Quay Gate. He remained there for the remainder of the siege. In his new home he would have heard the boom of the Jacobite ordnance firing from Stronge's orchard, followed, moments after, by the whistle of the bombs and balls passing overhead as they flew towards Shipquay Street.

After Whitney's conviction, the command of his regiment was given to Captain Monro, while the command of Parker's regiment went to Captain Lance.

In England, a second relief operation was about to get under way. On 18 April, Captain Jacob Richards, an engineer in King William's service and the son of Colonel Solomon Richards, had been ordered to Chester. He arrived seven days later and 'heard that Colonel Cunningham and Colonel Richards [i.e. his father] were returned from Londonderry'. It was a bad sign. He also learned that he was to sail to Derry at the first opportunity with some French officers (serving Williamites, despite their nationality) to assist in the defence of Derry. On Tuesday 30 April, Captain Richards reported from Liverpool, 'arrived here one Stevens, a messenger from King William, with orders to go to Derry and to make his report of that place. In the afternoon he embarked in a small vessel of about twenty tons.' The Williamites didn't know if the city had fallen. Stevens had the unenviable task of finding out.

Meanwhile, the bakers and brewers of Liverpool and Chester were put to work to supply provisions for the relief of the besieged. On 2 May Captain Richards received new orders: he was to 'embark with some regiments ordered for to relieve Londonderry', though these were yet to arrive.

Back in Derry the next evening, a party of Jacobite soldiers crept up to the Butchers' Gate under cover of darkness and fired on the city's pickets. The defenders had long believed that Jacobite sympathizers inside the walls were digging a passage under the ramparts, and this incident fuelled their fears. Governor Baker felt sufficiently concerned to search all the cellars near the walls on the pretence of looking for provisions. He found no sign of any excavations, but the notion that there were traitors inside the wall would linger right to the end of the siege.

Along with paranoia, feuds also flourished in the city's hot-house atmosphere: there was now a spectacular example of this. The parties were Henry Baker, the more dominant of the two Governors, and John Mitchelburne, the pre-eminent regimental commander. It is not known exactly why they fell out, but Baker grew sufficiently suspicious of Mitchelburne to order him to his chamber. In effect, he'd placed Mitchelburne under house arrest, but Mitchelburne was not prepared to go quietly. There was an argument, and both men drew their swords and fought. Baker prevailed and Mitchelburne was taken away.*

Meanwhile, in Dublin, James replied to Richard Hamilton's complaints in positive terms. In a letter dated 1 May he promised, 'with all possible diligence you shall have all I can send you to enable you to reduce that rebellious town'. While he waited for James to make good this promise, Hamilton was not idle: he was always looking for an opportunity to inflict damage on the enemy. In early May one seemed to have presented itself.

---

*No serious grudges seemed to be held after this. Mitchelburne was never tried, and later in the seige when Baker was ill, he nominated Mitchelburne to stand in for him as Governor.

As far as the Jacobites were concerned, the Williamite who had caused them the most grief so far was Adam Murray. Twice he had attacked them at Pennyburn, and as a result of those attacks two French generals had been killed. Now it was remembered that Murray's eighty-year-old father Gabriel was living quietly on the family farm a few miles away. This could be Murray's Achilles' heel. Hamilton issued orders for Gabriel to be brought to his camp at Brookhall. When he arrived, Hamilton explained that Adam Murray was in rebellion against the king and was inciting the people within Derry to resist. This behaviour had to stop, so Gabriel was to go to Derry under escort and tell his son to desist. If Adam failed to do as his father commanded, Hamilton would see to it that the old man was hanged.

Murray Senior was sanguine. He doubted this threat would sway his son to abandon his resistance, but he was willing to go. He was escorted to the walls and Adam emerged to meet him. Gabriel said his piece, then produced a Bible he had thoughtfully brought with him. He urged Adam to swear his fidelity to the Protestant cause and his opposition to the Pope. In spite of this effrontery, Gabriel escaped the rope. Richard Hamilton sent him back to his farm, where he remained, under Hamilton's protection, for the rest of the siege.

In Liverpool, the second relief force was still mustering. On 5 May Jacob Richards learned that his father and Cunningham were suspended pending investigation for dereliction of duty and that their regiments had been passed to Colonels Steuart and Sir George St George. He also learned that Major-General Percy Kirke, the Derry expedition commander, a soldier who had provoked immensely strong reactions in the course of his long but not always illustrious career, had arrived in the city.

Kirke was born in 1646 and entered the army when he was twenty. He received his first commission with the help of James, then Duke of York, in the Maritime Regiment, the forerunners of the Royal Marines, who were noted for their yellow coats. In

1681 he became commander of the 2nd Tangier Regiment. This put him on the track to promotion. The next year he became Governor of Tangier and remained in this post for the last three years of its brief existence as a British colony, assuming command of the Governor's Regiment. Their badge being the Paschal Lamb, they quickly became known as 'Kirke's Lambs'. Samuel Pepys visited Tangier in 1683 to oversee the winding up of the colony's affairs. Kirke, his regiment and his regime all appalled the diarist. The Governor was a drunk, and his boorish table talk was so repellent that Pepys withdrew from the mess with his companion, a future bishop, and thereafter dined apart. This didn't stop him hearing a catalogue of complaints about Kirke and his regiment. There were stories of Jews returned to the Spanish authorities (and certain torture at the hands of the Inquisition) because they could not raise the bribes that Kirke had demanded. There were stories of local women being raped, and houses being robbed by Kirke's soldiers. There were further tales of regimental courts that were improperly constituted, following which condemned soldiers were beaten to death. Yet Kirke had his defenders as Pepys freely acknowledged. The medical officer of the garrison, a man called Lawson, told the diarist that Kirke had done more for the garrison and its defences than all the previous governors combined.

Kirke returned to England with his 'Lambs' in time to fight for James at Sedgemoor. In the aftermath, he enthusiastically oversaw the meting out of punishment to Monmouth's rebels, for which James had rewarded him. When William landed at Torbay, Kirke and his regiment marched west to engage him. As he went, Kirke declared his intention to fight for James until he had shed his last drop of blood. In the event, like Churchill, he had already decided in the summer to defect. He crossed over and his new Dutch master rewarded him three days later with promotion to major-general.

This, then, was the officer selected to take the second relief force to Derry, with an allocation of four infantry regiments: his own Lambs, Sir John Hanmer's, and those previously of

Cunningham and Richards, now commanded by Steuart and St George. The naval commander was George Rooke. Some of these troops were already at Liverpool, while others were on their way there.

Back at Derry, the action now shifted from Pennyburn in the north to the south of the city. Five hundred yards in front of Bishop's Gate there was an area of rising ground. Its features included a ridge that ran along the top (this had obvious strategic benefits), a windmill and the city's gibbet. The Derry garrison had established an outpost there armed with a few fowling pieces. These weapons, flintlocks rather than matchlocks, needed no burning tow to fire them, which made them easier to use. They were also more accurate and had a longer range than matchlocks. Equipped with these weapons, garrison members had been sniping at the Jacobites. The casualties they inflicted were small, but the ceaseless firing obliged the Jacobites to be endlessly vigilant. The removal of this irritation was a good reason to take the hill, but equally compelling was the view it afforded. So far, the Jacobite artillery had been blazing away for days without making much of an impression. But James's promised heavy ordnance, if placed up on Windmill Hill, might inflict more serious damage.

The assault to secure the hill was launched on the night of Sunday 5 May. The forces involved were large: Brigadier Ramsey put three thousand men in the field – an entire brigade. With a force of this size appearing out of the darkness, success was inevitable. The garrison's pickets fled to the city bearing the bad news. Ramsey, knowing the defenders would not easily give up so precious a prize, ordered his men to consolidate. By sunrise it was done: they had transformed existing ditches into a sequence of trenches. These ran from the bog on Ramsey's left to the river on his right. This would prevent the rebels from working round the Jacobite flank and attacking from the side or rear.

Within the walls the outlook was grim. If the Jacobites were not ousted from the hill, their ordnance could soon demolish Bishop's Gate. An assault force – 10 men from each of the 117 companies – was assembled early on 6 May and set off towards the hill. The Derry soldiers found the Jacobites squatting down in ditches and behind old walls, only their heads showing as they squinted into the darkness. The attackers, their weapons primed, tow smouldering, unleashed a succession of fusillades. Great clouds of ball skimmed along the ground and crashed into Jacobite faces, ripping skin, smashing teeth and shattering bones. The Derry men then rushed the lines. The fighting was savage and intimate: the attackers used their muskets as clubs against the defenders to smash their skulls, crack their vertebrae, and pulverize their shoulder blades. In response to this onslaught, so sudden, so violent, so murderous, the Jacobites retreated in disorder. Brigadier Ramsey tried to rally his fleeing troops but failed.

By midday it was all over. The garrison had re-established control over the whole area for the loss of just three or four private soldiers and a single lieutenant dead, and twenty or so men injured. The engagement also yielded great booty, in the form of 'four or five colours, several drums, fire-arms, ammunition, and [a] good store of spades, shovels and pick-axes'. Colonel Mitchelburne – who, whatever his difficulties with his superior, had not been kept from the field – took two of the colours personally: they were yellow and showed a phoenix in flames and the motto *Dum Spiro Spero*. When he later became Governor, Mitchelburne had these hung in the Cathedral, and later still he had a bronze tablet erected in the Cathedral with an inscription commemorating their capture.

For the Jacobites, this engagement had been costly as well as futile. They had left behind in the trenches two hundred or so dead men with ball holes in their faces or chests, while a further five hundred had staggered back to their camp with appalling injuries. Of these, '300 of them within a few days died of their wounds'.

Worse for the Jacobites, the dead included a number of their meagre staff of officers, including the operation's commander. Brigadier Ramsey had been shot dead while he attempted to rally his men. This was a great loss, as Ramsay was 'reckoned the best soldier in the army next to Colonel Richard Hamilton' (perhaps not quite the compliment it seems) and 'much lamented by all who knew him'.

Besides their large number of fatalities, the Jacobites also had several officers taken prisoner, including Sir Garrett Aylmer, Lieutenant-Colonel William Talbot (son of Sir Henry Talbot, Tyrconnell's brother, who rejoiced in the sobriquet 'Wicked Will') and the venerable Viscount Netterville. If injured (and many of them were), surgeons treated them, after which they were confined in the house of Thomas Moor.

Once the bodies of the dead had been plundered, a drummer was sent to the Jacobite camp. The burial detail appeared on 7 May. They did their job, says Walker sniffily, 'very negligently, scarce covering their bodies with earth'. It must have been odious work to inter the dead of the heaviest Jacobite defeat to date.

As the corpses of his soldiers were being heaved into ditches or covered with earth, James's Parliament was meeting for its inaugural session in Dublin. The venue was the King's Inns, the suppressed Dominican priory where the Four Courts stand today on the Quays. Until now, James had tried to conciliate the Protestant and settler elements in Ireland so as not to alienate the English. However, Jacobite Irish Catholics – or, to be precise, Irish Catholics of Old English provenance – had rather different priorities from James's. Though they believed they had loyally served the Stuarts through the Civil War and after, the regicides still had the spoils – the land. They wanted this Parliament to undo the Acts of Settlement and Explanation and restore the land to the proprietors who had been in place on 23 October 1641. Clearly, then, the English Jacobite and Irish Old English aspirations were incompatible. Though this had been fudged thus far, this so-called 'Patriot' Parliament would lay bare these differences. The new body's composition would guarantee that.

In the spring of 1689, when the writs for this gathering were moved, most Protestant freeholders had already left Ireland. Those who had not were locked inside Enniskillen, Derry or other places in the north; they were not involved in the election process and did not return any representatives to Dublin. In those parts of the country that did send members the returns had been fixed. With the writs for election that had gone out in early spring soon after James's arrival in Ireland, Tyrconnell had usually sent letters recommending who should be chosen. The result was a House of Commons with 6 Protestants and 224 Catholics; of these about 60 had Gaelic Irish names while the rest were Norman or Old English. So the Lower House was emphatically Old English, and these men were much more interested in 'an English dependency under a Catholic oligarchy' than the restoration of James on the far side of the Irish Sea.

The House of Lords, with only 36 members, wasn't quite so weighted. To be sure, Protestant membership was attenuated – most temporal peers had left the country – but four Protestants who had remained on the island were present (the Earls of Barrymore, Granard and Longford, and Viscount Rosse). Moreover, the seven bishops summoned were all Protestant (James had not dared to summon any Catholic prelates, as that would have played disastrously in England), and though three were excused attendance on grounds of infirmity, the other four did attend. They were Anthony Dopping of Meath, Simon Digby of Limerick, Thomas Otway of Ossory and Edward Wettenhall of Cork and Ross. Their presence reflected not only the reality of Jacobite authority in Ireland (it wasn't absolute), but that, for some Protestants, despite all that had happened, William's seizure of the throne was constitutionally dubious. These eight Protestant lords would be the block, albeit only a small one, against the majority's ambition.

James attended the opening and made a speech to both Houses. He acknowledged that without the help of King Louis XIV he would not be in Ireland. He took care to thank the Irish for their loyalty, too. He then declared for liberty of conscience. This ideal, he confessed, had proved elusive, but he was determined, where he had the power, that in future there should be 'no other test or distinction but that of loyalty'. It was an admirable ambition, but quite how it would be achieved in the midst of a confessional civil war he did not say. He also spoke of 'relieving such as have been injured in the late Act of Settlement' but added the caveat that this would only be 'as far as may be consistent with reason, justice, and the public good of my people'. These were fine words. Unfortunately for James, the reality was that one of the great works of the session would be the repeal of the Acts of Settlement. The Commoners wanted them squashed, and, lest there should be any doubt, they promptly selected Nagle, one of the great enemies of the Settlement, as their speaker.

As the session got under way, and following hard on the reports of the losses at Pennyburn, news came of Windmill Hill's heavy casualties and the loss of another significant soldier in Brigadier Ramsey. Then horse litters started arriving from the north with their cargoes of officers wounded on the hill. The testimonies of these men added to the reports already circulating, and before long it was agreed throughout Dublin: Derry was James's slaughterhouse.

The last thing James needed in his struggle with Parliament was the news from the north. It gave his Irish supporters the moral high ground. They could argue, with justice, that they were fighting and dying to help him get his kingdoms back, so now he must grant them back their land. He was unwilling to do this as it would confirm his reputation in Scotland and England as a Catholic tyrant and make it that much harder to recover those kingdoms. On the other hand, the Irish – both those in Parliament and the soldiers in the field – expected nothing less. This was their understanding and they were not about to compromise. He was in a bind but as the pressure in Ireland was the most immediate it was there he would give ground.

CHAPTER FIFTEEN

Grinding on

On Wednesday 8 May, the day after the opening of the Parliament in Dublin, the Jacobite forces in the north were handed a further drubbing. The Enniskillen garrison was small but angry, and in this war animosity was a vital resource. Most recently they had been infuriated by a cattle raid orchestrated by the increasingly hungry Jacobite forces:

> On 2 May the Jacobite garrison in Omagh sent two men into the parish of Kilskerry within five miles of Enniskillen, and in the night the two men stole away with about twenty or thirty cows. In the morning the owners, missing their cows, and seeing their track go towards the road that leads to Omagh, did believe them stolen, and therefore sent to some of their neighbours to come and assist them in going in quest for their cows.
>
> Accordingly eight of them got together and went upon the trace of the cattle, and overtook them within a few miles of Omagh; but the thieves made their escape to that garrison. The men that followed the cows gave themselves no further trouble in following the thieves, but were

bringing the cows back with them to their own dwelling. But before they got about half way home they were overtaken by four and twenty dragoons from Omagh well mounted.

The men [from Enniskillen] having all but bad horses and few arms, three of them quit their horses and got into a great bog. The other five, thinking they had done no harm but followed their own goods, submitted and had quarter given them. The dragoons, leaving a guard with the five prisoners, followed the other three men, but to no purpose. For the bog that they got to lay near a mountain not passable by horse, whither they escaped and so got back home.

The dragoons returned to the prisoners, carried them a little way back with them, and then most barbarously murdered them all, cutting them so in the face with swords and bayonets, that their friends scarce knew one of them when they found them.

And this for the most part was the fair quarter that the Irish gave our men whenever they took any of them, which was the principal cause of our* so obstinate defence both of Derry and Enniskillen against such unequal odds.

In other words, the Protestants of the north saw no point in surrendering, because they were convinced they would be murdered if they did.

A day or two after these events, on 4 May, a message was received from Captain Folliot, the commander of the Protestant garrison at Ballyshannon, twenty miles from Enniskillen. He was under siege from Jacobites and needed help.

---

*The author of this account was a rector in Kilskerry, near Enniskillen.

A force was mustered, and on 6 May Colonel Lloyd (the Adam Murray of Enniskillen), twelve companies of infantry and a few troops of horse set out for Ballyshannon.

The Jacobites soon learned this force was heading towards them. They advanced from Ballyshannon to Belleek, three miles away, where they positioned themselves in a narrow pass flanked by a bog on one side and the River Erne on the other. To make it even more difficult for the troops from Enniskillen to attack them, they erected a barricade, then demolished a bridge.

On Wednesday 8 May Lloyd and his forces appeared before the position the Jacobites had so carefully prepared. The defenders egged them on, inviting them to come forward and fight. Lloyd's men, though, secured the services of a local who offered to show the Enniskilleners a path around the side of the Jacobite positions. From behind their barricade, the Jacobites saw they were about to be outflanked and, without having fired a shot, they turned and began to flee. The Enniskilleners chased after them and meted out ferocious treatment, partly in retaliation for the slaughtered cattlemen. Nearly two hundred Jacobites were killed. The rest were lucky to make it to Sligo and safety.

Hereafter, the local Jacobite forces, under the command of Patrick Sarsfield, were hobbled. His task was to ensure no troops from Enniskillen went to relieve Derry – the Enniskillen garrison was small, but had a reputation for violence, and Sarsfield's brief to keep watch used up precious men and resources that were sorely needed further north.

While the Jacobites were burying their dead in Belleek, the relief operation in Liverpool received encouraging news. On 8 May Stevens returned from Derry and confirmed the city was still in the hands of the Protestants. He also brought the interesting information that the defenders 'have several times beaten the Catholics from before the place [and had] killed a French general and several English men of quality'.

Kirke called a council of war, at which it was decided to send an advance expedition. It would comprise a lieutenant, an ensign and about forty soldiers, including gunners and miners. Captain Richards would command. This might have been poetic justice – sending the son to the site of his father's disgrace.* It might have been generous – giving him the opportunity to clear the stain from the family name. Or it might simply have been practical, as Captain Richards had served at the siege of Buda† in 1686 that saw the expulsion of the Turkish pashas who had controlled the town for over a century: he knew about sieges and was an engineer.

Two days later Richards received his orders. It was a short document but redolent with Kirke's terror of losing his expedition's ships. The orders started with a terse preamble telling Richards that he 'and the four French officers, with the gunners and miners, should immediately embark and repair to Londonderry in Ireland provided it be still in the Protestants' hands'. Article one then told Richards 'To go no farther than within cannon shot of Culmore Fort'. There he was to stay until he had ascertained 'what condition Londonderry is in; whether any batteries be raised to hinder the passing of ships, or whether any other means are made use of, as the choking [of] the channel or chaining it over'. He was to continue on to Derry only once he had ascertained it was safe to do so. Article two specified what he was to do if, as was more likely, he couldn't pass without running the risk of losing the ship. In this case he was to sail around the Foyle and the coast and learn what he could about the enemy. He was then to send a report of the intelligence he'd gathered back to Kirke.

---

*Although at this stage Richards Senior and Cunningham hadn't had their military careers terminated, the signs were there.
†The town on the Danube's right bank that, with Pest on the opposite bank, now forms Budapest.

His orders received, Richards must have presumed he was about to leave, but two more days passed before he boarded the *Edward and James* on Sunday 12 May. This merchant ketch – a small yacht with two masts – carried him and the forty or so soldiers out to the other ships of the expedition: a frigate, the *Greyhound*, and another ketch, the *Kingfisher* (sometimes called simply the *Fisher*). These were all vessels of shallow draught, and could reach Derry via the Foyle if conditions allowed. The next day, Richards transferred to the *Greyhound* and the little armada finally set sail for Derry.

In London, Kirke's tardiness had not gone unnoticed. As Richards was boarding the *Greyhound*, Lord Shrewsbury was writing to the Major-General to say King William was both unhappy and perplexed that he was still on Merseyside. Despite this, it was a further four days before Kirke assembled his troops on the quays, ready to go.

His forces weren't what had been promised. Colonel St George's regiment had mysteriously fallen away. This left Kirke with three regiments rather than four, although each was of reasonable strength: the Lambs numbered 666 men, Hanmer's 593 and Steuart's 660. On Friday 17 June the relief force set sail and promptly ran into contrary winds that drove it straight back to the Mersey. Here it remained because of the weather for the rest of the month.

Back in Derry, several officers proposed that Windmill Hill, now it had been retaken, should be put beyond the reach of the Jacobites. They suggested a line of defences from the bog to the river, and Governor Baker agreed. A system of outworks was constructed. L-shaped, these ran from the Double Bastion to the Windmill and then, describing a ninety-degree turn, to the river's western bank. With this, all the land south and west of Derry 'was taken in by the besieged to the distance of 260 paces' from the walls.

The Derry garrison should have felt confident now: they had

three victories to their credit and they had augmented their defences. Yet a succession of little incidents chipped away at their self-belief. Immediately after the victory at Windmill Hill, an officer on duty there was suspected of communicating with the enemy. Following this, two captains, both surnamed Closses, deserted to the Jacobites. Until then, the night guard had been drawn only from the regiment on duty. It was decided that from now on the guard must be made up of men from more than one battalion, so the units could watch each other as well as the enemy. It seemed that not every member of the garrison was a committed anti-Jacobite. The same was true of the civilians. One day in the middle of May, several citizens went out of the city 'without orders to parley with the enemy'. To stop this unsanctioned meeting, the Governors ordered a cannon fired at the party. The shot killed four of them. At this time Richard Hamilton was also regularly in touch with people within the walls, offering protection. Between twenty and thirty people a day were slipping across to the Jacobite lines. Naturally, the Governors did little to stop this exodus: it meant fewer mouths to feed. Hamilton, however, believed that the intelligence he gained from the refugees would help his cause more than keeping the maximum number inside the walls. Starvation was not yet part of his plan: he still believed the city must fall before his superior army.

Hamilton's masters knew better. In his letter of 10 May, having acknowledged Ramsey's death and promised more ordnance and troops, James was emphatic: because 'they may want provisions and may want to rid themselves of useless mouths, I think it absolutely necessary you should not let any more men come out of Derry' other than for what he termed some 'extraordinary occasion'. However, Avaux, who had long grasped that the only way to win was to starve the city and thereby turn the suffering majority against the 'No surrender' party, was soon reporting testily by letter to his master in France that Hamilton paid no attention to James's orders. He estimated the outflow

from the city was now running at between fifty and a hundred a
day. He was also starting to doubt the military capability of the
besiegers since the events at Windmill Hill. If there were more
military setbacks like this one, he continued, he was very much
afraid that the King of England 'will have all his troops killed in
detail before this place'.

After the fortification of Windmill Hill, there was a lull in the
fighting. Governor Walker puts this down to 'the enemy's want
of courage and our want of horse'. However, the bombardment
continued, and on most days there were skirmishes that followed
an unvarying pattern. The enemy would be spotted and men
would dash out from Derry, often under Captain Noble from
Lisnaskea, County Fermanagh, but not always. Sometimes private
soldiers would rush out without an officer. These engagements
were improvised and opportunistic: besides killing the enemy, and
preventing him having mastery of the terrain, they were used to
gather clothes, weapons, powder, ammunition and sometimes
information. After one skirmish, 'Captain Noble and others found
several letters in the pockets of the slain, giving them some intelligence, particularly about the surrender of Culmore'. There had
been no contact with the little fort since Benjamin Adair had left
with the kegs of powder and Governor Lundy. Now, 'We were
informed that Lundy, as he passed by [Culmore on the night he
escaped], sent a message to them that Derry was surrendered.
This, added to the discouragement they were under (having little
ammunition, and eight of the guns being before sent up to Town
by Captain Jemmet, on Lundy's orders), is said to have inclined
them to follow the example.' In fact Culmore had been well on
the path to surrender before Lundy left Derry, but the garrison
believed what they found in the letters.

However, much as the garrison's members abhorred the
betrayal, it was oddly reassuring to know Lundy had continued
to act basely after he fled, for 'this proved the justness of our
former suspicions'. At the same time, knowing Culmore was lost

must have added to the collective sense of isolation. Now, more than ever, hope focused on the relief expedition that was supposed to come from England. And the garrison needed something on which to pin its hopes, because the enemy's grip was tightening.

Until now, the principal Jacobite camp had been in St Johnston, but towards the middle of May they resolved to move closer to the city. They located their main camp on Balloughry Hill, two miles south-west of the walls, a second at Pennyburn and a third at Stronge's orchard. They also put guards on all sides of the city and along the banks of the river. 'After the placing of these camps, they brought their guns to Balloughry, and there successively discharged them all in the dusk of an evening.' Their troops then encircled the city and fired simultaneously, 'with a design (as we supposed) to strike a greater terror into the hearts of the besieged'. The siege was moving to a more intense phase.

This drawing closer of the Jacobites had many effects, most immediately on the gathering of intelligence. Over the preceding weeks, some individuals had been slipping in and out of the city to spy, on the pretext of visiting friends or relatives. Once the Jacobites were in their new positions, though, 'the besieged found it impossible to receive or convey any intelligence'. More seriously, the proximity of the Jacobites threatened the city's water supply. There were wells within the walls, but after so many explosions these had filled with earth. The Foyle was no good for drinking either as it was brackish. This left only one source of water: the St Columb's, or St Columcille's, wells. Unfortunately, they were in the no man's land beyond the outworks on Windmill Hill. The defenders, fearing the capture of these wells by the Jacobites, therefore constructed a redoubt to defend them. The Jacobites responded by constructing a trench from where they were able to fire on anyone who came to draw water. Some of those killed when doing so fell into the wells, and had to be dragged out to stop the water being poisoned.

This was but one aspect of the grinding, low-grade violence that characterized this period of the seige. There were, though, still occasional acts of courage (or atrocity) to punctuate the routine. On 10 May two hundred men under a Lieutenant-Colonel Blair slipped out of Derry and set off to attack Jacobite positions to the west. As they moved forward they were unaware that a party of Jacobites was creeping up behind and threatening to cut them off from the city. Colonel Murray on the walls, sensing disaster, mounted a horse, galloped out of Butchers' Gate and careered up Bog Street, the track leading west. He met a fusillade of fire, but, happily for him, all the shots missed and he was able to warn Blair. On 13 May a red-hot ball – probably heated in a brazier in the hope it would become incendiary – shot from across the river bounced up Pump Street, broke the leg of one boy and wounded another, then embedded itself in the church wall. The next day another was fired.

On 18 May a hundred men, led by Captain Noble and Captain John Cunningham, streamed out of Derry. They marched to a newly constructed Jacobite fort at Creggan and took it over. As night fell, a party of Galmoy's horse attempted to get between the fort and the walls. Noble and his men began fighting their way home. There were fifteen or sixteen fatalities (high by garrison standards) and Cunningham was taken prisoner. He surrendered, believing that quarter had been given, and was promptly murdered. The garrison sent a detail the next day to collect his body. According to Governor Walker, it was Jacobite policy to offer quarter and then act as if it hadn't been given. They had taken an oath, he wrote, 'not to keep faith with us, and to break whatever articles were given us'. He claimed he got this information from a prisoner who 'was troubled in his conscience that he had engaged himself in so wicked a design, and discovered it to us'. Walker also described going out himself to meet Lord Louth and Colonel O'Neil, who held a white flag, and being fired upon. Adding insult to injury, the Jacobites then 'denied they were concerned or knew anything about it'.

The Derry garrison benefited immensely from such incidents, which allowed garrison members to feel morally superior and reinforced their capacity to resist, whatever the circumstances. But this collective belief in the essential perfidy of the Jacobites did not make agreements impossible. As Mackenzie wrote: 'From 10 May until near the end of the siege, we had many little parleys with the enemy; sometimes to admit doctors to see the wounded prisoners, the Lords Netterville and Talbot; sometimes to admit provisions to them'. Clearly it was possible to suspend hostilities, and the garrison was happy to do so throughout the conflict. As usual, the story wasn't simply one of Jacobite Irish or Catholic bad faith and Protestant probity.

On 20 May Captain Cunningham was buried. The next day was devoted to God: both the Presbyterians and the Anglicans fasted and sermons were delivered. Over the following few days there were one or two sorties from the garrison, a couple of engagements, and the cannons were fired occasionally, to little effect. Outside the city, however, in the Jacobite camp on Balloughry Hill, there was a great deal of activity. Since the ships of Cunningham's relief expedition had sailed off, the Jacobites had been wondering about the second. They knew the English must return – they would not leave Derry to perish. The Jacobites calculated that the second expedition would most likely try to sail to the quays and unload provisions for the hungry city there. They had to devise a strategy to stop this. Some of James's advisers wanted to scuttle ships in the Foyle to block it. However, the besiegers were still convinced that the city would soon fall: if the river were made unnavigable, trade would be impossible when Derry capitulated. Given this, the Jacobites were left with one alternative: a temporary boom. The man entrusted with the task of building it was the French engineer, the Marquis de Pointis, who had now recovered from the wound he had sustained at Pennyburn.

He started work in the last week of May, choosing a spot near Brookhall, where the river was narrow. He bound oak timbers with iron chains and strung them across the river, but the oak sank, and before long the force of the water broke the construction. Pointis started again, this time with fir-beams, which he scavenged from houses in the district. The finished structure was two hundred yards long and five or six feet wide; it moved with the tide. Pointis thought an enemy sailing vessel, even with a following wind, would get stuck, which would leave the enemy sailors with no alternative but to try to cut the boom. To prevent this, he built forts on each bank of the river. On the left bank he dug a series of entrenchments, one above the other, creating a type of amphitheatre. These were very deep and also had impressive parapets. Crouching down inside, any Jacobite soldier guarding the boom would be safe from artillery fire, and as each tier could fire over the head of the one below they could bring massive firepower to bear. Pointis believed the English would be forced to surrender very quickly amid such an onslaught.

While the boom was being constructed, several men arrived from Scotland at the Jacobite camp at Balloughry. They proceeded to give Richard Hamilton advice he might have benefited from six weeks earlier. The way to force submission, they said, was to starve the defenders, and the first step towards achieving that goal was to stop them grazing their animals (especially their cattle) on the ground west of the city during the day, as they had been doing until now. Balloughry and Pennyburn, the visitors continued, were too far from Derry for the Jacobites to effect this. They needed to creep closer. Hamilton agreed, and over the next few days his troops built forts and dug trenches closer to the city than any of their earlier positions. Once this work was done, they would be able to menace the defenders as never before.

In the meantime, the fighting followed the established pattern, but with added urgency as the defenders tried to block these attempts to pen them in. On 27 May three hundred men (a large party by the standards of the garrison) went out to raid the enemy in their various camps. They attacked a new fort the Jacobites had just built towards Pennyburn, losing two men killed and four injured.

Informed by the principle of never letting the enemy rest, the combatants also continued duelling endlessly by cannon. On this same day two regiments of Jacobite horse and foot who were spotted resting in the distance were fired on from the walls and driven away. Meanwhile, the Jacobites continued to direct fire at the Cathedral, a prestigious target because this was where the enemy celebrated their obnoxious faith. Perhaps they had also learned that it was used to store powder. Unfortunately for the Jacobites their shelling wasn't so much wearing down the enemy as reinforcing their sense that God was on their side. On 27 May one of the Jacobite balls landed among the bells but did no harm, a second landed on the roof leads and disintegrated, while a third smashed through one of the Cathedral's windows, hit the floor and bounced out again. No one was injured. If ever there was a sign that the garrison enjoyed God's special favour, here it was for all to see, and they saw it.

A day or two later, Murray and a party of men rode out to Brookhall and attacked the Jacobites in their trenches. But the Jacobites were not in the mood to be intimidated. Following Murray's incursion they began constructing trenches in the bogs to the west of the city. To the defenders on the walls, this was provocation, so Murray led another sortie. The Jacobites fought back and, with no reinforcements coming – the Governors had decided not to send any – Murray and his detachment had to retreat. It was an uncustomary reverse, and the Jacobites maintained their new and threatening positions on the city's weak west side.

On 29 May the garrison learned that the Jacobites, with their new ordnance, were about to start bombardment in earnest. Baker and Walker ordered the powder in the Cathedral to be removed and stored in two dry wells in Bishop's Street. In the evening a drummer was sent up and down the lanes and alleys with a message for the thousands huddled in the city: every household was to have water to hand in case the enemy's bombing started fires. At least, since it wasn't for drinking, this water could be drawn from the Foyle.

The next day many 'dispatches of the enemy were seized from a post-boy making his way to Dublin'. These letters reinforced the garrison's self-belief. Since April, the Jacobites reported they had lost three thousand men, killed in the fighting or by sickness. The garrison's casualties were light in comparison. Also, many of the Irish Jacobite correspondents complained of exhaustion and never getting any proper rest because of the insecurity caused by the perpetual raiding. The Jacobite response had been to build hides. Only when they were below ground level could they feel safe from the garrison's guns and firearms. This was an army, at least on paper, that sounded as if it was resigned to defeat. And there was more good news for those inside the walls: 'From other parts we had account that a large army was daily expected from England and Scotland to raise the siege. For this our great guns were twice discharged, and our bells rung most cheerfully.'

However, the Jacobites, in their trenches or their underground hides, also finally had something to celebrate. James's promised ordnance had at last arrived. On the night of 30 May the Jacobites prepared to go on the offensive. They began building ditches to the west of Derry, then put one of their new cannons at Strawbridge's town and another at Tamneymore, on the other side of the river from Windmill Hill. The next morning their men ran through the fields in the early morning, surprising the defenders, and took a piece of high ground close to the network of outworks on Windmill Hill. Soldiers poured out of Derry and counterattacked viciously. After many casualties on both sides, the garrison pushed the Jacobites out of the ground they had taken.

Meanwhile, Captain Richards' little flotilla reached the lough mouth. Adverse winds kept them out, but the following day they were able to get into the lough proper and as far as Redcastle, where they anchored.

Before long, wrote Richards,

> Several people came off to us pretending to fly for their lives.
> They told us that Londonderry had made several sallies, and
> killed several people; that my Lord [blank in the original
> diary] were taken prisoners; that the whole number of Irish
> that is now before Londonderry is not above 10,000 men
> and 500 horse; [though] some say 7,000, others 15,000.
> They have invested it but dare not make any formal attack till
> they are stronger and have more battering artillery.

As intelligence went, this wasn't too bad, but it was slightly out of
date. The Jacobites were no longer waiting for their new ordnance, but were about to start using it. More seriously, the
witnesses knew nothing of Pointis's boom, and it would be another
week before Captain Richards heard about it. Torrential rainstorms
would keep him pinned where he was for the next six days.

'One of the difficulties of the garrison', wrote the historian Thomas
Witherow, 'was that they did not rely with sufficient confidence on
the wisdom and loyalty of some of their leaders. The experience
which they had of Lundy made them, perhaps, over-suspicious.'
From the start, Walker was a particular focus of animosity. It is easy
to imagine that a man with his showy temperament, who was also
in charge of the stores, would attract enemies, and he did.

'About the end of the month [of May], officers, having been
for some time suspicious of Governor Walker, drew up several
articles against him.' They accused him of a wide variety of
crimes. Around 18 April, the day James's forces had appeared
below the walls, he and others 'had privately sent a messenger
to King James, with proposals about getting the town to be
delivered up'. He had organized Lundy's escape, an action that
in turn precipitated Culmore's surrender. He had consulted
with other unnamed men with a view to closing the gates on
the garrison while they were fighting outside the walls, thus

ensuring their destruction. He had embezzled stores and sold the stolen items for personal profit. He had offered to betray Derry for £500 up front and £700 a year thereafter, an offer King James had approved. He had abused officers when they collected stores. He was also guilty of other personal vices that were glossed over.

These charges were widely endorsed. Of the 300-plus officers in the garrison, 100 signed them. Among the signatories were the now famous Captain Noble and the redoubtable Adam Murray, along with three of his fellow-colonels. Together, these officers wanted 'to prosecute him upon these articles, in order to [effect] the removing [of] him from all trust either in the stores or in the army'.

Governor Baker now had a problem. If tried and found guilty, like Colonel Whitney, Walker would see out the remainder of the siege from inside a cell. If he was cleared, he would remain at liberty and there would inevitably be friction between him and his detractors. Both outcomes were likely to split the garrison. Baker needed a formula that would show the signatories their grievances had been addressed while leaving Walker untouched. A motion was therefore proposed that 'the government of the stores, as well as the garrison, should be managed by a Council of Fourteen, of which he was to be President, and nothing be done but by them'. Baker readily consented to the establishment of the council, then persuaded Walker's detractors to set aside the articles. The new council appointed Mr Mogridge, who had helped to sink Lundy, as its secretary – there would be no likelihood of conspiracy or corruption with him around. It was also decided that the council could approve nothing unless seven members agreed.

The council might have caused fresh divisions, but it didn't. While appearing to extend democracy, in practice it left the status quo in place. Membership was limited to the regimental colonels, thus Walker was included, along with the Mayor, Gervais Squire, Alderman Cocken, representing the city, and

Archdeacon Jennings and Captain James Gladstone, representing the surrounding countryside. This was not a group likely to cause trouble.

The other impediment to the council becoming overweening was that it couldn't meet very often: 'the meetings of this Council were soon after, through the difficulty of the siege, especially the danger of the bombs, much interrupted, though the authority continued until the end of the siege'.

June began with the Jacobites trying to construct a trench opposite the gallows. The defenders on Windmill Hill poured fire down on their heads and drove them away. But all this military activity meant the defenders were running through their stores, and, unlike the besiegers, they were not being resupplied. Shortages were starting to show. On 2 June men from the garrison spent the day making cannon balls from the lead that had originally covered the Cathedral's steeple. Also on this day the Jacobites put into effect the Scots' advice. Until then, 'we [the garrison] had liberty enough for all our cattle and horses to graze over the bog, but now we are straightly besieged, and dare not venture without the island'. The garrison's sphere of control had shrunk to the land inside the outworks and the city walls. The siege had become a blockade.

With their new weapons, the Jacobites fired at the city, and the defenders returned fire: 'the great and small guns were not idle the greatest part of the day on each side'. Though the Jacobites were not very effective – they still seemed unable to damage the Cathedral – they were improving. The defenders had to fill barrels with earth and gravel and put them inside the Royal Bastion and the Double Bastion (at the south-western corner of the city) 'to secure the breast work from the enemy's battering guns'. In the midst of all this, ordinary human suffering went on as usual. Two men were lying in a hut on the Bishop's Bowling Green when a Jacobite ball crashed in and lopped off their legs.

The next day, lookouts saw ships on the Foyle, far beyond Culmore. The reconnaissance party under Captain Jacob Richards had finally arrived. There was, however, neither time to celebrate nor the opportunity to communicate. Such difficulties would be a theme in the weeks ahead. The defenders were locked up tight now, giving the Jacobites the opportunity to batter the city systematically with their new ordnance. The savage violence with which Abercorn had threatened the garrison in April was about to become a reality.

The strategy established now, and followed throughout June and July, was generally to fire cannon balls in the day, when the gunners could see their targets, and bombs at night, when it didn't matter where the ordnance fell as long as it was inside the walls. Occasionally, though, to keep the defenders on their toes, gunners reversed the pattern. These new bombs were much bigger than those lobbed into the city over the preceding weeks. Pieces weighing over 270 pounds and packed with 15 pounds or more of powder became common. When they exploded, the casing shattered, the jagged metal fragments mutilating anyone within range. Septicaemia often followed, then death. They also induced such terror that the besieged 'could not enjoy their rest, but were hurried from place to place'. From the beginning of June, the defenders at last experienced the same fatigue that comes from ceaseless and unending violence that the Jacobites had endured since the start. Between 3 and 9 June 159 bombs were lobbed into the city. Some citizens had miraculous escapes from the bombardment, such as a Mr Coningham, who saw a bomb land in his backyard dunghill and fail to explode. Others, though, were killed just as unpredictably. On the evening of 3 June Major Graham was leaning over the wall at Ship Quay Gate when a cannon on the other side of the river at Tamneymore was fired. The ball landed squarely in the major's stomach. Amazingly, he did not die until the next day.

*

The defeat at Windmill Hill had been one of the primary set-backs for the Jacobite forces, and in early June Richard Hamilton decided it must be avenged. To succeed at the site of an earlier failure would boost Jacobite morale, and the army needed a fillip, but there was more to Hamilton's thinking than this. The recapture of the hill was part of his strategy to keep the garrison penned as tightly as possible inside the city. Without land to forage or wells from which to draw water, surrender would come all the sooner. The Jacobites now also had a better chance of achieving this, because with the new ordnance had come reinforcements, six hundred men from County Down commanded by Colonel Buchan.

Over the days leading up to 4 June, Hamilton brought his forces from their various camps and placed them in front of Windmill Hill, but behind rising ground, where they couldn't be seen. They were about the distance of a good musket shot from the rebel positions. The assault force comprised about 12 battalions of infantry and 15 or 16 squadrons of horse, which should have meant a total of about 8,000 men, 450 of them mounted. But Hamilton's battalions were under strength – desertion, sickness and enemy attacks had seen to that – so the figure was probably between 5,000 and 6,000. As the troops mustered, plans were proposed. The newly arrived Buchan and Brigadier Dorrington, a grenadier commander,* argued they could carry the day, with a loss of no more than twenty men, with a frontal assault. Hamilton was dubious, but the colonel and brigadier persisted until he agreed.

Early on the morning of 4 June the Jacobite troops were roused and grouped. They divided their infantry into two units and their cavalry into three for the attack. At low tide and in three successive waves the cavalry was to attack the defences bordering the river. The ramparts there were lower

---

*Grenadier units were special formations of men usually selected for their size and height.

than anywhere else. Leading the first wave would be Edmund Butler, Lord Mountgarrett's second son. Before combat, he and his men took an oath in which they promised they would take the enemy's entrenchments. Meanwhile, as the cavalry breached the enemy's lines by the river, a party of infantry was to assail the entrenchments between the river and Windmill Hill, while the second, comprising grenadiers, was to hit those defences that faced the bogs to the city's west. This was to be a co-ordinated assault on both arms of the L-shaped defences that would pummel the defenders and precipitate their collapse.

Starting at seven, Jacobite soldiers made their way along the riverside on the south of the city. They were seen from both the walls and the entrenchments on Windmill Hill, so the defenders had time to organize. The author of *A Jacobite Narrative* ascribed this lack of guile to the Jacobites' sense of 'fair play'. Notions of honour, according to the writer, were ubiquitous among the Jacobites. This was simultaneously admirable and regrettable, he suggested.

In Derry a muster was sounded. The bulk of the garrison, eight thousand or so men, marched out and crowded into the outworks. As they disposed themselves through the redoubts and trenches, they formed three or four lines stacked one behind the other. The idea was that the front line would fire first. Then, when the smoke cleared, it would be the turn of the second line, and so on. Men not firing would be reloading. In this way fire could be maintained continuously, rather than, as usually happened, everyone firing together, which gave the attackers a couple of minutes to rush forward between fusillades.

Nearing ten o'clock in the morning, the Jacobites reached the gallows. Here they paused. Then the cavalry and infantry together gave 'a loud huzzah'. Their war cry carried north to the camps strung across Balloughry Hill, a couple of miles away, and when the camp followers heard it they shouted back. Over on the right the first echelon of Jacobite cavalry (about 150 men) dressed and armed, set off, trotting, cantering, then galloping. As they pounded on, they bent forward and kept their heads and upper bodies against the necks of their horses to protect themselves from enemy gunfire. The Derry garrison had been ordered to hold their fire until the last moment. When the vanguard of the Jacobite cavalry was only a couple of dozen yards away, the order was given. The first line of musketeers loosed a volley but it made almost no impact. As well as leaning over, the troopers wore cuirasses, thick chest plates. The musket balls simply bounced off. Captain Crooke, the defending officer in charge, quickly realized that they were aiming at the wrong targets: he told his men to fire at the horses. The second salvo had the desired effect and felled many of them, but Lord Butler and his echelon moved on, undeterred. With twenty-five or thirty troopers, the commander reached the enemy's positions at the edge of the water. Here they were confronted by a dry earth bank about seven feet high. The defenders were entrenched behind it. Butler spurred his horse up the bank and across the ditch behind. Colonel Purcell from Thurles followed, but his horse was shot beneath him as he scrambled up. Purcell had to jump backwards to save himself. Several other troopers made it over, only to find themselves in a maze of trenches. The defenders quickly sprang out of these and attacked them with muskets, pikes and scythes. Butler was wounded and taken prisoner. The troopers who had followed him fled to the river, hoping to get round the enemy's flank and away. Most never made it: in their heavy armour they drowned in the Foyle. Only 'three of these bold men with much difficulty made their escape', said Governor Walker. Coming from a man who was always quick to denigrate the Jacobites, this label of 'bold' was high praise indeed.

In the centre the Jacobite infantry had begun their advance in a sequence of lines. At the front was a detachment of grenadiers commanded by Captain John Plunkett. Behind came the colonels with pikes, then the infantry. The soldiers at the front had been issued with bundles of sticks which they held like shields in order to absorb the enemy's fire. They moved forward inexorably with their bundles held high. But then disaster: the vanguard reached the bank behind which the enemy was entrenched only to find it was even higher than the one the cavalry had faced. They needed scaling ladders but no one had thought to supply them. For the advance troops, unable to go forward or back, this was a calamity. The defenders reached down, 'grabbed them by the hair of their heads' and hauled them into their trenches behind. Here, they were either killed or taken prisoner.

Only the grenadiers came anywhere near to success. They had advanced over the bog near the Double Bastion and attacked the defences fiercely. The defenders retreated and the Jacobites swarmed through the forward trenches, empty now except for a small boy who had been pelting them with stones. These developments, however, were being keenly watched. Now Governor Baker sent his reserves towards the Bogside, as this was where a breakthrough was most likely. And after the men who hurried forward came women who 'also did good service, carrying ammunition, match, bread, and drink to our men, and assisted to very good purpose'.

From one end of the line to the other the Jacobites were now in disarray. Down at the water's edge, Butler's vanguard was destroyed. The echelons following, seeing the size of the enemy's bank, began to wheel about in an endeavour to escape. But this manoeuvre left them horribly exposed, for they were now side on to the musketeers, and therefore much larger targets. The defenders were still aiming low. Their musket balls skimmed along the ground and horses tumbled. Then, once the heavily armoured troopers had lost their mounts, the defenders, with their pikes, muskets and scythes, scrambled out of their redoubts, ran down the bank and attacked them in the field.

Once again, some troopers retreated to the water only to drown there.

In the centre the bulk of the Jacobite infantry, demoralized by the continuous firing and unable to advance, wheeled around and began to withdraw. As they did, their colleagues in the rear, realizing what this meant, also turned. The attack had turned into something that bore all the hallmarks of a retreat, with one exception: the Jacobites were moving more slowly than was generally the case when men fled. This puzzled the defenders until they realized many of the fleeing Jacobites were carrying dead men on their shoulders, which they did to 'preserve their own bodies from the remainder of our shot'. This was ingenious, if not exactly pleasant. Walker noted with characteristic sarcasm that these Irish Jacobite troops were of more use dead than alive.

Further inland, the grenadiers were now being so fiercely counter-attacked by Baker's reinforcements (and pelted with stones by the women) that they too had realized they must pull back. They abandoned the trenches they had taken and hurried across the bog.

By the afternoon the engagement was over. The Jacobites had not only failed to retake Windmill Hill but had once again suffered huge losses there. Walker said they left behind four hundred dead, but that was probably an exaggeration. According to Ash, about sixty were killed, plus double that number wounded or taken prisoner, which is probably closer to the truth. However, even taking the lower figure, the Jacobite casualties were ten times those of the defenders. The dead on the garrison side amounted to six private soldiers, plus Captain Maxwell. A Jacobite ball shot from across the Foyle pulped the latter's arm on the day, although he did not die until three weeks later. And there was an additional bonus: all those dead Jacobite cavalry horses. The carcasses were dragged back to the city, salted and eaten later.

The mood in the Jacobite camp on the night of 4 June was understandably sullen. Once again, the defenders had acquitted themselves better than the besiegers. The author of *A Jacobite Narrative*, for one, was pained by the discrepancy between the calibre of the two sides: 'You see here, as you have seen all along, that the tradesmen of Londonderry have more skill in their defence than the great officers of the Irish Army in their attacks.' But the Jacobite collapse and the rebel victory weren't simply on account of the latter fighting better than the former on the day – it was also a matter of planning. Why had the Jacobites not brought their artillery to bear on the entrenchments and pounded them before attacking? Why had they not sent pioneers in under cover of darkness to cut gaps in the defenders' works through which their cavalry and infantry could infiltrate? Why had they allowed themselves to be seen before they attacked? The answer to all these questions was that Buchan and Dorrington had overwhelmed Hamilton with their argument that they could pull off the assault with ease.

Pointis believed that their scheme had been 'contrary to every kind of judgment, [and] it was carried out contrary to every kind of rule and without paying any attention to what Mr Hamilton had ordered'. Hubris mixed with something not far from insubordination was at the root of the besiegers' woes. In the same dispatch Pointis had even harsher things to say about the consequences of the debacle. It had produced 'a general despondency amongst the troops that makes us very apprehensive if the enemy had the boldness to make the least sortie', and perhaps as many as three hundred soldiers had deserted following the fiasco. 'In a word,' he concluded, 'attacking must no longer be thought of . . . we shall have to wait on hunger.'

CHAPTER SIXTEEN

'In the Cup of Joy, Bitterness is Sometimes Mingled'

Angered by their defeat at Windmill Hill, the Jacobite gunners threw thirty-six bombs at the city in the evening, which 'plowed up our streets and broke down our houses, so that there was no passing the streets or staying within doors'. There was panic. The able fled to the walls, to the ground outside Ferry Quay Gate, to the ravelin beyond Bishop's Gate, or to the entrenchments on Windmill Hill. The sick left behind were those now most at risk. In this category were several men from Captain Ash's regiment, who were lying in the basement of Counsellor Cairnes' house when a bomb passed through the roof and the successive floors below. It landed among them and exploded, killing two and wounding many more. Another bomb dropped through the roof of the Markethouse and landed a couple of yards from a stockpile of forty-seven barrels of powder. It failed to explode.

The following day, 5 June, twenty-six bombs rained down, and many defenders were killed or wounded. The daytime bombs proved more lethal: at night, the burning fuses could be seen clearly and evasive action taken. But spending the night outside had other hazards. The great storms of rain and hail that were keeping Captain Richards' ships at Redcastle were also sweeping over Derry. The people, already debilitated by their appalling diet and lack of sleep, now had to spend much time in the open when they were wet and cold. They began to sicken, and the weak died. The only benefit of the bombardment was that 'The bombs, by throwing down some houses, furnished us with fuel, which we were in great need of.'

On 6 June large and small bombs were fired from cannons and mortars. Three hit the Markethouse, badly damaging the clock. The following day only eleven bombs were thrown at the city. The Jacobites were having to aim their fire at more pressing targets.

Since arriving off Redcastle the previous Saturday, Richards' flotilla had not moved. Now, on Friday 7 June, he decided he must sail on. The winds were still unfavourable, so the mariners of the three vessels dropped small anchors with hawsers attached, then pulled their vessels forward by hauling on the ropes. By this laborious process, known as kedging, the flotilla got to within three miles of Culmore before the tide turned and the ships had to drop anchor.

Keen-eyed lookouts up in the Cathedral tower spotted the masts far down the Foyle, ten or eleven miles from the city. Obviously, it was important to make contact immediately but, to do that, they needed a boat and all the city's vessels were gone: so, under the direction of Lieutenant Crookshanks, several soldiers from the garrison made one. It was a substantial vessel – as rowing boats went – with eight oars on either side. Under normal conditions a journey of ten or so miles with sixteen men rowing was quite feasible: this voyage though would not be under normal conditions. There was the boom and the riverside gun emplacements. And before either of these hazards there was the battery in Stronge's orchard from where the Jacobite gunners were watching. They saw the boat floated on the water, and then the men who were to take it on its maiden voyage piling in.

The boat must be sunk, they decided. Several salvoes were

loosed off, but remarkably – given the distance, a matter of only a few hundred yards – the gunners failed to score a single hit. Despite this good fortune, the boat made slow progress because the men had no room to row: the oars had been placed too close together. The rowers struggled back to Derry, where adjustments were made. A little later the crew boarded again and re-embarked on their journey. Again the Jacobites fired and missed, and again the crew could make little headway because the oars were still too close.

Meanwhile, on the *Greyhound*, Captain Richards was receiving various snippets of information from which he was supposed to construct a coherent picture. First, he could hear gunfire in the distance as the Jacobites tried to sink the boat. Then there were some gentlemen visitors: Newton, Gage and Hamilton. This trio had remained in their comfortable homes on the lough shore since the siege had begun. They had protections from Richard Hamilton, but had now come aboard (at considerable risk – if they were spotted with the enemy, their protections would be withdrawn) with news about the boom. This was exactly the sort of information Captain Richards had been sent to discover. Unfortunately, the three men could not agree on whether the boom was a plain chain, a set of cables floated with timbers or a chain of cables and timbers linked together, which Richards really needed to know.

At four o'clock in the afternoon, Richards noticed activity around Culmore fort. Through a telescope he saw some Jacobite soldiers pulling down an old house and loading the stones into a boat. A little later, an old Scot appeared on the shore. He waved a white handkerchief and was brought aboard the frigate. Shortly before night fell, a woman made a sign from the shore. A small boat was dispatched to fetch her and, despite a party of Jacobite dragoons appearing and firing, the mariners ferried her away, too. The Scot and the woman were interviewed. They were willing informers, though what they volunteered was of dubious value: 'Both these people said that our friends in Derry had sallied out and killed several officers and two or three hundred

Irish . . . [and] that the Irish had quitted Culmore.' Remembering the cannon fire from earlier, Richards concluded that he must have heard this battle, but what his visitors had actually described were the events of three days before when the Jacobites had been repulsed from Windmill Hill.

Having seen soldiers demolishing a house close by Culmore, Richards thought it unlikely the Jacobites had abandoned the fort, and he now consulted with the French officers. They agreed that when there was a fair wind the *Greyhound* should go within a cannon shot of the fort, as the first article of Kirke's instructions specified. It is unclear what Richards thought this would achieve, and furthermore, by following Kirke's orders he was undertaking a potentially suicidal operation: ships and forts were unequal adversaries. By now night had fallen, and all along the shore Richards saw great fires raging, including one in the house the Jacobites had demolished earlier.

When morning came, the wind was coming from the north-west, perfect conditions for the adventure planned the night before. The crew of the *Greyhound* rolled up their kit in their hammocks, then piled these bundles along the rails on the quarterdeck to protect the wheel and their captain from small shot. Everything that would not be of use in a sea fight was stowed in the holds. The yards were folded away, as were the below-deck partitions; this left a clear space where the ship's guns could operate without impediment. The mariners were ordered to their posts.

At eight o'clock the *Greyhound* set sail and later that morning came to anchor within cannon range of Culmore. Richards expected the Jacobites to fire immediately but there was silence. Perhaps Culmore had been abandoned after all. Through his telescope, however, he saw the Jacobites 'were very thick behind their walls'. They were frantically moving one of only two cannons he could see from its usual position, aiming straight across the river, to a new position where the *Greyhound* could be fired at.

With attack imminent, standard procedure began: the frigate fired a broadside at the fort. The Jacobites replied. Through his glass, Richards thought he saw one of the Jacobite guns was split. The two antagonists reloaded and duelling began. There was a good deal of noise, but little damage to either party. Richards climbed to the maintop, a platform at the top of the main mast, and saw the object of his quest – the boom, stretched across the grey water. It was immediately clear to him that the *Greyhound* would be unable to smash her way through.

On the western bank, over to his right, beyond Culmore, movement then drew his attention. He could make out the heads and backs of several horses dragging a heavy load – cannons, he concluded, that would shortly be firing at the *Greyhound*. Richards returned to the deck with this news. His plan now was to sail back to where they had started that morning and send the ketch to Major-General Kirke with a message about the boom. The anchor came up out of the water just as the wind dropped, while also shifting round to due north. The channel was narrow, and the *Greyhound* struck the shore opposite Culmore. The crew attempted a reprise of their kedging, but the tide was falling, and the *Greyhound* was soon caught fast with her starboard side to the bank opposite Culmore. The bulk of the hull was above the water, and the vessel was so heeled over that her heavy guns were useless. They were aiming at the sky.

The Jacobites, meanwhile, had hauled one battery into place north of Culmore and another directly opposite the *Greyhound*'s starboard side. There were eleven guns in all between the two shorelines, a formidable array of 24-pounders, 8-pounders and 3-pounders. The Jacobites had also marched up three or four battalions, several hundred men, who were facing the *Greyhound*'s starboard side.

Richards had a message sent back to the *Edward and James*: he was in trouble. Forty soldiers were brought by small boat and landed on the *Greyhound* to assist.

Around midday the two antagonists started blasting away at each other: the Jacobites with their cannons and small arms; the mariners with their small arms. The ship was soon in dire straits: over the course of the afternoon, the Jacobites put seventeen holes under the *Greyhound*'s waterline and fifty in her upper works, masts and rigging. Amazingly, only two men were killed, but several were badly wounded – among them Captain Guillam – by splinters, as was typical in naval encounters, and small shot. By seven in the evening the tide was flowing. The crew had 'got out most of her guns and several barrels of provisions, to make her as light as we could' and the *Greyhound* ought to have been able to limp away, but with water to a depth of four or five feet in the hold, she couldn't right herself and lift. Captain Boyce of the *Kingfisher* (who was now commanding) and his warrant officers agreed the situation was hopeless; they would evacuate the wounded and set fire to the *Greyhound*. The wounded were put in small boats and rowed away while the mariners remaining made ready to burn the ship, but the casualties had gone only a few hundred yards before the wind shifted through 180 degrees from north to south. The remaining crewmen seized their chance: they loosed the sails and the ship righted herself. Heavy in the water and listing badly, she nevertheless managed to sail out of range of the enemy's guns. Total disaster was averted.

However, within half an hour the *Greyhound* had taken in so much water that the crew thought she must sink. They took her out of deep water, ran her ashore again, and spent the night patching her up. By nine the next morning 'all her shot-holes were mended', her masts hauled back in place 'and her rigging spliced'. For Captain Richards, relief that the *Greyhound* hadn't sunk was tempered by the loss of all the instruments and clothes that he had brought with him on the mission. Some of his possessions had been shot to pieces. The seamen left on board had looted the rest. They were so badly paid that whenever the opportunity to make money came their way, they seized it with both hands.

*

The *Greyhound* sailed over to Scotland for a refit and Captain Richards returned to Ireland on the *Portland*. His ship met Kirke's fleet at sea off Inishowen, the peninsula bounding the left-hand side of Lough Foyle. Richards boarded his commander's vessel, the *Swallow*, and gave him a full account of everything he had seen, heard and done. His biggest piece of news concerned the boom. Richards, though an assiduous diarist, did not record Kirke's reaction, although, given the latter's subsequent inaction, we can presume it troubled him greatly. If ever there was a device calculated to lose a man his ships, it was a boom strung across a river at its narrowest point overlooked by enemy cannons. Kirke was already overcautious and determined that, however the city was relieved, his fleet must be preserved. What Richards told him confirmed what was already a core belief.

Meanwhile, around Derry the fighting continued. On 8 June, while the *Greyhound* was being blasted, thirty-five bombs were hurled at the city, spoiling houses, killing people and hurting 'many more by shattering their legs and arms to pieces'. But the next day was St Columcille's Day. Out of respect for the saint, and because of the high regard their troops had for him, the Jacobite generals directed that there should be no shooting. The next day being Sunday, there was no shelling then either – it had been Jacobite practice from the start to eschew shelling on the Sabbath. The bombardment started again on the Monday.

On Wednesday the 13th an unusual star appeared in the daytime sky. This was interpreted, with a nod to the Star of Bethlehem that presaged Christ's birth, as a sign that the fleet was about to come. Sure enough, at around six o'clock, lookouts spotted something in the lough: at last the main fleet had arrived from England. It was about twenty strong, the warships having been left at sea to guard the mouth of the lough.

It had arrived as conditions inside the walls were sliding from bad to worse. On 20 April, at the start of the siege, each company

of 60 men had been issued with a barrel of beef and a ball of meal.*
After that, a ration had been distributed every seven days: on 4
May each company was issued with a barrel of beef, 120 pounds
of meal and 56 pounds of butter; on 8 June the ration contained
no meat for the first time since the siege began. In spite of the
desertions and casualties, the city remained overcrowded, and
people were still sleeping in shifts. There wasn't enough fuel, the
weather was unseasonably cold and there was ceaseless shelling.
Water was short: St Columb's Wells were within the enemy's
range and the water in the wells inside the walls was muddy. The
result of all this was a debilitated population through which disease had begun to rampage.

At the sight of the fleet, the Cathedral bells pealed and a
beacon was lit at the top of the tower. Three cannon shots
were fired, to which the fleet replied. This distant rumble must
have sounded wonderful to the besieged citizens. They had signalled their dire hunger, and from the reply they believed they
were understood. By eleven in the evening the fleet had
reached Redcastle. The city was only a few hours' sailing from
deliverance. The coming of Kirke's armada 'gave us at the present the joyful prospect, not only of the siege being soon raised
but of being furnished with provisions, which then grew very
scarce, as appears by the allowance our men then had from the
stores'.

Naturally, it had the opposite effect in the Jacobite camps:
'Upon the appearing of the ships, the enemy seemed to be in a
mighty consternation. We observed a great motion in their camp
of pulling down tents, as we heard, in order to decamp . . . and
many of their common soldiers, as the country people informed
us [after], changed their red coats and ran away.' One Jacobite
soldier, a man called Dolan, deserted and crossed to the enemy
on Windmill Hill. Anxious not to be taken for a spy, he

---

*It is not recorded what the civilians were given.

described the Jacobite reaction to Kirke's fleet: the entire army 'were resolved to march away at night, for fear of the English, whom they heard were in the ships', he said. He also maintained the Jacobites had had to bury at least thirty men every day since King James had appeared below the walls. This amounted to nearly seventeen hundred, and, of course, did not include the dead left behind on the battlefield after engagements. The dead men Dolan described had perished through either disease (for the Jacobites were also highly susceptible because of fatigue, exposure and appalling diet) or battle injuries.

With their own casualties in the thousands, the Williamite relief in the lough, the intransigent garrison inside the city, not to mention the defiant Enniskilleners down the road, it was no wonder the Jacobite instinct was to retreat. Though he couldn't know it, Kirke had a unique opportunity when he first arrived. Morale on the Jacobite side had collapsed, while on the garrison side it had soared. An officer of different temperament might have capitalized, but Kirke was cautious. Instead of risking his ships, he adopted a wait-and-see policy.

On Saturday 15 June the last of the weekly ration was handed out. Out on the Foyle the *Dartmouth*, which had been fetching fresh water, returned to the fleet. Early on the morning of the following day the same ship headed towards Culmore and dropped anchor just over a mile from the fort. In Derry all the cannons on the walls and in the Cathedral tower fired three times, to encourage the vessel to finish her journey. The whole fleet replied with rounds of cannon fire – once again acknowledging but not understanding. Next, the *Dartmouth* hit the bar on the approach to Culmore. It was precisely this that she had been sent to investigate, and it was an hour before she freed herself and was able to sail back to the fleet.

In the evening Major-General Kirke summoned all his pilots to a meeting. He wished 'to know if anyone would undertake the piloting [of] the *Swallow*, or any other fourth rate ship over the bar . . . None would positively undertake it, but several promised to do their best.' So the commander had two impediments blocking his passage to Derry: the bar and then the boom.

Down at the theatre of war, events on the Foyle began to have their predictable effect. On the Jacobite side, 'the terror was soon over, when they saw them [Kirke's fleet] make no great attempt to come though they had both wind and tide to assist them'. The tents that had been pulled down were erected again, and 'the enemy now begin to watch us more narrowly. They raise batteries opposite to the ships, and line both sides of the river with great numbers of firelocks. They draw down their guns to Charles Fort [close to the boom], a place of some strength upon the narrow part of the river where the ships were to pass'. From here they could 'oppose the ships coming up to our relief' and sink them in the water. For the defenders, on the other hand, 'when we saw them lie in the Lough without any attempt to come up, it cast a cold damp on our too confident hopes, and sunk us as low as we were raised at the first sight of them'.

Frequent attempts were now made by the garrison to signal to the fleet. By burning braziers, waving flags and once again firing cannons, the garrison tried to communicate something of the city's distressed condition in the hope that it would sail to Derry's aid. Long before this time, the navies of Europe had worked out systems for signalling based on cannon-fire, flags, lights or even the movement of sails. Unfortunately, no one in Derry knew any of them. So the brazier-burning, flag-waving and cannon-firing, which the city-dwellers thought were unequivocal signs of distress, baffled the mariners, and provoked them to come up with all manner of spurious explanations. 'This morning,' wrote Richards, 'we saw flying on Derry's steeple, a much larger flag than was wont, hoisted upon a very large flag-staff.' This was hoisted and lowered four times while a gun was fired twice. The sages of the fleet decided this flag was a captured Jacobite colour that the garrison was anxious to show off to the

Jacobites, or the fleet, or both. Interpreting the phenomenon as a display of military prowess rather than despair, they stayed put.

Behind the walls, hope sank further, and the garrison discovered that, in the words of a nineteenth-century historian with a talent for the homily, 'In the cup of joy, bitterness is sometimes mingled.' A glimmer, though, lay in the fact that the home-made rowing boat had finally been fixed – men could now row without impeding one another. Despite the obvious dangers, particularly that afforded by the boom, the garrison decided to send it downriver, 'with the intent to make to the fleet, and give the Major-General an account of the sad condition we were in. [It] set out with the best of our wishes and prayers.' The Jacobites along the banks heard the rowlocks groaning and the oars dipping in the water. They fired into the darkness with gusto and the rowers had to turn back. A few nights later they set off again and the same thing happened. A new plan was devised: they would row the boat upriver and drop off a couple of boys with a letter for the garrison in Enniskillen.

However, before they did this, the instigators of the plan decided to confuse the enemy. They let it be known that they intended 'to rob the fish-houses on the Isle' (probably near Newbuildings). Since deserters, who trickled out of the city every day, ensured 'that the enemy received constant intelligence of our proceedings', they could rely on this being communicated. What is puzzling is that both destinations – the fish-houses and the wood where the boys were to be dropped – lay upriver. Why didn't they say they intended to sail downstream? This would have been credible: they had tried it before, after all. Perhaps the hope was that the Jacobites would wait at the wrong destination while leaving the rest of the river up from Derry unguarded. If this was the intention, it was a miscalculation.

On the night of 18 June the boat was launched at close to midnight. There were twenty or so men on board, including Alex Poke, one of the garrison's best artillerymen, as well as a couple of lieutenants, two captains, and the two boys who were to take the message. Colonel Murray and Captain Noble were in command. The boat moved through the darkness, but as it passed Evans' Wood the Jacobites fired a great gun they had planted there in anticipation and only narrowly missed. The Jacobites also poured small shot at the boat from both shores. The continuous firing inflicted no physical damage, but it made an impression on the boys. By the time the boat reached the drop-off point, Donnalong Wood, 'they were so terrified they dared not venture ashore'. The order was given to turn about 'and it now being early in the morning, our men discovered two large boats behind them, which the enemy had sent out and manned with dragoons to cut off their return'. As the adversaries closed, each side began blasting at the other (not easy, as the combatants were using muskets in moving boats). Neither party suffered any hits.

Ammunition was limited and stocks were soon expended, but one of the Jacobite boats now came up close to the Derry boat with the intention of boarding it. However, 'our men [the Derry men] were as quickly in upon them, beat back some of them into the water, and killed 3 or 4 others, besides a Lieutenant in the enemy's boat, whereupon the rest threw down their arms and called for quarter. We took thirteen prisoners in this boat.' The second Jacobite boat, 'seeing the ill success of their friends, made off with what haste they could'. The Derry boat, with its prisoners and spoils, a quantity of weaponry, rowed on.

Once again, shot rained down from the two shores. Some buried itself in Murray's helmet and bruised his scalp ('and for a while indisposed him for service') and one of the prisoners was also wounded; otherwise, no one was hurt.

The captives were landed near the Ferry Quay Gate and handed over to the night guards there. They were marched through the gate and away to jail. Murray and Noble, meanwhile, crossed the river to Tamneymore (opposite Windmill

Hill), where the Jacobites were moving one of their cannons. The Jacobites, greatly surprised by the appearance of the enemy, abandoned their gun and fled. Murray and his men chased them until they reached the top of a hill. From there they saw more Jacobite soldiers to their rear who were attempting to cut them off from their boat. The raiders fled back to the shore, jumped into their boat and rowed away quickly. They had enjoyed a productive night, notwithstanding the fact that they had failed in their principal purpose, but that couldn't alter the bleak facts of their position.

With food so short, the decision had been made to abandon the weekly handouts, which were thought to encourage profiteering. Instead, food would be distributed every few days. On 19 June, the same morning that Murray and the others returned, each soldier was issued just a pound of meal and one and a half pounds of wheat. It was a tiny ration.

The sight of the ships just a few miles away but seemingly not prepared to venture closer, coinciding with serious food shortages, created frustration and rage among the population. Most of these citizens vented their anger in the same direction: at one of their own leaders.

At some point early in June a trumpeter had come from the Jacobite camp on behalf of Mrs Talbot, wife of Colonel Talbot, injured during the first battle of Windmill Hill. Since then, he had been a prisoner in the city. Mrs Talbot was offering £500 for his release. This was a lot of money.

To discuss the offer, 'A sort of Council was held in Governor Baker's chamber' in the Bishop's Palace.* Adam Murray made a good, practical suggestion: Mrs Talbot would be better sending bullocks rather than cash. Colonel Walker, on the other hand, 'urged acceptance with some violence and threats against those that opposed it, and ordered the bier that would carry him [i.e.

---

*Baker had been sick for some time and was now too ill to leave his room.

Talbot] away to be this day brought to his lodgings'. After further discussion it was decided to accept the cash ransom. Only 'Governor Baker, perceiving it to be ill resented by the garrison, declined'. Perhaps he was liberated from greed by the nearness of death.

Out in the street, word spread of this decision, and, in Captain Ash's charming phrase, 'The rabble of our garrison took a vagary.' They 'would not hear of money, saying they would have prisoners for him, or nothing'. A mob formed, located the bier that was to carry away Talbot 'and made a fire of it in the main guard'. Next they went looking for Walker. The clergyman hurried back to the Bishop's House and hid in fellow-Governor Baker's chamber. Unable to find him, the mob turned on the Jacobite prisoners scattered around the city. Any who could walk were seized and thrown into the jail. (William Talbot couldn't walk, so he escaped this fate.)

Having discharged their civil obligations and put the prisoners where Walker couldn't sell them, the mob began to think about their own needs. They were hungry and several people known as hoarders were relieved of their stores. The mob then broke into 'Mr Walker's own lodging, where they found beer, mum and butter'.* Not having found Walker at home, they guessed where he was hiding. They set off for Governor Baker's, some with the aim of putting the clergyman in jail, others, who were armed, intending to shoot him or hang him. When the mob arrived at Baker's door the better-liked Governor staggered out, 'though indisposed, to pacify them [promising] no ransom should be taken for the prisoners, [and] entreated them for his sake to pass by what Mr Walker had done, and suffer the

---

*Mum is defined in the *Oxford English Dictionary* as 'a kind of beer originally brewed in Brunswick'. The principal ingredients of the drink included wheat-malt, oat-malt, ground beans and a variety of spices, such as marjoram and bay berries. It was renowned as a formidable antidote to scurvy, lingering distempers and deprivation of the blood and bowels; in short, 'the most useful liquor under the sun'.

prisoners to go to their own lodgings again. All of which they, with difficulty, consented to'.

Walker was therefore saved physically, but his reputation was in tatters. His secret was out – he was a drinker. By evening, the mob's feelings having abated, the promises they had made to Governor Baker could be put into effect: some of the Jacobite prisoners were allowed to return to their quarters.

The following day feelings were calmer still and the other prisoners were allowed to return to their quarters too. A remnant of the rabble was still around, however, and they pulled down the bomb-damaged Markethouse, then carried off the timber.

By 21 June, Governor Baker was so ill that it was decided to choose a man to act in his place until he recovered. A council of war was convened at the house of John Mitchelburne, where the colonel had been confined since his altercation with Baker. The council decided to ask Baker whom he'd suggest, and they sent Colonel Lance to the sick-room in the Bishop's House. The name they brought back was Colonel Mitchelburne's. The colonel had held a commission in the army of Charles II, then in James's.* He was the most experienced officer left, so it was little wonder the council consented.

The choice also boosted Baker's standing, proving he could forgive and forget. That he could rise above the personal and act on behalf of the whole by choosing the right man for the job was both noted and admired. That same day, one and a half pounds of wheat were issued to each garrison member.

By a neat coincidence, there were changes in the leadership on the other side of the walls, too. The bellicose Rosen, who now rejoiced in the title 'Marshal General of His Majesty's Forces', returned to the Jacobite camp. On his arrival, wrote

---

*Later, the Prince of Orange would commission him as a major in Skeffington's Regiment, with whom he had come to Derry.

Walker gleefully, he was most unhappy to discover 'how little they [the Jacobites] had prevailed against us'. The marshal 'expressed himself with great fury against us'. First, 'he would study the most exquisite torments, to lengthen the misery and pain of all he found obstinate, or active in opposing his commands and pleasure'. Then, he 'swore by the belly of God, he would demolish our town, and bury us in its ashes, putting all to the sword, without consideration of age or sex'.

Inside the walls, reaction to Rosen's appearance was sanguine. The threats, 'as well as his promises, in which he was very eloquent and obliging, had very little power with us,' asserted Walker. The defenders derived the spirit and the resolution necessary to defeat any fear or temptation from God. They were devoted to the defence of their city, their religion and the interests of King William and Queen Mary. And as an emblem of their belligerence, they now had the 'Bloody Flag' as it was known. It was Mitchelburne's idea: it was crimson coloured and was flown first from the Royal Bastion, the part of the city's fortifications closest to the enemy's lines, and later mounted on the Cathedral. The message it signalled was simple: Rosen and his troops were of no consequence:

That Crimson Flag, which on the steeple flies,
Tells Rosen, that his forces it defies.

This was the public position, at any rate. In reality the authorities were rattled, as is illustrated by the order they now passed: it became an offence either to attempt to surrender the city or to move the garrison to sue for surrender. The penalty was death.

The man who had caused this reaction – Rosen – would have been gratified: he believed brute force achieved results. In the meantime, though, he stayed his hand and left Hamilton in command. Rosen himself would concentrate on preventing Kirke's forces from landing, but he did make some changes to the way the forces were arranged around Derry. The Jacobites had shelled the city from the east and had attacked from the south twice. Rosen, however, saw the west as the weakest side, so he had three mortars and several pieces of ordnance transferred from the east to the west, where they could fire at Windmill Hill. He also had trenches cut near there, from where Jacobites could harass the outguards and make drawing water even more dangerous. He then had culverins (long cannons) set up opposite Butchers' Gate and started blasting away at it. He organized for a trench to run from Bog Street towards the Butchers' Gate with the intention of manoeuvring directly under the gate's bastion to blow it up. Every night the Jacobites worked at extending this trench.

The defenders responded by deploying extra guards. They began to countermine the enemy's trenches in front of Butchers' Gate, under the zealous command of Captain Schomberg, son of William's commander-in-chief designate for the Irish campaign. They also erected wooden screens there, paid for by public subscription, for protection against the enemy's constant firing. The fighting was about to enter a new, dirtier phase.

CHAPTER SEVENTEEN

Nastier and Nastier

Although his pilots did not want to venture up the Foyle, Kirke's mariners continued to act as if they soon would. Depth soundings were taken around the lough, and 'Several debates . . . concerning going up to break the Boom' took place, though 'nothing was resolved on'. Clearly, more needed to be done, if only to give the hundreds of Redcoats idling aboard the ships the impression that the leadership was purposeful and determined. At 8 a.m. sharp on 19 June all officers and commanders were summoned to Kirke's quarters aboard the *Swallow* for a council of war. The idea was to concentrate their minds on 'the several obstacles . . . against . . . attempting . . . going up to Derry'. These obstacles comprised the awesome boom; the numerous sunken boats filled with stones that littered the lough; and the curious absence of communication from Derry, which was interpreted to mean that behind the walls 'they were neither pressed much by the enemies or by want of victuals and provisions'. They decided that the fleet would 'continue here in Lough Foyle till more forces join us from England and Scotland', unless, of course, they received a message from Derry, 'which if desperate might make us take measures for their relief'. This rider was less a statement of policy and more a form of words that would insure the expedition against future criticism. If Kirke and his officers were subsequently accused of dereliction of duty, they could point to this.

The next day, Captain Richards was posted to the *Dartmouth*, '(it being the advance ship) to observe what the enemies did'. Kirke joined him, and together, from the maintop, they observed the boom, noting how it heaved up and down with the tide like a sea monster. This was a spectacle that surely must have gladdened the major-general: his decision to stay put had obviously been correct.

Inside the walls, on top of the problems of the revitalized Jacobites and Kirke's non-appearance, there were shortages of everything. All iron bullets were gone, and the defenders had to make do instead with pieces of brick coated in lead. The lack of food was now so acute that some citizens had

> ordered the gunners (who for the most part lived in town)
> to make diligent search for provisions, which they did to
> good purpose. For digging up cellars and other places, they
> got much provision under the ground, which some that
> went away, and others during the siege, had hid. And many
> that saw how sincerely concerned they were for the safety of
> the place brought forth their provisions of their own accord.
> By this means the garrison was furnished with bread
> (though the allowance was little) until the end of the siege.

On 21 June William Talbot finally died of his wounds. Walker noted the fact, then went on to observe that when Talbot died, 'we lost the benefit of our bargain'. In spite of everything, he was still hoping for the ransom. Talbot's body, with his wife in attendance, was interred. After the funeral, the Council of Fourteen met to decide what to do with Mrs Talbot. As the widow of one of Tyrconnell's relatives she might be a useful bargaining chip.

Ultimately, it was decided to let her go and a party of officers escorted her back to the Jacobite lines.

Meanwhile, in London, the House of Commons was impatient to hear good news from Ireland, and grumbling about the tardiness of the relief. One MP cried: 'Are those brave fellows in Londonderry to be deserted? If we lose them will not all the world cry shame upon us? A boom across the river! Why have we not cut the boom in pieces? Are our brethren to perish almost in sight of England, within a few hours' voyage of our shores.' The upshot was a resolution that William be moved to permit some Members of the House to inspect the books of the Committee of Irish Affairs and discover why the army had not been ready earlier for service in Ireland and why Derry was not yet relieved. William agreed, and a committee was established to investigate. In the meantime, the officers who were thought to be to blame were arrested: Lundy was sent to the Tower and Colonel Cunningham to the Gate House.

Back in Ireland, aboard the *Swallow*, Major-General Kirke still wasn't making the sort of progress the Members of Parliament desired, but one of his earlier strategies was at least about to lead to some action. On the day of the fleet's arrival in the Foyle, Kirke had asked for volunteers to go to the city, promising 3,000 guineas to the individual who succeeded in doing so. James Roch, recovering from wounds sustained in action in Bantry Bay when he heard of the offer, was attracted by the colossal sum of money but wasn't sufficiently fit to undertake the hazardous journey. That chance went to two other volunteers, who were dropped ashore. Only one of them returned, with a sorry tale. He had reached the Jacobite lines, where the guards had turned him away. Then, somehow, he had lost his companion. Making his way back towards the ships, he had bumped into some Jacobite soldiers who told him a spy had just been hanged. He assumed the man was his missing accomplice.

Despite this unhappy conclusion, Roch, now recovered from his injuries, was still anxious to try. He had no illusions about the danger involved, but the reward justified the risk. The money, presumably, was also the lure for James Cromie, another volunteer. Cromie apparently knew the countryside and would show Roch the way. The former was a Scot, while Roch was Irish, which later caused some eyebrows to rise, including Mitchelburne's. The acting Governor could not believe that in the entire fleet only an Irishman could be found for so important a mission. What Mitchelburne really meant, of course, was that Roch must be a closet Jacobite whose real purpose was to help the enemy. But if this were the case, he went about his mission in a very odd way.

On the evening of Monday 24 June Roch (presumably carrying a letter from Kirke for the garrison) and Cromie boarded a small boat which took them to where the River Faughan ran into the southern shore of Lough Foyle, a spot that was very distinctive. This was important because it was here that the boat would return to collect the men.

Roch and Crombie disembarked at about ten o'clock in the last remnants of daylight. They were about five miles below Derry and they picked their way upstream along the shore. Slipping undetected past the Jacobite lines, they reached a fishhouse three miles above the city between midnight and one o'clock. But they were on the wrong side of the river - on the east bank, and Derry was on the west.

Promising Cromie, who could not swim, that he would send a boat from Derry to collect him, Roch removed his clothes, piled them on the bank, and slid into the Foyle. Although it was summer, the water was cold and the currents strong, but Roch kept going. Finally, at about 4 a.m., he was observed struggling ashore by the night guards. Several of them ran down and surrounded him. They gave their frozen visitor liquor to warm him, but then, assuming he was a Jacobite spy, began to interrogate him. Roch, knowing his fate would be the noose if no one believed his story, had arranged with Kirke that at midday exactly he would make a sign: a flag would be waved from the steeple and four guns would fire. The fleet would then answer with a pre-arranged signal to confirm that Roch was who he said he was. Hearing this, the guards gave him some clothes and took him away to await the signals. At noon, Derry signalled as they'd been told to, the fleet responded as Roch said it would, and his bona fides were established.

Now the city had someone who could speak with authority of the fleet. 'He told us there were thirty ships below Culmore and that they expected the remainder very soon', then proceeded to give the garrison 'an account of the ships, men, provisions and arms in them for our relief'. This was surely welcome news. Malnutrition had damaged the immune systems of everyone behind the walls, but it was only after the fleet was sighted that 'the fevers, flux and other distempers grew rife, and a great mortality spread itself through the garrison, as well as the inhabitants'. On one especially bad day in June fifteen officers had died. On the day Roch arrived, Walker included the size of the garrison, for the first time, in the statistical records he was keeping. At the start there were 351 officers and 7,020 private men. The latter now numbered 6,185. That represented a loss of 835 men, the majority of whom had died of disease. The ration issued to each soldier on the same day was a pound of meal, a pound of tallow (produced by melting animal fat and traditionally used for candles, not food) and a quarter-pound of beef, which was supposed to support him until the next issue, on 4 July.

This was the context in which the letter Roch carried from Kirke was now read. In it, Kirke assured the garrison 'in the kindest manner, that everything in Scotland, England and Ireland was prosperous, and that succours beyond their wishes were speedily to join them'. However, he then added a chilling caution to husband their provisions, which was 'more alarming to them than all the menaces of their enemies'.

Walker now insisted that the exhausted Roch must return to the fleet, and he wrote a letter for Roch to take back with him: it stated that there was enough food for only four more days.

Roch spent 25 June resting, but at about 9 p.m. he returned to the quay below Ferry Quay Gate. Walker's letter was put into a bladder and tied to his hair. He removed his clothes and began to swim, his destination the bank where he had left James Cromie. From the city's walls, eight guns were fired, which was the signal that Roch and Cromie had agreed with the fleet would be given when they were starting the journey back to the pick-up point. Three of the fleet's guns replied.

At about midnight, roughly twenty-four hours since he had left, Roch, frozen and exhausted, reached the spot on the east bank from where he had set out the night before. As soon as he got ashore 'he found that his clothes were taken away, by which he supposed himself discovered'. He was right: the Jacobites had found Cromie and were waiting for Roch. The soldiers came out of the trees, armed and on horseback. Roch was unarmed, naked, tired and on foot. But, in his own words, he 'was resolved, however, to carry back the letters for the General . . . and accordingly travelled naked for three miles . . . pursued by the enemy [and] was forced to take shelter in a wood where the horse could not follow him'. This was because the wood was full of briars, and, as Roch plunged forwards, the thorns caught on and tore his skin. Emerging from the wood, he ran into a party of the enemy's dragoons. One swung a halberd at his face and smashed his jaw. Roch ran on, still eluding his pursuers, and finally reached a rock from which he jumped thirty feet into the Foyle below. He started swimming back towards Derry. The dragoons, still in pursuit, followed him, on horseback, into the water. They shouted an offer of £1,000 if he handed over the letters they guessed were inside the bladder tied to his hair. Roch refused, so the dragoons fired at the head disappearing into the darkness. They hit their target in the arm, chest and shoulder, but they didn't kill him. Roch swam on for several hours, and early the next morning made it back to the quays below the Ferry Quay Gate. He scrambled ashore and passed out.*

Cromie, meanwhile, had been hauled off to Stronge's orchard. General Rosen, when informed a spy had been caught, 'charged the Chevalier de Vaudry to frighten and interrogate him strictly'. The Frenchman set to work. Cromie, who spoke French, was 'a man of good sense', in Rosen's words. He must have struck his interrogator as a gentleman, and their conversation ranged widely. The Chevalier learned, besides details of Cromie's mission, something about Scotland, from where Cromie had come about ten days earlier; something about the regiments aboard Kirke's fleet, and that the ships contained huge quantities of arms, ammunition and provisions; and that the formidable Count Schomberg was to command the forces preparing to ship to Ireland. None of this information was especially useful, but the Chevalier did manage one coup. He got Cromie to agree, 'being in hazard of his life . . . to give the besieged a discouraging account', one calculated to undermine their morale. Another gambit in this psychological campaign would be tried first, though.

On Wednesday 26 June, while Cromie's erstwhile accomplice Roch was recovering from his ordeal in Derry, the Jacobite Colonel O'Neil requested a parley. As the defenders rank and file believed any contact with the enemy led inexorably to betrayal, permission had to be sought from as wide a constituency as possible. The officers were consulted and consented, so Colonel Lance and Lieutenant-Colonel Campbell went out to meet O'Neil near the gallows, which allowed those on the walls to watch. O'Neil told them James had sent instructions to Rosen. There was a new offer on the table, one of exceptional generosity. If the city surrendered, all would be free to go home, and

---

*This extraordinary, if possibly exaggerated, story created a favourable impression when it was presented to Parliament several years later. In recompense for his efforts, Roch received a gift of land on the Everard estates in County Waterford.

James would recompense everyone for their losses. Those who
wanted to pursue a military career, and were prepared to take the
oath of allegiance, would be free to enter his army, where they
would be treated in exactly the same way as Catholics. Finally,
anyone who wished would be free to go to Scotland or England.
Lance and Campbell promised an answer the following day, and
O'Neil returned to his camp.

The Jacobites might have imagined that these terms were
then given serious consideration inside the walls, but of course
they were not. Relief was the pre-eminent preoccupation, and
somebody was still needed to reach Kirke and tell him to hurry
up. Step forward McGimpsey. This plucky citizen, referred to
only by his surname in all the accounts, had volunteered some
days earlier – before Roch had made his epic journeys – to
swim to the fleet. Now it was decided to let him try. Three letters for Kirke were prepared. The shortest, from Walker,
reported Roch's safe arrival in the city and his unsuccessful
attempt to return to the fleet, then summarized the offer just
received from O'Neil. The terms, he said, had been categorically
rejected, at least for the time being. However, 'if we have not a
speedy supply and that in a few days not exceeding six' the city
would be forced to yield through no fault of its own. (It was not
clear why the survival period had jumped from four days, which
was what he'd said in Roch's letter, to six.) As a final inducement
to Kirke to relieve the city, Walker promised, 'the booms across
the river are certainly broken'.

Adam Murray, John Cairnes and James Gladstanes signed the
second letter. With no proper meat, the citizens had been eating
horseflesh, it said, which was now almost gone too. Starvation
was the norm, and people were sick and dying in great numbers.
Finally, the signatories declared with magnificent gusto, 'our
case calls for help, help, help from God and from you. The Lord
Himself guide, lead, and protect [you] in this great work where
our lives, even many thousands of lives both old and young,
men and women, lie at stake.'

Governors Walker and a still ailing Baker signed the third letter. It started with a brief first-hand account of the situation in and around Derry, and of how the appearance of the fleet had filled the Jacobites with such astonishment that they

> resolved to raise the siege. In order thereto, they took down their tents, removed towards Finn Water their mortars, and sent to other garrisons their sick and wounded men. But perceiving that you did not endeavour to land, and that no aid or succour came (as we expected) they took new courage, brought back what things they removed, [and] reinforced themselves.

When they returned, they blockaded the city even more tightly than previously. Next, now writing that the city's provisions would not last above *eight or ten* days, they implored Kirke to take pity on the besieged and send a small vessel or two laden with foodstuffs of any kind, but especially biscuit, cheese and butter. They also asked for a small barque with a supply of coal. To reassure Kirke, they promised that there were 'but one small field piece, and [only] a few little drunken Dicks at Culmore, for all the rest of the guns were removed hither, [and] the ships may come up to our quay (we hope) without any hazard'. The rest of the letter was devoted to the city's martial achievements, the prestigious prisoners captured and number of enemy killed.

Just before ten o'clock on the evening of 26 June, McGimpsey went to Ship Quay. The three letters were put in a bladder along with some musket balls and tied around his neck: in the event of capture, the plan was that he would break the string and the bladder would sink to the bottom. The Jacobites mustn't find out how perilous the situation was behind the walls. McGimpsey was also given a couple of bigger bladders filled with air, to use as water wings. He slid into the river and set off to swim downstream. His destination – the fleet on the far side of the boom – was eleven or twelve miles away.

Unaware that he was on his way, Kirke and his officers also knew nothing of Roch's exploits or Cromie's capture. They knew only that on the previous night eight guns had been fired in the city, the pre-arranged signal that Roch and Cromie were on their way back. It was now time to send the pick-up boat to the point where the Faughan entered the lough. The detail crossed Lough Foyle and approached the appointed spot. When the mariners were within about a pistol shot of the shore a voice called out to them from the bank, beckoning them closer. Unknown to those aboard, a party of Jacobites, alerted by Cromie's intelligence, was waiting to ambush them. The lieutenant on the boat called back, requesting the password. The respondent said he couldn't remember. (Either the wily Cromie had not passed it on or the Chevalier had forgotten to ask.) The lieutenant asked the man on the shore for the name of his ship. He had forgotten that, too. The lieutenant wondered now why he heard only one voice when there had been two volunteers. The voice in the darkness replied that he had not seen his colleague since he went into Derry. The lieutenant suggested that the man should wade out into the water so that he could be picked up. The man declined. Moments later, there was a fusillade of musket fire from the shore. Miraculously, no one on board was hit and the boat returned to the fleet. The lieutenant made a report of what had happened, by which it was judged 'either one or both of the men are taken in their return to us'.

Meanwhile, still several miles away, McGimpsey was struggling towards the boom. Sometime in the night he drowned and the next morning his body was spotted in the water and heaved out by the Jacobites. The big bladders were still fastened to his arms, and the small bladder was still around his neck. The letters were carried to headquarters. Rosen wrote to James that 'we have fished this morning a drowned man who floated on the river with . . . the three letters enclosed, by which your Majesty may see what state the town is in now'. The news that the enemy was starving even while their relief bobbed at anchor boded well for the proposals O'Neil had delivered the day before. However, when Colonels Lance and Campbell met O'Neil and gave the city's answer, it was a defiant no.

But Richard Hamilton, still officially in charge of the siege, was not to be rebuffed so easily. He knew for sure that the city was on its last legs, and with the right offer couched in the right terms it just might pass to King James, so he had formal terms drafted. Knowing how much General Rosen was feared as well as hated, and suspecting this might have been why O'Neil had been rebuffed, Hamilton began, 'General Rosen has no power from the King to intermeddle with what Lieutenant General Hamilton does, as to the siege, being only sent to oppose the English succour'. Then he said he was prepared to give the besieged whatever security they demanded if an agreement were to be brokered. His core terms were the very least his enemy would demand – 'free liberty of goods and religion'. All who wished to could stay in Derry under his protection. All who wanted to return home could leave, and enjoy an escort and victuals. He also offered to return the cattle plundered from settlers and taken 'to the mountains'. As for those who had commissions from William of Orange, they need not be apprehensive either, as 'it will be in the King's interest to take as much care of his Protestant subjects as any other, he making no distinction of religion'. This held as true for those in Enniskillen as for those in Derry. Hamilton was willing to employ in his army any men who would freely swear to serve James faithfully.

The garrison gave the appearance of considering Hamilton's proposals, but in reality they used the time to search for protein. The garrison was now subsisting 'upon horse flesh, dogs, cats, rats, and mice, greaves of a year old tallow and starch,* of which they had good quantities, as also salted and dried hides, et cetera'.

Meanwhile, the Jacobites kept up the pressure. On the

---

* A fibrous by-product from tallow production traditionally used as dog food or fish bait.

evening of 27 June they fired ten bombs at the city. One hit a house in Bishop Street where two barrels of powder had been stowed. Fourteen people were killed – six grenadiers from Ash's regiment, four horsemen and four women. Another bomb hit Ash's own room, smashed his lantern, and continued on to the street, where, he observed, 'it did no other harm, thank God!'

The Jacobites also upped the psychological pressure. The following day they signalled with a flag for parley. Lieutenant-Colonels Fortescue and Blair travelled over the river to Stronge's orchard, where they met some Jacobite officers. The latter told them they were mistaken about Major-General Kirke and the prospect of imminent relief, and invited them to hear it from the horse's mouth. Cromie was brought forward. The prisoner '(being so sworn to do) repeated to them the words that had been put into his mouth'. However, unknown to the Jacobites, the Derry garrison had of course heard a very different tale from Roch. When they put this to Cromie, his response was as blunt as it was revealing. He said that the two testimonies would obviously differ because 'he was in the enemy's camp, [while] Roch [was] within the walls of Derry'. The visitors now tried to negotiate Cromie's release, but the Jacobites were only prepared to exchange him for prestige prisoners (whom the city would never release). The lieutenant-colonels returned to Derry alone and Cromie's subsequent fate is unknown.

Though Cromie hadn't disheartened the rebels as they had wished, the Jacobites had another means to undermine the garrison's hopes of deliverance: McGimpsey's corpse and the three letters that told of the city's plight. They erected a gallows on the east bank in clear view of the city and strung up the body, then 'called over to us to acquaint us it was our messenger'. Here was incontrovertible proof that Kirke must still be ignorant of the conditions inside the walls. The Jacobites hoped this gruesome spectacle would further damage rebel hopes, and threw twenty more bombs over the walls for good measure.

This combination of parleys and violence, however, was unavailing. The garrison 'unanimously resolved to eat the Irish, and then one another, rather than surrender'. But they wouldn't tell Hamilton this yet. He could wait a little longer for a response to his terms.

McGimpsey's corpse was strung up on a Friday and the same day Lord Clancarty arrived with his regiment to reinforce the Jacobite forces around Derry. He was a nephew of a Jacobite grandee, Lord Mountcashel. Avaux described him as 'a young madcap and a little dissolute'. Besides his soldiers, Clancarty had also brought his reputation. 'We were often told that some great thing was to be performed by this Lord, and they had a prophecy among them that a Clancarty should knock at the gates of Derry,' wrote Walker. This was a widely held belief among the peasantry, and was certainly believed by the new arrival himself. Before the day was over, he intimated, he would be knocking.

Inside the walls rumours circulated and there was a sense of foreboding. Governor Baker, still unwell, decided he should be on the walls to direct the troops.

At about ten o'clock on a summer's evening, while the Jacobite artillery still shelled the city, Clancarty led his men – about two hundred strong – across the bog. They arrived at the outworks in front of the Butchers' Gate and lobbed grenades into the trenches. The few defenders who were in place climbed out and ran back inside the city. At this moment a Jacobite shell that 'had missed its aim fell among his [Clancarty's] men . . . The light of the combustibles ignited and thrown about by it discovered the assailants' who were not simply in the trenches outside the gate but right up to the city wall. One was calling back for fire to burn the gate. Simultaneously, and more worryingly, miners were flooding into a cellar under the Gunner's Bastion a few yards north-east of Butchers' Gate.

The garrison reacted quickly. Sixty men, led by Noble and Murray, slunk out of Bishop's Gate and crept along the outside of the wall until they met a covering party Clancarty had posted to protect his miners. Then 'they thundered upon them'. At the same time, the soldiers on the walls unleashed volleys of case shot at the heads of the Jacobites below.* Ash had never before heard 'so many shots fired in so short a time'. Clancarty and his troops fled back across the bog to the Jacobite camp. They left behind perhaps thirty dead men, including three officers, as well as the miners. The defenders' casualties were negligible: one man killed and one wounded.

The reaction within Derry was a combination of delight and knowing superiority. The prophecy, as the besieged gleefully pointed out, had foretold only that a Clancarty would knock at the gates of Derry. It hadn't said that he would get inside. Once again, they crowed, the enemy had proved they were superstitious and credulous.

But the defenders had their own equally vivid superstitions. Each and every midnight an 'Angel, mounted on a snow-white horse, and brandishing a sword of a bright colour, was seen to compass the city by land and water'. This nightly visitor sustained morale and reinforced the garrison's belief in the certainty of their salvation, What both phenomena showed was that, although this appeared to be a modern war fought with the latest seventeenth-century weapons, ideas from earlier periods still had currency.

The rebuff of Clancarty and his men was a successful operation, but whatever it did to boost morale was soon undone. After his night out on the walls Governor Baker had a relapse. Two days later, on Sunday 30 June, he died. Walker, despite his tendency to claim all the credit he could for himself, paid generous tribute to his colleague: 'his death was a sensible loss to us and generally lamented, being a valiant person. In all his

---

*Traditionally pieces of old iron, stones, nails and other sharp objects.

actions among us he showed the greatest honour, courage and conduct, and would it suit the design of the journal, might fill a greater share of this account with his character.' Also extolled were the dead man's prudence and resolute conduct. He was held in considerable affection by the garrison, and Ash said that he was 'greatly beloved and very well qualified for the government, being endued with great patience and moderation, [and] free from envy or malice'.

The pallbearers at the funeral included Walker and Mitchelburne, and the coffin was interred in one of the vaults of the Cathedral. Mitchelburne took over permanently as Governor, though without official confirmation from the council. There was too much fighting to allow it to meet.

In his quarters in the Jacobite camp, General Rosen knew nothing yet of his adversary's death. He was worried: the troops he had brought up were appallingly equipped. For the most part, the arms issued to the infantry were faulty, and, as there was not a single gunsmith in James's army, they couldn't be fixed. The cavalry was even worse off. They were mostly without pistols, muskets or boots, and many of their mounts lacked tackle. The horses were also in a poor condition. Walter Butler's regiment had been sent from Dublin without swords, powder or ball, while Bagnal's were without shot, even though the officers had requested an issue before they had set off.

Those already quartered in the camps around Derry when Rosen had arrived were just as ill equipped, as well as being under strength due to death and desertion. The very best battalion, he said, in a letter remarkable for its measured sarcasm, had only two hundred men and of those only fifty had swords, belts and bandoliers. It should have numbered six hundred. The cavalry and dragoons, the jewels in the Jacobite military crown, were hardly better: even the strongest company had only twelve or fourteen troopers rather than the usual forty.

Compounding the lack of men were problems of terrain and communication. There was only one road around Derry and it was so bad that it was difficult to move artillery on it. Then there was the river: the besiegers had to station troops on both banks, thereby diminishing the forces concentrated against the rebels. These were further diminished by the obligation to have troops a full thirty miles away to the south, under the Duke of Berwick, to prevent the Enniskillen garrison marching north to relieve their brethren.

Then there was Kirke and his troops to worry about. Rosen, from what he had learned from Cromie, believed that Kirke was waiting for Schomberg to come with three regiments of cavalry and two of infantry, troops that would be as impressive as the reinforcements from Dublin were useless. He wrote: 'There is no doubt but this expectation has kept him from making any attempt to throw provisions into Derry, as he might easily have done, by hazarding some vessels for that end.' But these troops would surely arrive soon, and then the Doomsday situation for the Jacobites would unfold. Men of fighting age who'd had pro- tections and been living quietly would flock to the enemy colours. The relief army would head for the city. The garrison, inspired by the reinforcements, would sally forth. The under- manned, underarmed, undertrained Jacobite forces would be caught between the two forces and this unequal contest would end in catastrophe.

But if Derry surrendered before Schomberg arrived, all this could be averted. The question therefore was how to force a surrender. The blockade was hurting: the letters taken from McGimpsey showed the city was starving. Unfortunately, the authorities were still defiant, bolstered no doubt by the tanta- lizing sight of the relief just a few miles away. Had the Jacobites been stronger now might have been the time to storm Derry and settle this by force. But after months of fighting the besiegers were too weak for this. That left only blackmail – the threat of something so awful that surrender would seem prefer- able. So Rosen wrote a letter to the garrison. His language was courteous but the message was terrifying. He wrote that they

had until six o'clock on the evening of Monday 1 July (the next
day) to surrender on the terms offered by General Hamilton. If
they declined, he would issue orders 'for the gathering together
of those of their faction, whether protected or not and cause
them immediately to be brought to the walls of Londonderry.
[Then] it shall be lawful for those in the same (in case they have
any pity on them) to open the gates and receive them into the
city.' Of course, the rebels could decline to admit anyone, but if
they did, they would have the pleasure of watching their friends
and relations starving to death. In addition, Rosen wrote that he
intended to lay waste to the countryside, to guarantee that any
forces coming from England would be unable to survive.
Finally, he reminded the defenders that this was their last
chance. If they turned him down and his army subsequently got
inside the walls, as he assured them they would, his soldiers
would 'have orders to give no quarter or spare either age or
sex'.

The letter was sent, and Rosen now issued his supporting
orders, as he assumed he would not be believed until he was
seen to be doing what he had threatened. He commanded
Jacobite troops of dragoons to round up all Protestant non-
combatants who could be found within ten miles of the city
and have them brought to him so he could send them to the
walls to die. He also ordered all of James's other northern commanders, from Sligo to Carrickfergus, from Coleraine to
Belturbet, to send every man, woman and child related to
anyone behind Derry's walls. He had learned that a considerable
number of the wives and children of the Derry rebels were in or
around Belfast, so ordered an especially close search be made
there, and that all men, women, boys and girls sent to him.
These orders specifically discounted protections and directed
commanders to feed those rounded up only the minimum necessary to sustain them on the journey to Derry. To maximize
the impact of the spectacle, Rosen wanted the prisoners to look
as woeful as possible.

On the same day he wrote to James that he intended to exterminate all Protestants and enclosed a copy of this communiqué to Derry. The letter explained he had no alternative, and that the enemy was unworthy of mercy and deserved to die. If James disapproved, Rosen asked for the command at Derry to be passed on to Richard Hamilton or some other officer.

Inside Derry, the start of July saw new orders for the night guard instituted. All soldiers were ordered to sleep in their clothes, with their weapons near by and a candle burning. Officers had to congregate at Mitchelburne's house and stay there, awake, most of the night. They had candles, tobacco pipes and ale to help them through. Sergeants and lieutenants congregated elsewhere. In the event of an attack, the officers were to go to their company quarters and lead their men to wherever they were directed to go by the Governors or colonels. At 4 a.m. each night two great guns would be fired. This was the signal for the change over. Those who were up all night would go to bed and volunteers, burghers and citizens would take over. They had to stay until 7 or 8 a.m. If they failed to answer the roll twice, they would be fined; on the third offence they would be turned out of the city. Officers who failed to report, without good explanation, were, on the third offence, to be deemed disaffected, broken in front of their regiment and imprisoned for the rest of the siege. These orders were posted on the ruins of the Markethouse, the four gates and the Windmill. The garrison was jittery.

In the countryside around Derry, Jacobite dragoons got on with the business of rounding up non-combatants. Some of the soldiers, besides starving the prisoners, added extra degradations of their own invention: they stripped them and held them in cattle pounds or dilapidated houses. It was still wet and cold, and the exposure was often fatal, especially to pregnant women.

Inside the city, Rosen's letter was being considered with a

mixture of contempt, indignation and disbelief. Surely he was bluffing, trying to intimidate the garrison into accepting Hamilton's proposals. The deadline came and went and nobody was driven to the walls, which confirmed the suspicions in Derry. A letter was drafted, dated 2 July, and signed by the two Governors, Walker and Mitchelburne. It was addressed not to Rosen but to Richard Hamilton, and began with an excuse: they would have written sooner and responded to those written terms Hamilton had offered at the end of the previous week, but for Baker's death and 'the disturbance given us from the camp'. Then they turned to the matter of Rosen's document. They asked why anyone in Derry should believe Hamilton's terms, when Marshal Rosen appeared to be in charge and had just abolished the protections given to every Protestant living in the north. They expected favour from King James and General Hamilton, they said, 'yet we expect no mercy nor favour nor keeping of conditions with us from the said Marshal or his countrymen with him, if he and they shall have power'. They had also noted that the commission by which James had authorized Hamilton to act was dated 1 May. However, since then, a Parliament had met in Dublin, 'whereof our lives and estates were forfeited'. This was true. In mid-June the Acts of Settlement and Explanation had been repealed and all land restored to the representatives of those who had possessed it on 22 October 1641. After this an Act of Attainder was passed, listing 2,400 traitors who had joined the Williamite project. As well as those in open rebellion – it included several men currently serving on Derry's walls – it named some who were never in revolt, such as Bishop Hopkins and Colonel Robert Lundy.

Because of the Attainder, Walker and Mitchelburne felt they could ask Hamilton to extract from James 'a new commission to treat with us', along with James's promise that he would abide by what Hamilton agreed. This was essential, they argued, in order that neither Rosen nor anyone else could 'break what articles shall be made for our advantage or that we shall be oppressed by them'.

The letter was sent to Hamilton, but before he could reply he was overtaken by events. Rosen's deadline had passed the previous day.

CHAPTER EIGHTEEN

Threats Fail, Kirke Demurs

Throughout Tuesday 2 July, the prisoners the dragoons had collected were herded into the besiegers' camps to be prepared for their coming ordeal. Meanwhile, the Jacobite artillery, for the first time in weeks, did not shell the city.

Inside the walls it was decided to take advantage of the lull. The Jacobites who had been killed on Windmill Hill in early June were still lying where they had fallen. The corpses were now swollen and flyblown. The bodies of the men who had died more recently when Clancarty had knocked on Butchers' Gate were also lying where they had fallen. It was decided to organize a burial detail. All the ordinary private prisoners (such as the men Murray had captured on the river) were taken from the jail (only officers were quartered around the city) and put to work. They buried their fellow-soldiers, then returned to prison.

On the Foyle, Kirke's fleet still rode at anchor. Since Roch had failed to return, Cromie had been captured and McGimpsey had drowned, Kirke had not attempted to send in another messenger, but he was still gleaning information. Not far from where he was moored near Whitecastle there was a parson's house where some Jacobite dragoons were quartered.

A number of Protestant civilians also lived there, among them
a husband and wife who were supplying information. Their
intelligence came in letters, which were always left under the
same stone on the beach. When there was one ready for collection, the couple would promenade on the shore. A detail
would go in at night and collect the document. Through this
channel, Kirke had learned of how Clancarty had knocked at
Butchers' Gate.

Now, at noon on 2 July, a Mr Hagason signalled from the
shore. Captain Withers went ashore and spoke to him, returning
in an hour. The news from Hagason was bleak, if predictable. As
Richards reported laconically, in Derry 'they were weary of this
siege, for there was nothing but hunger and slaughter in it'.
There was also a terrible want of provisions.

After dinner, Kirke called a council of war. The principal
item on the agenda was Inch Island. Parallel to Lough Foyle,
but separated from it by the Inishowen peninsula, lay Lough
Swilly. Inch was halfway down this adjacent waterway and
although it was a long way there by water, the journey overland from Inch to Derry was only ten or twelve miles as the
crow flies, and a little longer by road. Henry Hunter, an ex-
soldier who had been disarmed by Jacobites the previous year,
had visited Kirke and told him that Inch might be a good
place to hospitalize his sick. Then Captain Hobson had sailed
there in the frigate the *Bonaventure*. Several Protestant residents
of the island had come aboard and told him a Jacobite quartermaster was on the island gathering provisions for the army.
(The island was fertile and rich with grain.) A lieutenant and
one of the Protestant gentlemen went ashore, ambushed the
quartermaster and relieved him of his papers and £5 before
returning to the ship. The papers turned out to be letters from
the general officers of the Jacobite camp, which revealed that
they were in dire need of provisions. Their horses especially
were starving. It appeared they had no ready sources of food or
fodder, other than Inch.

Kirke and his council therefore knew that Inch was a rich source of food and that the Jacobites might seize it. If Kirke could occupy the island first, he would cut off the besiegers' best supply of food. Furthermore, Kirke's mariners had been living in cramped, unsanitary conditions on board for weeks. Some shore leave would boost morale.

The *Bonaventure* had also brought assurances from the Protestants of Inch. There were several hundred of them, and if Kirke's troops took the island, they were ready to join his forces to fight the Jacobites. Finally, Inch was so close to Derry that it might be possible to launch an overland relief expedition from there, perhaps in conjunction with the Enniskillen garrison. Even if that were not possible, the expedition's very presence on the island would force the Jacobites to commit troops to watching it, thereby relieving some of the pressure on Derry.

A decision was reached: six hundred men would be sent by boat to occupy Inch, prevent the Jacobites gathering food, and protect local Protestants. They would build a fort, then the balance of the relief force would join them. The expedition would not leave immediately, though. It would go once the *Greyhound*, currently on reconnaissance in Lough Swilly, had returned.

During the evening of Tuesday 2 July, the first two hundred Protestants who had been taken into custody were herded towards the city. They were mostly naked, cold and hungry, and as they stumbled forward they moaned horribly. Many Jacobite officers added to the cacophony by weeping: this didn't seem like warfare to them.

From their places on the walls, the guards saw the masses coming down the hill towards Butchers' Gate.

Our men at first did not understand the meaning of such a crowd, but fearing they might be enemies, fired upon them. We were troubled when we found the mistake but [then] we found that none of them were touched by our shot, which

by the direction of Providence (as if every bullet had its
commission what to do) spared them, and . . . killed 3 of the
enemy.

The prisoners reached the walls, two hundred shivering, famished co-religionists. This was the moment when they were
supposed to plead and the garrison was supposed to let them in.
However, when he had devised the scheme, Rosen had failed to
factor in the attitude of the prisoners. They had worked out his
plan: they knew he wanted to force them into a city that was
already starving and thereby hasten its surrender. But they
believed that would be a calamity, because once the garrison had
been disarmed there would be a massacre and they would all die.
So they called out to the guard to resist all pity and to keep them
locked out.

Rosen had also miscalculated the effect of this spectacle on the
garrison. It didn't produce disorder and collapse. On the contrary, the garrison was 'warmed with a new rage and fury against
the enemy'. Instead of opening the gates so the refugees could
flood in, the garrison scooped up and lodged in the jail the
prestige prisoners who had been scattered around the city, about
twenty Jacobite officers in all. Next, they notified the enemy that
they would hang the officers if the refugees outside the walls
were not sent home. A gallows for this purpose was immediately
erected on the Double Bastion between Bishop's and Butchers'
Gates. Finally, Hamilton was told 'the prisoners might have
Priests to prepare them after their own methods for death',
although, as Walker added tartly, 'none came'.

The Jacobite prisoners were at least allowed to make appeals.
The first, directed to Marshal Rosen, had no impact. He was
intent on finishing what he had started, and the next day
another thousand Protestants were driven up to the walls. In
addition, thirty bombs were thrown into the city to keep up the
pressure.

Down the coast, there was also military activity. When Kirke was told what was happening, he put ashore two boatloads of soldiers. They attacked the parson's house where the dragoons were quartered and plundered it, then escaped with forty refugees, who were later sent on to Scotland. The Jacobites were alarmed, and, fearing the long-awaited and much-dreaded relief operation had finally started, they sent three battalions from their camp near Culmore to investigate. They found, of course, that no great landing was under way.

Back in Derry, the Jacobite prisoners, having received no reply from Rosen, now wrote to Richard Hamilton. This was a short communiqué, shorn of all circumlocution. Driving the prisoners to the walls, they explained, had incensed the Governors and the garrison. As a consequence, they (though not the ordinary private soldiers) had been condemned to die unless the prisoners under the walls were withdrawn immediately. They did not blame the garrison or the Governors, they said; the latter had treated them with every imaginable civility. Nor, they added quickly, did death concern them: they were happy to die for James with their swords in their hands. It was being hanged like common criminals that pained them. They begged Hamilton, as a man who abhorred the shedding of innocent blood, to intercede with Rosen.

Hamilton's reply was cavalier and brutal: the Protestants under the walls had only themselves to blame because they had wilfully sabotaged their chances of getting into the city. As for the forthcoming executions of the Jacobite officers on the new gallows, there was nothing he could do about it. The only consolation he could offer them was that they would be revenged.

Over in London, of course, no one yet knew of these developments. The authorities were still considering Kirke's letter of 19 June, in which he had said that as Derry had sent no distress signals and the boom looked unbreakable, he would await reinforcements. King William noted that Kirke had decided on his course of action because he had presumed the boom could not be broken or breached. But this was conjecture: Kirke must establish the truth. He must talk to his naval officers about smashing the boom, and obtain an accurate account of conditions inside Derry. Then he must calculate the number of reinforcements required. When written down, William's message to the major-general was unmistakable: Kirke had better get on with his mission – the relief of Derry.

This letter was dated 29 June, but it wasn't sent then. Before dispatching it, Schomberg added a postscript on 3 July: King William had already sent reinforcements of horse and foot. It seemed he had finally grown tired of Kirke's inactivity.

On the evening of Wednesday 3 July, the prisoners who had been under the walls were moved to Windmill Hill and parked on the far side of the lines. Once darkness fell, the garrison took in some of the fitter males from the twelve hundred prisoners and sent out some of their own sick and a number of their womenfolk. By this point, the garrison must have believed they were going to emerge victorious from the stand-off.

In his quarters Hamilton was pondering. This was now the second evening that prisoners had been outside the city and the garrison still had not cracked. It was becoming clearer to him (and also presumably to Rosen) that they would never be admitted. If the situation were allowed to run on, they would certainly start to die and once that happened the garrison would string up the Jacobite officers. Also, this affair was playing very badly with the Protestants in his army. They were enraged by Rosen's barbarous treatment of their co-religionists and had expressed their feelings vociferously over the previous thirty-six hours.

In the meantime, news of what Rosen was doing had reached James in Dublin. He was furious, denounced Rosen as a 'barbarous Muscovite' and characterized his practice as a 'cruel . . . contrivance'. Melfort wrote to Rosen, but the letter gave no indication of James's fury. In its opening address it described Rosen as 'Trusty and well-beloved', and continued using a nice mix of flattery and reproach: with 'regard [to] your project of pillaging and ravaging the neighbourhood of Londonderry in case you are obliged to raise the siege', James approved. On the current scheme with the prisoners, though, Melfort suggested that Rosen could not have seen any of the declarations 'in which we have promised our protection not only to those who choose to submit to us . . . but also to those who choose to return to their habitations'. Rosen therefore must immediately release all the prisoners and send them home. James also dispatched couriers to all the commanders to whom Rosen had previously written, countermanding the marshal's orders.

The following day the messengers were still trundling north. However, before they reached their various destinations, Rosen and Hamilton agreed that the scheme was doomed to fail. A new order was issued: the Protestant prisoners were to be issued with food and money, and let home.

That evening, Roch was ordered by the Governors to wave a flag three times at the fleet to indicate the city's continuing distress. At the same time the Jacobites began herding their prisoners prior to their release. However, the keen-eyed among them spotted these were not all the same prisoners that had been put against the walls two days before. Some of the younger men were missing and in their place were women and some sick folk. They were easy to spot: they were emaciated, covered in sores, and they stank. The Jacobites returned them to Derry.

The defenders immediately dismantled the gallows and the Jacobite officers were allowed to return to their quarters. A disaster had been averted.

The next day Captain Richard set off with a detachment to Inch. Nine bombs fell on Derry, some exploding in a graveyard, disinterring the dead. And James's letter of rebuke reached Rosen. The marshal replied immediately: he had received James's letter and was honoured. It showed him that James was 'full of benevolence towards the rebels of this kingdom', but unfortunately that had only encouraged their insolence. With his scheme at the walls, Rosen continued, he had hoped to persuade these troublesome people to surrender, but he had not got as far with it as he would have liked. Only a small number of people had been put in place 'before the enemy had the cruelty to fire upon them and to refuse them every kind of assistance'. At which point, now that they comprehended the difference 'between your Majesty's clemency and the cruel treatment of their own party', he had sent them home.

James, when he received this letter, remained appalled. Indeed, he was so appalled that subsequently he applied to Lord Dover at the French court to have Rosen recalled to France. With his blackmail scheme at Derry, James explained to Dover, Rosen had done fantastic damage: nobody believed what James and his people promised any more. Rosen was the best recruiting officer the Williamites had.

In the meantime, James had other, even more pressing, concerns. On the day that Rosen wrote his letter, Melfort was generating one for Hamilton. On 2 July the garrison had questioned Hamilton's authority to treat with them, so Hamilton had requested a new commission and full authority to negotiate. This was what Melfort was writing, and he sent it with a mission statement: Derry must be settled, whatever it cost, so that the Jacobite army could move on to Scotland, where Dundee was calling for them. Hamilton was therefore told to negotiate whatever terms he judged fit, and James would ratify them. If the negotiations looked like foundering, Hamilton was to grant those inside the walls a royal pardon for all that was past and protection for the future.

Yet, what was given with one hand was taken back with the other: Hamilton was also instructed to concede only the minimum consistent with the overriding aim of securing the city. Furthermore, he was told to tell the rebels that if they did not yield to his propositions, they would be excluded for ever from partaking of James's mercy. Issuing ultimatums prior to complex negotiations is always a mistake, the more so when the opposite party has already withstood several months of siege. James concluded that he had no doubt Hamilton would 'have the honour to finish the business of Derry with success and without employing any of these extraordinary means the King has expressly [forbidden]'.

The letter propelled Hamilton to initiate negotiations with Derry's Governors. Subsequent historical accounts have tended to emphasize the city's doughty and fearless resistance, but the garrison and the population were tired, thirsty and hungry. The will to resist may have survived, but not the ability. Mortality rates were soaring, the garrison was shrinking and the survivors were so weakened they were now largely unable to fight effectively. This was the background to Hamilton's overtures.

The victims inside the walls now were not only children and the old, but hardened soldiers. On 4 July the roll, according to Walker's records, numbered 5,709: 476 fighting men had died since his last tally nine days before. As before, disease had claimed the majority of the dead. And, of course, non-combatants were dying too, presumably in even greater numbers.* That day Walker issued to each company two pounds of ginger, and to each man a pound of meal and a pound of tallow (by now euphemistically called 'French butter'). These ingredients, spiced with ginger (or, later, pepper and aniseed), seemingly made excellent pancakes.

By 7 July the besiegers had grown either more determined or less well mannered: that day, for the first time on a Sunday, bombs were hurled at the city. The next day the besiegers battered Butchers' Gate again. A fourteen-pound ball punched through and felled a man in the street behind. Walker conducted another roll-call which revealed that in four days 189 men had died. The number of private soldiers now stood at

---

*No precise records were kept of civilian deaths.

5,520. He issued aniseed and tobacco to each company, while the ration to each man was again a pound of meal and a pound of tallow.

John Hunter of Maghera, who served throughout the siege, was so weak that he fell under his musket when going out to the walls one morning to fight. In addition, his face, through lack of food and drink, was black. His suffering was profound, but for the non-combatants who did not receive rations the situation was far worse. On 9 July, as the soldiers were tucking into their tallow pancakes, the ordinary people were scouring the city and the tiny acreage outside the walls held by the garrison for herbs and weeds. The horse meat had run out at the end of June, and the main source of protein now was dog.

There were other miseries, too: the weather was still vile; the water from the wells was contaminated; the lanes were filled with faeces and urine. For those who were unable to go beyond the walls, there was nowhere else for their waste. And there was no let up in the bombardment. Butchers' Gate was so pounded that the defenders, fearful the structure might shatter, had to pile timber and earth behind it.

To the west, the small flotilla arrived peacefully at Inch and anchored a mile above Rathmullan. 'Captain Richards had landed on the island a little above Burt Castle with an ensign and 20 men and staked out a redoubt on the great strand about a mile away, taking in the whole breadth of the strand that was fordable.' The position he chose was a commanding one. The enemy would have to pass this place if they wanted to land on Inch.

In Derry no one knew of this. They did know that ships had been leaving Lough Foyle, because they had seen them going. As had the Jacobites. Hamilton, in his quarters, saw the glimmer of an opportunity. A fleet appeared to be deserting the city for a second time. A breach in Butchers' Gate seemed imminent. The citizens were obviously in distress. The time seemed to be ripe for Hamilton to secure Derry's surrender.

Back when the siege had started, the ordinary soldiers had been the most determined to resist, while the officers, who were in a much better position to know how weak Derry really was, had always been more willing to negotiate. However, after eighty-three days, Hamilton believed (and with some justice – he had the testimonies of numerous defectors and McGimpsey's letters) that the 'No Surrender' ethic was collapsing, and that the war-weary, famished soldiers would now be amenable to an offer. He had to circumvent the recalcitrant officers and appeal directly to the suffering people, so he prepared a document outlining the terms that he hoped would do the trick. Next, he arranged for copies of it to be smuggled into the town. Then he had a copy put into a shell containing no explosive, which was fired into the city. The shell shattered on impact, and, as the smoke and dust cleared, there were Hamilton's terms.

The document was addressed not to the authorities but to the soldiers and inhabitants of Derry. Hamilton began with assurances that he was sincere and that his powers from King James were real. His terms were simple: those who chose to do so could serve James, while any who wished to leave Ireland could have passes and go. The rest could return to their homes, where they would be free to practise their religion, spared from persecution. If anyone doubted the powers vested in Hamilton, then twenty citizens were welcome to visit his camp and see the document signed and sealed by James, which certified that whatever Hamilton negotiated would be binding. Forgo obstinacy and abandon misery, Hamilton urged his readers in conclusion. Things would only get worse, and, when the time came and the city's garrison could no longer resist the Jacobite forces, his offer would no longer be on the table. They had to make peace now or face certain annihilation later.

On the same day that Hamilton's communiqué appeared, Jacobite cavalry units menaced Captain Richards' position on Inch. Whenever they appeared, he drove them off with cannon fire from the little battery he'd established. Throughout the day, these shots were heard in Derry, but no one had the slightest idea what they signified. All they knew was that most of the fleet had left Lough Foyle. They had had no further communication with the fleet since Roch came. And there was almost nothing left to eat.

In light of all this, the decision was taken open negotiations with Hamilton. If nothing else, this would at least buy the garrison time, during which the relief might appear. A timetable was agreed. Each side would nominate six commissioners and tell each other who these were the next day. The city's commissioners could speak only to their opposite numbers or Hamilton himself. The city would also send out demands. If they must surrender, then everyone should know the terms beforehand. The two sides would meet in two days' time, 13 July, and discuss them.

The commissioners appointed were Colonels Lance and Hamill, Captains White and Dobbin, Alderman Cocken, who was now a captain, and the chaplain of Walker's regiment (and his most bitter critic), the Reverend John Mackenzie. An anxious document, signed by thirty-four luminaries, including Walker, Mitchelburne, Murray and Ash, explained how the six named individuals from the city were shortly to be sent to the Jacobite camp. There they were to discuss the possible rendering of the city into James's hands by the terms attached.

For those scenting submission even the most cursory perusal of the documents would have been reassuring. The commissioners were not negotiators but advocates. They had no room for manoeuvre, and the terms they were supposed to advocate amounted to nothing so much as a defenders' wish-list that comprised nineteen separate articles. Everyone in Derry, as well as those who had been in Sligo or Enniskillen, or anywhere else in Connacht or Ulster, and who had taken up arms against the Jacobites, was to have a free pardon. They were also to see the return of all their lands and personal property. Churches and tithes were to be returned to the clergy of the two provinces. Protestants were to have freedom of religion. All persons in the city were to be at liberty to go wherever they wished: to Dublin or any other part of Ireland, England or Scotland. Provision was to be made by the Jacobites for the care of the sick and wounded. No one in the city was to be compelled to take an oath of allegiance to James or made to serve in his forces. If William landed an army in Ireland, those from the city who remained on the island were to be left unmolested. Any debts owed to the king – outstanding Crown rents for their properties, for example, which hadn't been paid while the siege had been ongoing – were to be waived, and no interest charged. The Irish soldiers, especially the half-pikemen and their followers, were to be disarmed and prevented from roving the country and robbing or killing Protestants. Moreover, the Jacobites must guarantee they would stop 'using reproachful language to . . . Protestants'. When the garrison quit the city, the troops would leave with drums beating, colours flying, their match alight and their weapons in their hands. Any troops who wished to do so were to be free to join the English fleet. Anybody from Derry who wished to go to Britain was to be free to do so. All officers and gentlemen might retain one servant each and wear their swords. These onerous terms had to be confirmed by 26 July by an Act of the Irish Parliament or by King James under the Great Seal of Ireland. Commissions were to be appointed on behalf of the city and every county in the two provinces to ensure the terms were not infringed. Meantime – that is, until 26 July – there would be no more fighting: to ensure this, the protagonists would proffer hostages. Hamilton's would be kept on the English ships, the garrison's in one of the Jacobite camps near Derry. In the event of relief before 26 July both sides would return their hostages and hostilities could resume, but if the terms were accepted and the city was not relieved by that date, then the Governors would surrender Derry to Hamilton, with all its stores, armaments and ammunition.

On Thursday 11 July James wrote to Hamilton to say he had to have Derry. Jacobite artillery pounded Butchers' Gate all day, and four bombs were thrown into the city when evening came. The Jacobites were anxious not to give the impression that they had lost heart because of the forthcoming negotiations. The defenders wanted to send the same signal, so that evening the garrison went on the offensive. Five or six men were drawn out of each company and then marched out of Bishop's Gate, towards the gallows. The intention was to discover if there were large numbers of Jacobites in a camp there. The besiegers, seeing the enemy coming, mustered. The garrison party, not knowing they had been observed, marched around the field above the gallows with their colours flying. The reconnaissance mission had turned into a display of ornamental triumphalism. For the Jacobites watching from their trenches this was an irresistible target: they leaped out and fired.

Mitchelburne, who was leading the party, ordered the men back to their trenches, but instead they fled 'as if the Devil drove them' all the way back to Bishop's Gate. Here they stopped: the gate was shut. Mitchelburne and his officers caught up and issued an unequivocal order: all soldiers were to return to the ditches they had been ordered into after the enemy salvo. The soldiers refused to obey, preferring to remain 'thrusting and thronging at the gate, which was kept shut a long time'.

Insubordination on such a massive scale had never happened before. It was a worrying sign: perhaps the garrison was now so exhausted, famished and jittery that they would listen to what Hamilton had to say.

The next day, the city sent out its terms. Though there would be no hostilities once the negotiations were under way, they had technically not yet begun, so the Jacobite artillery bombarded the city as normal.

On Inch, meanwhile, Captain Richards had positioned four guns on a piece of rising ground. Whenever Jacobite parties appeared, he fired these to drive them away. He had marked out the land for trenches and redoubts and made a start on them. For labour, he used a combination of Redcoats, the six hundred or so who were on Inch, and the Protestant refugees who had flocked there from the surrounding countryside once Richards and the troops had arrived.

By three in the afternoon two redoubts were nearly constructed and the four field pieces were put between them. There was still more work to do – trenches to be dug, battery platforms for more guns to be made – but the forces on Inch could now effectively protect themselves in the event of attack. With this reassurance, they could finally turn their thoughts to Derry, which, after all, was why they had come to Ireland. A letter was prepared which explained that Inch had been secured and troop reinforcements were expected soon from England. All that remained was to find someone to take it to Derry. A little boy was entrusted with the task of getting through the Jacobite lines and delivering it.* The letter was hidden inside one of the gaiters that held up his stockings and off he went. By the following morning, he still hadn't arrived in Derry.

The commissioners, meantime, were leaving the city and heading for Windmill Hill and the negotiations. There they met the six Jacobite commissioners: Colonels Sheldon, Gordon O'Neil, Sir Neil O'Neal, Sir Edward Vaudry, Lieutenant-Colonel Skelton and Captain Francis Marrow. The Jacobites had erected a tent for the meeting and everyone filed inside. There were tables and chairs, and a meal was served. By the time the proceedings started, Hamilton had arrived. Both sides argued forcibly, but the city commissioners had the advantage because they flatly refused to negotiate. Hamilton, on the other hand, had received orders from James that he was to secure the city on any terms. He therefore agreed to one article after another.

Inside the walls, Governor Walker took advantage of the quiet to conduct routine business. He took the roll-call: since the last,

---

*In spite of his bravery, the boy's name was not recorded.

five days earlier, the garrison had lost a further 186 men to hunger and disease. He issued the day's ration to the city's fighting men: half a pound of meal, half of beef and half of shelling, or grain husk. Disaster seemed to be imminent.

But then the little boy appeared on the other side of the city from where the negotiations were taking place. He explained his business to the guards and was brought before Walker, to whom he gave that long-awaited and infinitely desirable item: the bona fide letter from the relief forces. The boy also said the city should signal immediately, with seven rounds fired from the Cathedral tower, with three more fired at midnight, and a lantern hung from the Cathedral flagpole. But, with the commissioners negotiating and hostilities suspended, the city couldn't fire its guns at that moment. As an alternative, Walker wrote a letter. Its principal thrust was to rebuke: why hadn't the relief force sailed up to the city? He then informed Kirke that the enemy had offered honourable terms, and that there was only enough food for another fourteen days' resistance – until 26 July – after which, if Kirke's forces didn't come, the city would have no alternative but to surrender.

The letter was rolled up tight, put into a little bladder, then inserted into the little boy's rectum. This was certainly a better place to hide the document he carried, if somewhat less comfortable than behind his gaiter. The boy left the city for Inch and arrived there safely at about three o'clock in the afternoon. The letter was extracted and read.

Back in the city, Walker was now facing a dilemma. He knew that the citizens must have seen the boy on his way to meet him and there would be questions, but the relief was relocating to Inch, not coming immediately to Derry, and Kirke was awaiting more troops from England. This could offer no hope to the tired, exhausted and hungry citizens of Derry. Only the promise of immediate relief would boost their morale. So Walker couldn't allow Kirke's letter to circulate, at least not in the form in which it had arrived. Fortunately, he was never afraid of sharp practice. He decided to transcribe the letter for the garrison, changing it as he did. He skilfully left as much of it intact as he could, and amended the meaning with just a few new words. The original had 'mentioned Major-General Kirke's having sent *some* to encamp at Inch'; Walker amended this to '*4,000 horse and 9,000 foot*'. For the garrison, such a huge force so close would be as good as a promise to smash the boom. The transcribed letter was distributed.

Meanwhile, the negotiations continued, but by early evening there was an impasse. Hamilton had agreed to all but three of the articles. First, the surrender date of 26 July: Hamilton said the city must surrender by noon on Monday 15 July. Second, he insisted that his hostages could not be put on to Kirke's ships. They had to be kept in Derry. Third, when the garrison sallied forth after surrender, Hamilton said only the officers and gentlemen might bear arms. The ordinary soldiers must march out unarmed.

Hamilton's strictures on the location of the hostages and proprieties of the garrison's exit seem curiously pernickety – he could have given way on these – but his insistence on the garrison's surrender by Monday was essential. Much could happen in two weeks: Schomberg and his troops could arrive; the Enniskilleners could punch up from the south; the forces that Hamilton knew were bedding down in Inch could attack. Therefore, Derry's date of 26 July could not be permitted.

It seems that, although the city's commissioners had no mandate to negotiate on any of the terms, they were just as reluctant as Hamilton for the meeting to end in deadlock and for hostilities to recommence. So they apparently argued for an extension. Probably, of the two sides, they were the more desperate. They persuaded the Jacobites to prolong the truce until noon the following day, Sunday 14 July, then returned to Derry. They immediately went before the Governors and the Council of Fourteen to report what the Jacobites would – and, more importantly, would not – accept.

At this meeting Walker argued that the city should surrender on Monday, as Hamilton had demanded. This was a shocking about-turn: publicly, he'd always been implacably opposed to capitulation. His colleagues were bewildered for two reasons: surrender was so out of character for Walker; and, more recently, what about the letter Walker had just distributed? It had been read by several of those present, and they reminded the Governor of its details: a truly awesome force was at Inch. They could march to Derry in a matter of hours and smash the Jacobites to smithereens. Why talk of surrender now, when the relief was finally so close at hand?

A man of less character than Walker might have concocted some spurious reason for his change of heart. To his credit, Walker told the truth: the good news in the letter was a fiction of which he was the author. Though more troops were expected from England, at the moment there was no army of thirteen thousand in Ireland. Worse still, Kirke had no immediate plans to relieve Derry. All the city could expect was more hunger and death.

It had grown late, and another meeting was scheduled for the next morning at eight o'clock. After a night's sleep, the authorities would decide whether to concede to General Hamilton's demands.

On Sunday 14 July Walker's unhappy letter reached Kirke aboard the *Swallow*. He immediately penned a reply that was sent to Inch for forwarding to Derry. On the same morning the Governors and the Council of Fourteen met again, as arranged, to decide on the city's fate. Walker still thought Derry should accept all three of Hamilton's terms. His colleagues were prepared to be flexible on the march out, but they were adamant that the Jacobite hostages must be kept on Kirke's boats and that the city could not be surrendered until 26 July. A resolution to this effect was agreed.

The commissioners arrived at the Jacobite camp and delivered their answer. There was further discussion but neither side would budge. It was stalemate: Hamilton had lost his last real opportunity to acquire the city without force.

The city's commissioners left the Jacobite camp in the early afternoon to return home. They were no sooner back at their lines than the enemy bombardment resumed. Throughout the afternoon and evening the enemy's guns fired, though 'blessed be God, [they] did little mischief'. Eighteen bombs were hurled into Derry, where hopes were refocusing on the forces at Inch. In the evening, as had been requested the day before, guns were fired and a lantern hung from the Cathedral tower. This wouldn't bring the relief any faster – but something else was happening that just might.

During the day, Captain Richards at Inch had received a startling piece of news: the guns were gone from the Foyle and the boom was broken. The provenance of this information remains obscure, and the boom was probably at least still partially intact. But it seemed important, so a messenger was dispatched to Kirke at once. The next morning, the messenger was back. He had not been able to deliver his message because Kirke was at sea, sailing round the peninsula to join Richards in Lough Swilly.

CHAPTER NINETEEN

Desperate Times

Eighty-nine days had passed since James had summoned the city to admit him. Both sides were like exhausted, punch-drunk pugilists: they went through the motions but were unable to inflict any more damage.

On 16 July Jacobite grenadiers attacked on the west of the city and seized some trenches in front of Butchers' Gate. The defenders stoned the enemy from the walls with such virulence that the grenadiers withdrew.

The Jacobites, it had been noticed, had a new fort near the Royal Bastion. If this were destroyed, it was reasoned, Butchers' Gate would be less likely to be assaulted. Captain Noble would lead out a party; then, once this fort was out-flanked, Adam Murray could attack it with his men. Noble and his troops failed to get around the fort, but Murray's troops attacked anyway and were repulsed, with Murray himself being shot in the thigh.

On 17 July Walker counted his troops again: 220 more had died. The ration issued was half a pound of meal, half of shelling, half of tallow and three pounds of salt hides; it was supposed to last five days. Throughout the day, the bombardment continued.

Six bombs fell before dark, and eight at midnight, the first scoring a direct hit on an old man called Thomson. His body broke into pieces.

The next day, the Jacobite artillery once again pounded the breastwork of the Gunner's Bastion and Butchers' Gate. The Duke of Berwick meanwhile attacked Rathmullan, a village on the Swilly not far from Inch, where some of the relief force had gone to seize cattle. His 1,500 troops were repulsed by a force of about 120 men who had barricaded themselves into the village.

At this point, Kirke was still at sea, endeavouring to sail to Inch. But his reply to Walker's letter had already arrived at Richards' camp. The little boy who had made the journey before was summoned to deliver it to Derry. This time, it was sewn inside a cloth button. On the night of Thursday 18 July the boy re-entered the city and was escorted to Walker and Mitchelburne. The latter recognized the handwriting – he had served under Kirke in Tangier.

The letter began with a promise that Kirke would do his utmost to relieve the city. Unfortunately, he went on, it was impossible to do this by river. Consequently, he had already sent troops to Inch, and would soon be relocating there himself. He had stores and victuals for Derry, he continued. He was also supplying Enniskillen, and, at some future point, in conjunction with the Enniskillen forces and the six thousand troops he expected from England, his plan was either to attack the Jacobites from there or entice them to attack him, thereby diverting attention from Derry. But all this was would take time, so he advised his readers: 'Be good husbands of your victuals and by God's help we shall overcome these barbarous people'.

The Governors drafted a reply: they had only five days' food left; starvation had already felled five thousand members of the garrison; the rest were so weak they could barely creep to the walls; men died every night at their posts. The city had been offered honourable terms, but, despite having no expectation of aid, it had rejected them, thus throwing away the inhabitants' best chance of survival if the Jacobites succeeded. The enemy had vowed to spare no one once they breached the walls, which they would surely succeed in doing if the relief didn't come. And, frankly, the citizens were perplexed that the boats could ride at anchor and do nothing, even with a favourable wind. As for the obstacles of the riverbank batteries and the boom, these, the Governors assured Kirke, were no longer a problem: the guns had been removed and the boom was broken. His ships could sail to Derry without hazard.

The letter was sewn inside the button and the little boy was sent on his way. This time, he was stopped by a party of Jacobite troops, who marched him back to their camp for interrogation.

In the five days since the negotiations had broken down, a total of 106 bombs had been thrown at the city, and on Friday 19 July the Jacobites battered Gunner's Bastion and Butchers' Gate yet again. Then came a setback. As Massé, the French engineer general, went to lay a gun in a battery he had constructed, he was killed by a cannon ball from the city. The same ball also took off a captain's hand and wounded a gunner and three soldiers. A second, fired an instant later, killed two more soldiers and produced a wind so hot it burned a Major Geoghogan's face so badly that he nearly lost an eye. Thirty-six French artillerymen had been sent to Derry, but over the months sickness and death had reduced the number serving to five. Massé's death meant there were now only four.

Despite this level of attrition, the Jacobite programme of intense shelling was at last having an effect inside the walls. What had been a coherent and committed garrison was fraying at the edges. From this day onwards, a court martial would be held every day 'to rectify and set right misdemeanours in the garrison'. Among its other responsibilities, the court was charged with calling to account the storekeeper and those connected with the collection of excise duty and the city rents. With everything now so expensive, money had become a new source of friction.

Kirke finally made the Swilly towards midnight. He fired thirteen guns so the people at Inch would know he'd arrived. They fired seven in return. The exchange could be heard in Derry.

The next day, in Dublin, James wrote to Hamilton, suggesting a brisk attack. However, if this failed, the blockade must be continued. Hamilton was also to lay waste to the country around Derry in case troops arrived suddenly from England. Hamilton was to send his sick and wounded as far towards Dublin as he was able. Finally, in what was James's most open admission that failure loomed, he wrote, 'if after all, as God forbid, you should be forced to leave a place that has cost us so many men and so much time then you must think to guard the passage of the river on this side as well as can be'.

Hamilton didn't need to be told: that very day he was preparing for this eventuality anyway. He needed to protect himself from the criticism that would inevitably be directed at him should the siege be aborted. One likely source of bile was Rosen, so on the subject of the marshal he informed James that he 'kept his bed and was much out of humour, and was resolved to meddle with nothing'. Hamilton also shared some bleak figures with James: the last time he had counted he had about six thousand men, but he estimated that a further thousand had died since then; and they were about to run out of provisions, it 'being extremely bare about Derry'. The enemy now had a distinct advantage: the relief fleet had arrived, and he surmised they planned to hook up with the Enniskillen garrison to strike at his troops. So Hamilton's position was that he commanded a demoralized army insufficiently strong for the task, and the enemy, once they rallied their forces, would crush him. He would have to withdraw, but, to protect himself later, he had to make the decision look consensual. Therefore, on the day he wrote this adroit if pessimistic letter, he convened a council of war to obtain the views of his generals on the siege and its likely success or failure.

Brigadier-General Carney believed the Jacobites hadn't a

chance of storming the city successfully. John Wauchop, Dominick Sheldon, Thomas Buchan, Brigadier Girardin and the Duke of Berwick concurred. Unless famine did the job for them, there was no way the Jacobites could take the city. To these lugubrious conclusions, Hamilton added his own. There were forces on Inch and a dangerous garrison in Enniskillen. The conjunction of these would be fatal, so keeping them apart was becoming the most pressing objective. Each man gave his opinion in writing and signed it. This depressing collection of documents was immediately dispatched to James in Dublin.

Morale was much higher at Inch, where Kirke went ashore to view the work Richards had effected. There were entrenchments, redoubts, a gun battery with six three-pounders and two six-pounders, a magazine, cattle and provisions. Work remained to be done, but this was already a formidable military installation. Kirke pronounced the works a success and ordered the entire relief force to disembark and take up quarters at Inch. He was then told that the guns were gone from the river and the boom was broken. At about five o'clock in the afternoon the little boy walked into Inch and told his story. He had been interrogated by the Jacobites but had told them nothing and they had released him. He handed over the button, and the letter was extracted and read. Of course, it confirmed that the guns were gone and the boom was broken. Kirke was delighted and impressed with the boy: he promoted him to ensign on the spot.

Now, prompted as well as chastened by all the documents he'd received, and with great secrecy (he believed spies at Inch might betray him), Kirke finally set in motion the relief operation. In his fleet he had three tiny merchantmen of shallow draught, and he issued instructions to their masters. They were to pack their holds with provisions, take aboard forty musketeers each, go to Lough Foyle and sail on to the city.

The three victuallers were loaded, which took until nightfall.

Then Kirke boarded his own ship, the *Swallow*, and set a course for the Foyle with the three smaller ships. They arrived at the mouth of the Foyle on the following day, 21 July, where they were joined by the *Dartmouth*, a frigate commanded by Captain John Leake. With the *Swallow* too large to make the river passage, Kirke gave Leake the task of escorting the merchantmen on their dangerous journey. Leake, knowing he'd have to escort his charges past the boom, cadged the *Swallow*'s longboat, a little vessel with a crew of nine. Because it was agile and manoeuvrable, he judged it would greatly assist the task ahead. Leaving the *Swallow* behind, the three merchantmen and the *Dartmouth* sailed upriver. Their instructions were to lie off Culmore until conditions allowed them to go on to Derry.

CHAPTER TWENTY

At Long Last, Relief

On Monday 22 July, by which time he could probably see the beleaguered city from his mooring on the Foyle, Kirke started to have second thoughts about Inch. He issued new orders: a small party was to be left on Inch to hold it while the rest of the troops were to re-embark. He sent off these orders, along with a letter that had arrived from William and Mary addressed to Marshal Rosen. News of Rosen's attempt to accelerate the city's surrender by herding non-combatants under the walls had reached them. In their letter they warned Rosen that, unless he desisted, Catholics in England could expect the same treatment.

As the vessel set off with these letters on its journey of several days, another messenger simultaneously left Inch for Derry. He was an ex-garrison member who had been sent by Governor Baker to England in May to denounce Lundy to the authorities and had come back with Kirke. Assisted by his knowledge of the terrain, and perhaps by the collapse of Jacobite morale, he skirted around enemy lines, entered the city later in the day, and delivered his message to the Governors. In four days the Enniskillen garrison would combine with the troops at Inch to raise the siege. Derry need only hold on until 26 July.

Although the messenger had evaded the enemy with ease, the Jacobites had not completely fallen to pieces. Elements within the besieging army were still determined to press the siege, in particular the artillerymen, who resumed bombardment. According to Walker forty-two twenty-pound balls were thrown at the city before nine in the morning, and a further six in the evening. Between the two bombardments, Walker counted the garrison: a further 141 soldiers had perished. For the first time, their total had dipped below five thousand.

In Dublin, James received the awful dispatch from Hamilton and the other officers on the impossibility of victory. He responded immediately:

> Seeing that Derry cannot be taken by force with such a
> small number of men as it is besieged by, our will and
> pleasure is that, as soon as you receive this, you prepare for
> raising the siege, and then actually raise it . . . unless you be
> of the opinion that, in continuing the blockade, the town
> will be forced to surrender for want of provision, which in
> all appearance must happen very shortly.

Inside Derry, even while civilians and soldiers were dying in their hundreds through starvation and disease, jealousies and vendettas, rages and feuds continued to flourish. Inevitably, Governor Walker, on account of his manner and his responsibility for the stores, remained the principal hate figure. He had already received a warning from a friend in the Jacobite camp that a plot was afoot to harm him. Not long after this a rumour spread through the garrison that he had a hoard of food: while the mob starved, he was eating like a king. Mutiny seemed imminent.

Walker solved this problem with one of his characteristic schemes: he persuaded a friend, a soldier from the garrison, to play Judas. The soldier was to join the mutineers and state that he thought Walker was hoarding. He was then to have Walker's house searched, find nothing, and spread the word to this effect. This was done and the rumour died.

But Walker's troubles were not over. Next he was accused of collaboration. The roots of the trouble lay back in May. Another friend of Walker, a Mr Cole, had been taken prisoner by the Jacobites. Two months later he was brought before Richard Hamilton, and the General ostentatiously enquired of the prisoner what sort of person Mr Walker was and who his friends were. Cole replied that he himself was one of the Governor's friends. Unaware that this might be a trap, Cole continued, unabashed: he hoped, because of this relationship, that he might be sent back to Derry with a message, and so gain his freedom. He thought right: Hamilton gave Cole a private message for Walker's ears only – it was a message that would suborn the city's surrender – and issued him with a pass. When Cole returned, he should have gone straight to Walker but, believing his offer to play messenger was merely his conceit to get the enemy to let him go, he didn't. However, he remembered the message well enough, and shared it with some members of the garrison.

In the hysterical atmosphere behind the walls, Hamilton's secret message became a cast-iron certainty: Walker was about to hand the city to the enemy and was to be handsomely rewarded for his efforts. The first Walker knew that something was wrong was when several garrison members sarcastically 'saluted him by some great names and titles'. He was much troubled: hungry, angry men and women scenting a sell-out were apt to turn murderous. He began to make enquiries, and soon traced the canard back to Cole. Walker interrogated him and extracted a full account. Once he had the story, he was able to convince the garrison that, while the slippery Hamilton had offered a bribe, Walker had not accepted it, nor even heard of it until after the rumours had started. The garrison grudgingly believed him.

Hunger and exhaustion were also wreaking havoc with the

garrison's temper. On Tuesday 23 July Captain David Ross, one of the officers running the daily court martial, visited the quarters of Adam Murray, who was still recovering from his thigh wound. Ross had orders to search for saddles belonging to Sir Arthur Rawdon. Samuel Lindsay, one of Murray's horsemen, objected to the search and there was an argument. Ross drew his sword; Lindsay produced a gun and shot him dead.

On the same day two turbulent persons were overheard planning a coup. With others they intended to sabotage the guns (by plugging with spikes the vents through which the powder was lit), beat the drums and make terms unilaterally with the Jacobites. The pair were arrested and the scheme foundered, though among the garrison it was one more reason for anxiety: there were still turncoats in their midst.

The relief flotilla on the Foyle was still waiting for the right conditions, but the masters of the vessels had been evolving a plan, which suggests it was now obvious to them that the reports of the boom's demise had been exaggerated. When finally the time was right and the winds were favourable, the *Dartmouth* would move first. She would engage Culmore and the batteries there. The *Phoenix* and the *Mountjoy*, accompanied by the *Swallow's* longboat, would follow. They would slip behind the protective curtain provided by the *Dartmouth* and continue to the narrower section of the river above the fort. Here, there were new hazards: Newfort on the Culmore side; Charlesfort, where the boom touched the bank on the west side; and Grangefort on the east. Assuming she survived whatever was fired from these, the *Mountjoy* would then, under full sail, run herself against the boom, in an attempt to break through. The longboat, well barricaded and its seamen armed with axes, would follow. Their task was to sever any remaining rope or timber, clear away the debris, then haul the merchantmen through the gap. At this juncture, the *Dartmouth* would signal the *Jerusalem*, the reserve ship in the operation, that one of the ships was through and it was safe to weigh anchor and follow. In the meantime, the *Mountjoy* and the *Phoenix* would sail on to Derry. When they reached the quays, they would unload their stores. The blockade broken, the Jacobites would be forced to retire.

From the city, the vessels aboard which these plans were hatched were clearly visible as they rode at anchor beyond Culmore. But from behind the walls there was no sign that these ships were any different from all the others that had idled on the Foyle for weeks. So the city had no idea that provisions were coming. As a result, the court martial ordered that all black cattle – probably dairy cows – that had been kept in houses should be slaughtered for the needs of the garrison. Eating the animals that had provided milk would be a last, desperate step.

Members of the starving garrison had also noticed cattle grazing between the city and Pennyburn, the property of Jacobite soldiers. It was decided that, at four the next morning, when the Jacobites would be sleeping, five hundred men would sally out. They would then drive the cows back to the city.

Before they went, Walker addressed the whole garrison with a stirring speech calculated to maintain spirits that might otherwise have crashed:

> 'Tis truth they [the enemy] boast their numbers and
> strength. But we have God's justice on our side – God that
> with this small handful of men has baffled all their counsels
> and their force . . . Oft in our sallies we clear their trenches.
> We have looked their bugbear General in the face and
> broken their boasted idols in pieces. We have laughed at
> their infallible granadoes. Their pretended Almighty bombs
> do not affright us.
>
> Our consciences are clear in what we do and the
> Almighty God will to the last defend us. Keep up your
> hearts, dear fellow-soldiers, if you have any respect for your
> wives and children, your estates, your liberties, but above all,
> if you have any hope to enjoy that holy reformed religion

you profess. Take courage. Tis for that chiefly we are hunted and persecuted. And it is for that chiefly we shall to the last glory to suffer, and which in the meantime to the last drop of our blood maintain and defend.

At this point he raised his voice and shouted, 'So help us God.' The garrison were so moved they shouted back in unison, 'Amen.' For the short term, at least, Walker's words had had the desired effect: they had to struggle on for a little longer.

Early on Thursday 25 July, the five hundred men assembled in Shipquay Street, close to the gate. Walker addressed them again. Though he might have recommended surrender earlier in the month, he also knew how to hide his anxieties and inspire his listeners. He conflated, on the one hand, rape and compulsory religious indoctrination, and, on the other, chaste marital congress free from violence and fidelity to the Protestant religion. This was obviously unsavoury but also deeply effective because it played on his listeners' deep terror about what would happen in the aftermath of a Catholic triumph. The fact that the Irish rebels half a century earlier, in 1641, had largely not raped was neither here nor there. It was believed that they had and would again.

When he had finished, the men were divided into three groups: one would leave by Ship Quay Gate, one by Butchers' Gate, while the third would wait by Bishop's Gate in case the windmill was attacked. Between them and their quest were an orchard and ditches full of soldiers. These must be neutralized before the cattle could be grabbed. The raiders crept around defences and fell on the enemy from behind. The boys minding the cows, on hearing the commotion and realizing, perhaps, that they were the real target, fell back quickly with their animals. For the troops in the trenches, the only option was to fight, though they were ill prepared for the onslaught – most didn't even have their match lit. One account speaks of only three soldiers out of hundreds able to fire his gun.

Unsurprisingly, given the bile Walker had just poured into the ears of his soldiers, the attackers, for all their weakness, were as unforgiving and zealous as ever. The Sieur de la Pannouze, an old French captain in the regiment of Lorraine who was trapped in his trench, was smashed twenty times on the head and body with musket butts and left for dead. Hearing the fighting, the soldiers at Bishop's Gate rushed round and joined their colleagues. Those Jacobites who were lucky enough to get away fell back, and the garrison flooded into their trenches; but the Jacobites had no intention of ceding their positions without a further struggle. Soldiers from the fort in Creggan were mustered and counter-attacked vigorously. The garrison's soldiers were so weak through hunger that they had insufficient strength to fight back. They retreated with the prisoners they had taken, as well as the plunder they had seized in the trenches – tools, arms and, most importantly, bannocks made from oats and mutton - but no cattle.

Estimates of the dead varied enormously: perhaps as many as three hundred Jacobites died, and between thirty and sixty of the garrison. Hamilton reported to James that the dead Williamites' pockets were stuffed with starch, which he took as a sign both of their great wants and of the breakdown in trust: everyone was so hungry and food so scarce that no one would risk leaving their ration behind when they went out to fight.

At Inch there was also activity. The package of post from Kirke had finally arrived. The royal letter of warning for Rosen was given to a drummer to take to the Jacobite camp: Kirke's orders were opened and read by Colonel Steuart, who in turn showed them to Captain Richards. Like his commanding officer, the engineer was horrified, believing 'that if we followed these orders we should ruin our interest here, expose some thousands of souls to a cruel enemy, and unavoidably lose the island'.

Meanwhile, the *Mountjoy*, the *Phoenix* and the *Jerusalem* had not gone unnoticed. As Richards was digesting Kirke's appalling orders, Hamilton was reporting the merchantmen's presence in a letter to James. They were resolved, Hamilton was sure, either to sink or reach the city by the first wind. Naturally, Hamilton took steps to ensure the former. He had four guns that had been pulverizing Derry moved to the Foyle's banks. In addition, he deployed two thousand men with small arms along it. When the ships appeared, Hamilton hoped, this firepower, combined with the boom, would stop them. If the merchantmen got through, that would be the end of hunger behind the walls, Derry would never surrender, and the siege would be finished.

On this same Thursday Governor Walker recorded that another 81 men had died in the still starving city.

Back on Inch, Colonel Steuart convened a council of war at which Kirke's extraordinary new orders were read out. The assembled officers bridled: they wanted to stay. Richards drafted a letter to Kirke to explain that the troops were better off on Inch than they would be back on the ships. Furthermore, the refugees would be vulnerable to attack if the Redcoats abandoned them, which was indefensible because of the contribution they had made: five companies of sixty men each had been recruited from them. Finally, through their presence on Inch, the enemy had been unable to gather food and forage from a place close to their camps. It was a cautious, diplomatic text – less an outright refusal to obey orders and more a catalogue of anxieties that the Inch officers hoped Kirke would address before he forced them to act – and it was immediately dispatched.

On Friday 26 July the siege entered its ninety-ninth day. In Derry, every citizen and soldier was required under oath to give a true account of the provisions he or she had. Each person was allowed to keep sufficient for themselves and their family for one week, and the rest they had to pass to the authorities.

The next day's roll-call was the worst of the whole siege. Since the last, a mere two days before, a staggering 436 soldiers had died. This was nearly 10 per cent of the total garrison.

The death rate among non-combatants was also accelerating: there were so many corpses that the city had run out of places to bury them. For want of anywhere else to put them, the bodies of the dead were now being thrown into cellars and left to rot.

In the streets, there was not a dog to be seen: they had all long since been killed and eaten. Though there were no reports of cannibalism, Walker recorded a lively anecdote that implied it was not far off. Around this time, he says there was a certain fat gentleman in the city who began to fancy that members of the garrison were looking at him in a strange way. Fearing he might be eaten, he hid for three days.

With so little left to eat, there was no alternative but to slaughter the surviving livestock. The twelve cows ordered to be slaughtered two days earlier, along with sixteen horses (almost but not quite all the animals left, as we shall see), were killed. The cows' blood was sold at fourpence a quart and the horses' at twopence a quart. The butchery done, Walker issued each member of the garrison with a half-pound of meal and one and a half pounds of beef.

On Sunday, the 101st day of the siege, Walker's reading of the situation was bleak: 'for we only reckoned upon two days' life, and had only 9 lean horses left, and among us all one pint of meal to each man. Hunger and fatigue of war had so prevailed among us, that of 7,500 regimented, we had now alive about 4,300, whereof at least a quarter were rendered unserviceable'.

The *Dartmouth* and the three merchantmen, meanwhile, had been lying on the lough now for a week. The masters remained anxious to effect the relief, but they needed a strong wind from the north to speed them past the batteries and give the *Mountjoy* enough power to smash the boom. The wind was blowing in the right direction but it was too weak.

Back in the city, where the northerly had been registered as keenly as it had been aboard the vessels, the crimson flag on the Cathedral steeple was struck. Eight shots were then fired from the steeple. The crimson flag was waved again. The intention was to send the message that, 'if they came not now, the wind blowing fair, they might stay away for ever'. The ships on the lough fired back, which was interpreted to mean they would come on the flood tide.

In the afternoon Governor Walker preached in the Cathedral. He was confident, he said, that God would not, having miraculously preserved the city for so long, suffer the enemy to win. On the contrary, He would deliver them, of this Walker was certain, and in the meantime it was only incumbent on his listeners to remain true to their faith.

By early evening it seemed that the long-anticipated and much-desired moment had come. The wind was now blowing more strongly. (In some accounts it was even described as a gale.) At six, the *Dartmouth* and the *Mountjoy* weighed anchor. The *Phoenix* (in a refinement to the plan) had orders not to follow until the *Dartmouth* was trading shots with the fort at Culmore, and the *Mountjoy*, with the *Swallow*'s longboat, was past and on her way to the boom. As arranged before, the *Jerusalem* was to wait until the boom was broken and one of the ships was through.

As the *Dartmouth* creaked towards Culmore, great and small shot rained down on her. Leake told his gunners to hold fire. He concentrated instead on manoeuvring his ship's bow on to the wind, in which position she wouldn't move. Then he could offer protection to the *Mountjoy* and attack the Jacobites effectively. The *Dartmouth*'s guns began firing and the *Mountjoy* and longboat slipped behind her protective bulk. The *Phoenix* received her signal to follow and weighed anchor.

In Derry, the cannonading was heard, and hopes rose that the relief was under way at last. Soldiers and citizens crowded on to the ramparts and peered down the Foyle. Suddenly, on the river's narrower upper reaches, they came into view – the *Mountjoy*, the longboat and then the *Phoenix*. It was the beginning of the end.

Invisible to those in Derry, though very much audible, Leake had brought his vessel to anchor within musket range of Culmore. From this position his ship's guns had continued to pound the fort. Several Jacobite cannons were blown off their mountings, while the gunners found it hard to stand beside those that were not.

Improbably, the wind suddenly eased, so now there was only the flood tide to carry the *Mountjoy* slowly but inexorably towards its target – the boom. As the ship crept forward – watched anxiously by thousands on the walls – the Jacobites poured cannon fire and small shot at her from both banks, while the musketeers on board returned fire. The *Phoenix* was similarly bombarded. A dense cloud of smoke formed. It was so thick that, by the time the *Mountjoy* and the longboat drew close to the boom, the action was hidden from those watching on the walls. They couldn't see the seamen with their axes as they began to cut away the wooden lengths that formed the body of the boom. The *Mountjoy*, carried forward by the tide, then hit the chain. Unexpectedly, it curved like a tightening bowstring and then recoiled, pushing the ship back with phenomenal power. The smoke cleared and the spectators on the city's ramparts saw the outcome of the rebound: the *Mountjoy* had been pushed up against the east bank. Her stern buried at the river's edge, she was stuck fast. Worse, within moments, Jacobite cavalry, scenting victory and shouting jubilantly (these cries, according to Walker, were 'the most dreadful to the besieged that ever we heard'), swarmed along the shore towards the stricken vessel, then jumped from the bank and splashed into the shallows. Clearly their intention was to board the *Mountjoy*, a sight that 'struck such a sudden terror in our hearts, as appeared in the very blackness of our countenances'.

Aboard the *Mountjoy*, the master stood on the deck, sword drawn, cheering on his men. His soldiers and crew let the Jacobite cavalry come within a pike's length, then three cannons loaded with partridge shot – much the same as case shot – fired.

The tangle of metal hurtled through the air and felled several troopers. An enemy bullet, coming the other way, smashed into the master's head. According to Macaulay, 'he died by the most enviable of all deaths, in sight of the city which was his birthplace, which was his home, and which had just been saved by his courage and self-devotion from the most frightful form of destruction'. As he fell there was panic in the shallows and on the bank behind, despite this lucky shot. The Jacobite cavalry turned. The French officer in command ordered them to regroup and continue the attack. They refused and fled.

Now the rising tide loosened the ship from the sandbank on which the keel was caught and sent the *Mountjoy* lurching back into deeper water. From there she headed back towards the boom. This was now broken – the chain had snapped as the *Mountjoy* rebounded. Seamen from the longboat had been busy hauling debris from the water and had cleared a path: the *Mountjoy* passed through, followed not long after by the *Phoenix*. James McGregor saw from the Cathedral tower that the boom had been breached and fired the large gun to signal that the ships were coming.

The wind now fell away almost completely, so the longboat had to attach a line to the *Mountjoy* and begin the slow, exhausting process of towing her to the quays. The *Phoenix*, being lighter, was able to make headway with the little wind there was. She overtook the *Mountjoy* and when she reached Pennyburn the citizens raced out in boats and helped to tow her. The *Mountjoy* enjoyed the same treatment. (Where these little boats came from is a mystery, since not long before the garrison had felt the need to construct their clumsy rowing boat from scratch.)

As the ships crawled towards their destination, the Jacobite guns continued to fire. Cannons were pulled along the shore to keep pace with the ships and maintain the barrage. Meanwhile, dreading the Jacobite shooting would hinder unloading, hundreds of citizens hurried with empty casks and hogsheads to the

Ship Quay. These were hastily filled with earth and piled into protective walls that would block the enemy's fire. It was ten o'clock at night, not yet fully dark, when the ships finally docked. The garrison's soldiers around the walls and the citizens on the quay shouted at the tops of their voices.

On board the *Dartmouth* Captain Leake, who'd been duelling with Culmore all the while, heard the shouts and saw that the ships were through. His vessel had not just shepherded the merchantmen past but had battered down the upper part of Culmore's walls, a remarkable victory for a ship over a fort. He moved away to a little estuary and anchored. His total casualties were one dead soldier and one wounded soldier. The *Mountjoy* suffered slightly higher casualties: along with her master, four mariners and five or six soldiers had been killed, and a lieutenant had been wounded.

Docking completed, the master's body was taken from the *Mountjoy* and the business of unloading was begun behind the protective wall of earth-filled barrels.* The citizens and soldiers lit celebratory bonfires around the ramparts and throughout the night, while the flames flickered and the bells pealed, the Jacobite gunners fired continuously. One shot killed the luckless Alexander Lindesay and his daughter, friends and neighbours of Walker from his Tyrone parish who had been refugees in the city throughout the siege. But such individual tragedies could not dampen the collective mood. As Ash recorded, it was 'A day to be remembered with thanksgiving by the besieged in Derry as long as they live[d]. For on this day we were delivered from famine and slavery. With the former they were threatened if they stayed here, and the latter, if they went away or surrendered the garrison to the enemy.' For the victors, at any rate, this indeed was what the event came to represent. At the very last moment disaster had been turned into triumph, and who could

---

*The master was later interred beside Governor Baker in the Cathedral.

doubt, under these extraordinary circumstances, where God's favour lay?

The next morning, Monday 29 July, soldiers from each company were appointed to carry the provisions that were still in the holds of the *Mountjoy* and the *Phoenix* and take them to the store-houses. These soldiers were at some risk as the Jacobites continued firing from their trenches (even though their officers must have known that the siege must now be raised). Perhaps it was the best remedy for the despondency that gripped them.

In the meantime, James received notification that the boom had been snapped and enemy ships were unloading on Derry's quays. He issued orders for the cannons, ammunition and the three thousand sick to be sent away to safety, and the country around Derry to be wasted. He stressed the importance to Richard Hamilton of retaining Coleraine even as he retired beyond Charlemont.

On 30 July the Jacobites continued firing at the city even as preparations were being made to leave. Some of their soldiers, preferring desertion to retreat, made their way to Inch, for Richards reports that 'Early this morning several people came to us from the Irish camp and did assure us that they saw our ships go up with provisions to Derry quay on Sunday night last past.'

Only forty-eight hours had elapsed since the blockade had been broken, but already myth-making was under way: according to the account that was given to Richards, a longboat approached the boom with a witch aboard, and, with three magic strikes of her hatchet, she had severed it.

The next day, Kirke appeared on Inch again. He made no mention of the letter his subordinates had drafted – to all intents and purposes a precursor to disobeying his orders. He knew that he'd enjoyed a stroke of luck. But as he confirmed the news of Derry's delivery to his officers at Inch, he didn't really know the half of it. The Gods were smiling on the Williamites.

Earlier in July, Kirke had supplied the Enniskillen garrison with six hundred firelocks for their dragoons, a thousand muskets for their infantry, eight small cannons and twenty barrels of powder, along with seven or eight of his best officers. The man in charge of this little unit was a Staffordshire soldier, Colonel Wolseley. He and his colleagues sailed round to Ballyshannon and then up the Erne. They arrived at Enniskillen when the ominous news was just breaking that Viscount Mountcashel had reached Crom Castle. Mountcashel's army was supposedly part of a three-pronged attack. The others were to be led by Sarsfield, coming from Sligo, and the Duke of Berwick, coming from Trillick, an overwhelming combined force that would surely crush the Enniskillen garrison.

However, this plan had been amended. Rosen had feared the Enniskillen and Inch garrisons might unite and relieve Derry together, so he had pulled Berwick and his troops back to the Finn River to block the movement of troops from the south. As a result, the arrangements for co-ordinating Sarsfield's advance with Mountcashel's had broken down. Thus, the three prongs had shrunk to one – Mountcashel's. His cannons were currently battering away at Crom Castle. The troops inside had only small arms, insufficient for any sort of sustained defence, and their commanding officer, Colonel Crichton, had already applied to Enniskillen for relief.

Gustavus Hamilton, Enniskillen's Governor, was ill, so Colonel Wolseley had taken charge. He sent Lieutenant-Colonel Berry to Lisnaskea with a few hundred dragoons, horse and foot. His orders were to stop the enemy occupying the town. In a brisk skirmish at 9 a.m. on 31 July, Berry's troops met the Jacobite force sent to occupy the town: some two hundred Jacobites were killed, and thirty (mostly officers) taken prisoner. A couple of hours later, Wolseley, with the rest of the troops, joined Berry's men. Their arrival coincided with the news that Mountcashel and his army of about four thousand men had reached Newtownbutler, a few miles away. Wolseley's force was perhaps half that, and they were short of rations; in their haste to leave Enniskillen they had neglected to bring any.

Wolseley put the question to his troops: did they wish to advance and engage the enemy or march back? They voted to go forward and fight. Wolseley gave them their battle cry: 'No Popery!' He was clearly in no doubt about the confessional nature of the conflict.

About half a mile from Newtownbutler, Wolseley's army came to a bog crossed by a single narrow road. The Jacobite infantry were waiting on a hill on the other side. The Enniskillen troops advanced, the Jacobites resisted, the engagement was in the balance. Then Mountcashel ordered some of his cavalry to wheel right and support his threatened right wing. But when the message was delivered, it had become: 'Right about face and march.' The cavalry obligingly made the move, but to the infantry this looked like retreat, so they retreated too. The Enniskilleners knew weakness when they saw it and hastened after the enemy.

Now the Jacobite forces made their second catastrophic mistake: they moved on to a bog covered with trees. It looked like the best place to hide, but it had a terrible disadvantage: the only way out was the way they had come in, because behind the bog was Lough Erne.

The Enniskillen troops entered the wood, anxious to finish off their enemy, whom they knew they had now cornered. What followed was butchery. One captain, William Smith, swiped so hard with his blade at the head of a Jacobite fugitive that the upper skull, complete with brains, was cut off like the top of an egg. Two thousand of Mountcashel's men were slaughtered in the wood over the course of the afternoon. Another five hundred fled into the lough and drowned. Only one man swam to safety. Four hundred, mostly officers, were taken prisoner. When Mountcashel himself emerged from the wood with five or six officers, a party of Enniskillen troops at first mistook him for one of their own. He fired his pistol at them and they realized their mistake. His horse was shot from under him, then half a dozen Enniskilleners rushed forward with every intention of clubbing Mountcashel to death. Some blows were delivered, but before the job could be finished one of his colleagues called out that he was the general. So Mountcashel was spared and carted away to Newtownbutler.

It had been a good day for Wolseley and his troops. Besides wiping out an entire army and bagging their general, they had taken all the drums and colours, as well as a great deal of *matériel* that the Jacobites could ill afford to lose, including seven cannons, powder, and many cannon and musket balls. They themselves lost only about twenty men killed and forty injured.

In the evening, when his wounds had been patched, Mountcashel was asked by his victorious captors why after his cavalry had performed their disastrous retreating manoeuvre he had chosen to follow his men into the wood instead of slipping away? Mountcashel explained that his troops were the best King James had, other than those in Derry, but once they buckled the Stuart project in Ireland was finished and the kingdom was lost. He went into the wood to die, and he regretted that he hadn't.

Whether this battle was the precise moment that James's position became untenable is debatable. But it was certainly a huge disaster for the Jacobites and a great triumph for the Williamites. It also crowned the achievement of the Enniskillen garrison.

That evening, back in Derry, Jacobite units set fire to several properties in the countryside around the city. That night the besiegers burned the tents and huts that had ringed Derry for over a hundred days. Then, before daylight, they moved off, striking south for Strabane and Lifford, a well-armed party of cavalry at their rear. The weather was stormy, with a strong wind and pouring rain. When dawn came, they were retracing their steps towards the fords across which they had burst in April with such high hopes.

As they did so, a deputation from Derry arrived at Inch to

wait on Kirke, the hero of the hour. They gave him an account of the raising of the siege, thanked him and invited him to visit. But in the midst of this good humour and gratitude there were already signs that Kirke's interests and those of the settlers he had just liberated did not coincide.

Though the Jacobite army was retreating, little knots of marauders were loose in the country and still burning Protestant houses. Colonel Crofton came to Inch and asked Kirke to send a couple of hundred Redcoats out into the surrounding countryside to prevent these depredations. Kirke refused, and the orgy of arson was allowed to run on unabated.

The bulk of the Jacobite train made it to Strabane and pitched camp. Here, Richard Hamilton and his staff, and later the entire army, heard of the disaster at Newtownbutler. Now, suddenly, it seemed a hastier retreat than had been planned was required, but for that ordnance and other encumbrances must be abandoned. The Jacobites broke up several big guns and threw the pieces into the river. A quantity of small arms went the same way. Then the army headed off, south-east, leaving behind the sick and wounded.

The siege was over. Walker claims the Jacobites lost between eight and nine thousand soldiers and about a hundred officers. This was certainly an overestimate, just as the figure of two thousand given by the author of *A Jacobite Narrative* was an underestimate. Their actual casualties were somewhere between the two.

According to Walker's own computations the Derry garrison was down to 4,300 by the end of July, making its total loss nearly 3,000. He doesn't give a figure for the number of non-combatants who starved to death or died of sickness, but it must have run into thousands, too.

The besiegers prosecuted the siege at a cost; the defenders resisted at a cost. The city 'won' (if only just), but it was hardly the resounding military triumph of, say, the battle at Newtownbutler.

However, its psychological significance would prove eternal, encyclopedic. As a narrative, it would offer a point of common convergence for all the traditions in Ireland. Of course, it would have polar effects on the two sides, depressing those who identified with the losers just as much as it would delight those who identified with the victors. But for both, the siege was an event without parallel in Ireland's history.

CHAPTER TWENTY-ONE

Aftermath

On Friday 2 August Colonel Steuart and Captain Richards left Inch and went to Derry. They came, said Walker, 'to congratulate [us on] our deliverance', although Richards records that he was more concerned 'to give the necessary orders for the repairs' than with protocol.

Two days later, Kirke rode from Inch to make his ceremonial entry into the city. He dismounted at Bishop's Gate. The Mayor, Gervais Squire, and Alderman Cocken greeted him in their civic robes, along with other worthies, including Walker and Mitchelburne. They offered the keys of the city, the civic sword and the mace to Kirke, gifts 'the Major-General very courteously returned'. Preceded by the sword and mace, flanked by the Governors, Kirke entered the city and began to move along Bishop's Street. The garrison was drawn up on either side of the road with the non-combatants behind. Everyone cheered, the cannons on the walls fired; the mood was festive, jubilant, ecstatic. However, behind this glaze of joy there was misery. Standing (if they could) at the windows and doors of the damaged houses, cheering with everyone else, were the sick. Some of these people were racked with typhus, others with plague.

Laid out, wherever there was room, were the dying, delirious and semi-conscious, swimming in dirt, sweat, faeces, urine and vomit. Kirke did not enter any of the citizens' houses, going into Mitchelburne's instead. There the authorities had prepared a reception: 'The Governors treated the General with a very good dinner considering the times,' and their hospitality stretched to sour beer, milk and water, and even a little brandy.

Kirke later returned to Inch, and the next day Walker visited him there for dinner. The minister was anxious to return to his religious duties, so he offered Kirke his regiment – a tactful move. The commander, equally diplomatically (and tact was not usually his strong point), invited Walker to dispose of his regiment however he wished. Walker ceded command to a Captain White, presumably irritating a few majors in the process.

The next day, Tuesday 6 August, having left a rearguard of 150 men, Kirke quit Inch and set off with the rest of his force for Derry. On arrival there was another bacchanal of celebratory gunfire. Kirke was quartered in the Bishop's Palace, but for the body of his troops Derry was declared out of bounds because of the various diseases raging inside the walls and they made camp on Windmill Hill. In the evening Kirke convened a council of war for all field officers to discuss the regulation of the garrison, the civil government and cleaning up the city. Thursday 8 August was designated a day of thanksgiving. A sermon was preached by a certain John Knox 'on the nature of the siege and the great deliverance, which from Almighty God' the city had enjoyed. Later the entire garrison was arranged on the ramparts and there was another feast of gunfire.

On the same day Kirke issued the first of several onerous proclamations: he prohibited the taking of goods out of the city by anyone without a licence and ordered all those who were not enlisted and had previously resided in the country to quit Derry within four days. The licences would prove almost impossible to obtain, while the order to leave proved inflexible, so non-combatants had to quit the city, often without even their bedding or clothing, and return to homes that had been destroyed.

Kirke also embarked on a ruthless demobilization programme for Derry's citizen army. His first move was to reduce the garrison's eight regiments to six. Walker was perturbed, but the disingenuous Kirke assured him of his care and favour to the men. Walker was relieved to have this assurance before he left. At a council meeting on 8 August he had been 'prevailed on to go to the King William and to carry an address from the garrison'. The address was drawn up, and the next day he sailed to Glasgow. Mitchelburne was left in sole charge in the city, and Kirke gifted to his old comrade from Tangier the cattle he'd had rounded up from the surrounding countryside 'upon pretence of their belonging to the enemy'.

On 12 August Kirke's demobilization project went up a gear. The entire garrison was told to muster in the field outside the walls. The soldiers went cheerfully: there was a rumour that Kirke intended to distribute a cash bonus among them. However, once they were drawn up they learned that the number of regiments was to be cut again, from six to four. Next, Kirke named new captains for most of the companies, a good number from his own entourage. The result was 'that a great many of those Captains, who had not only raised and armed their companies almost wholly at their own charge, but had done the greatest service in the defence of the town, were either disbanded or reduced'. When one of the captains who had served during the siege complained, Kirke threatened to have him hanged from the new gallows he'd erected in front of the ravelin. Most of Murray's regiment, who perhaps knew that engaging Kirke was pointless, disappeared into the country, taking their carbines and pistols. Kirke promptly had their saddles seized, then confiscated Adam Murray's horse, which the latter, with difficulty, had managed to keep alive throughout the siege. Finally, those members of the garrison who remained found their daily rates of pay drastically reduced (theoretically – as yet they'd received no money).

Perhaps on account of the mass desertion of Murray's men, Kirke followed his amalgamations by instructing all sentries to confiscate arms that any garrison member attempted to carry out of the city. He also prohibited a subsistence allowance to the sick or the wounded out of stores. These men went into the surrounding countryside to beg. With the landscape devastated and a good few houses empty, they didn't do well, and several died. Little wonder that some of those who had signed the address that Walker was currently carrying to King William began to wish that they hadn't signed, packed, as it was, with praise for Kirke.

Walker arrived at Glasgow on 13 August and was immediately enrolled as a Burgess and Guild Brother of the Corporation, posts that gave him the freedom of the city. He was in Edinburgh the next day and was awarded the same privilege, this time on parchment with letters of gold. He also met Alexander Osborne, the Presbyterian minister Tyrconnell had sent into the north after Richard Hamilton's army in March. Osborne wanted news of friends and colleagues in Ireland, and Walker obliged, without mentioning that he was going to libel Osborne as a Jacobite spy in the book he was soon to publish.

By 22 August Walker was at Chester, where, news of Derry's ordeals having arrived in advance, adoring and curious crowds followed him in the streets. London, where he went next, offered the same pleasures of celebrity in even greater measure. He was met at Barnet by Sir Robert Cotton and conveyed to the City in the latter's coach, with hundreds of bystanders running alongside, desperate for a glimpse of the hero. He had an audience with King William, at which he wore – how modest – not military uniform but the habit of his calling. William drank his health, commissioned Sir Godfrey Kneller to paint his portrait and promised that the bishopric of Derry would be Walker's as soon as it fell vacant. Other honours heaped on the Rector of Donoughmore included a banquet courtesy of the Irish Society, honorary degrees from Oxford and Cambridge, the thanks of the House of Commons and a cash grant of £5,000.

Walker soon found himself caught up once again in the affairs of his old colleague and sometime superior Colonel Robert Lundy, who was still languishing in the Tower of London, 'upon suspicion of treasonable practices against His Majesty's Government'. Some weeks after Walker's arrival in the capital, a committee was appointed by Parliament to inquire into the events in Derry. Lundy was brought before the members and interrogated. His replies were weak and the testimonies of others made him appear foolish. For example, Lundy admitted that at the fateful council of war with Cunningham he had told the English officers that there was no more than ten days' worth of supplies in the city. Cornet Nicolson and Sir Arthur Rawdon both testified to the committee that Lundy had known this was untrue. To the members of the committee, Lundy looked like a liar, while Colonels Cunningham and Richards looked like dupes who should have known better.

The committee was unsparing in its verdicts on the trio. The colonels were judged guilty of negligence, for which, in the language of the times, they were broken and dismissed from the service. But for Lundy, whom they thought more heinous, they had something far more serious in mind: they recommended 'That Colonel Lundy be sent over to Londonderry to be tried there for treason'. If he were found guilty, Lundy knew he would hang, so he began a campaign to prevent the trial, and lobbied those with influence. On 23 September he wrote to Lord Melvill, a relative, and asked the question: if he really were a traitor, then why on the night of 20 April, when he reached Culmore, did he not double back to the Jacobite lines, which were only a couple of miles away? If he were a Jacobite, they would have protected him and rewarded him. The fact that he sailed to Britain could mean only one thing: he was no traitor. He asked Melvill to make William aware of this and to point out that, as he was not a traitor, he should be freed from jail. Otherwise, he and his family faced ruin. Alternatively, he wrote, William could give him a handsome allowance, as life in the Tower was very expensive. Lundy also wrote to Lords Shrewsbury, Dorset and Monmouth to the same effect.

It was at this point that Governor Walker re-entered the life of Robert Lundy. The hero of Derry came before the Committee that had investigated Lundy and offered some unexpected help to his old commander. He argued against sending Lundy to Derry for trial on two counts: one, because 'most material witnesses against him were dispersed'; and two, more surprisingly, because in Derry 'he had a faction for him'. Walker believed that these two factors would lead to Lundy's inevitable acquittal. It was an opinion that carried a good deal of weight, but Lundy wasn't out of the woods yet.

Walker had other business before the House besides helping his erstwhile superior. Derry needed remuneration, and plenty of it, if the ravages of war were to be rectified. He had already asked the Irish Society for their help, since 'most of the houses in Derry were demolished by the military operations of the enemy', and he had touched the great livery companies for a hundred pounds each. This was better than nothing, but much more was needed, so two months later Walker presented a petition to the House of Commons soliciting support for the two thousand widows and orphans that he calculated the siege had created, along with the eighteen conforming and seven non-conformist ministers, or their families (if they had died), who had served the city so well.

The House called Walker back the following day and the Speaker informed him that the Members had voted £10,000 for the relief of those in Derry who were suffering, along with the thanks of the House, which he was asked to carry back to Ireland with him. Walker promised to pass on their thanks. The money was never paid.

Walker's account of the siege was published while he was in London. It generated controversy and undermined the reputation he enjoyed as a doughty fighting cleric of unimpeachable probity. The first cause of offence was the self-laudatory puffs that littered the text: 'Mr Walker receiving intelligence that the enemy was drawing towards Derry, he rides in all haste thither and gives Colonel Lundy an account of it'; 'Mr Walker took his post at the Long Causeway as commanded by Colonel Lundy'; 'Mr Walker found the gates shut against him and his regiment: they stay all night without the gates'; 'Mr Walker found it necessary to mount one of the horse and make them rally, and to relieve Colonel Murray whom he saw surrounded by the enemy'. Making this trope all the more objectionable, the real heroes – men such as Murray and Noble – hardly feature. In Walker's defence, he never claimed to be writing an objective history. This was his personal account, so obviously his story and his experiences would be at the centre. But Walker the author did not seem to appreciate that resistance was collective and that to glorify himself while omitting almost everyone else was, at the very least, tactless.

The second cause of offence was his attitude to nonconformists. Although he had been in his rectory in County Tyrone when Tyrconnell's unwilling intermediary Mr Osborne had addressed the Council of the North, this did not stop Walker from accusing Osborne of being 'a spy upon the whole North, employed by my Lord Tyrconnell'. As it happened, Osborne was acting for Tyrconnell, but he was an emissary rather than a spy, and he had been forced into his role. If he were acting surreptitiously for anyone, it was for the Council of the North, to whom he provided intelligence on the Jacobite forces while encouraging them to resist.

Besides slandering an individual like Osborne, Walker also denigrated nonconformists as a group. For instance, in the middle of his account, he wrote, 'there were eighteen clergymen in the town of the communion of the church who in their turns, when they were not in action, had prayers and sermon[s] ever[sic]day'. The nonconformist ministers, he continued, 'were equally careful of their people, and kept them very obedient and quiet', meaning, in other words (and this was how it was interpreted), Presbyterians were usually troublesome and disobedient. The greatest insult to the nonconformists, though, was the appendix, where Walker gave the names of the conforming clergymen in Derry during the siege. At the bottom of this list, he added casually that were also 'several nonconformist ministers, to the number of seven, whose names I cannot learn, four of whom died in the siege'. With this, Walker was, in effect, refusing to acknowledge the huge contribution nonconformists had made during the siege. And, with Presbyterians forming the majority in both the city's garrison and the refugee population, he offended many people.

The clamour against the *True Account* was so loud and so vicious that Walker hurriedly published *A Vindication of the Account of the Siege of Londonderry*. As a work of rebuttal it was lively but hardly convincing. For instance, of Osborne, Walker said, 'Mr Walker will be very ready to give that gentleman all opportunity of justifying himself, and shall make him all imaginable satisfaction if he has done him wrong'.

He was even more mealy-mouthed on his failure to list the names of the nonconformist ministers: 'Mr W. allows they might very justly reproach him, if he had designedly omitted' them. But he claimed he hadn't: he had searched long and hard but still, despite so much effort, he could not recall the names, not even when one was John Mackenzie, the chaplain of his own regiment. Walker's lacklustre excuse convinced no one: it was obvious he did not want to remember them.

As for John Mackenzie, the chaplain in question, he was oblivious of the controversy provoked by Walker's two texts. He was back in Derryloran, the parish in County Tyrone where Cookstown is situated. It was not until December that he was able to read a copy of Walker's *True Account*. He was understandably appalled and determined to put his own account before the world. With the assistance of the bookseller John Dunton, his *Narrative of the Siege of Londonderry: or, the late memorable Transactions of that City, Faithfully Represented to Rectify the Mistakes and Supply the Omissions of Mr Walker's Account* appeared in the spring of 1690. Mackenzie's account did indeed make good many of Walker's omissions. It was also a better, much more detailed book. However, for all that, it was also malicious: the author took every opportunity to denigrate Walker. For instance, Mackenzie suggested Walker was never a Governor of the city, however much he liked to pretend he was. According to his detractor, Walker was really just a glorified quartermaster, appointed by Governor Baker to oversee the stores. These were stores, moreover, to which Walker on occasion helped himself – a hugely damaging allegation against any man after a siege. Mackenzie ridiculed Walker's martial exploits, accused him of being overfond of the bottle and, worst of all, characterized him as a man in the same mould as Lundy: a coward, maybe even a closet Jacobite, who would have surrendered the city if he had not been challenged.

Shortly after Mackenzie's *Narrative* appeared an anonymous author charged to Walker's defence. This individual (probably John Vesey, nonconformist turned Episcopalian, Archbishop of Tuam and friend of Walker) published a short book with the uncompromising title *Mr John Mackenzie's Narrative of the Siege of Derry a false LIBEL. In defence of Mr George Walker. Written by his Friend in his Absence.* This was a marvellously vicious tract, one of whose sharpest barbs was the assertion that Mackenzie was a feeble writer and unable to marshal sentences couched in proper English. Mackenzie's work was categorized, rightly, as a work of hate, 'a long-winded paraphrase upon a short text and the whole substance of the book may be resolved into two lines, viz. *All the brave and glorious actions in that siege were performed by the Dissenters and Colonel Murray at the head of them, [while] all inglorious actions and treacherous attempts are to be imputed to the other part of the garrison and principally to Dr Walker.*'

Mackenzie was unabashed, and replied with a further pamphlet, modestly titled *Dr Walker's Invisible Champion foiled, or an Appendix to the late Narrative of the Siege of Derry: wherein all the arguments offered in the late Pamphlet to prove it a False Libel are Examined and Refuted.* This was little more than a rant, and, had Walker got Mackenzie into a courtroom, he might well have succeeded in obtaining redress. It would certainly have provided a fitting climax to their feud.

The Jacobites might have failed to seize Derry but they were still armed and dangerous, and King James's writ still ran over great tracts of Ireland. King William sent Schomberg with an army to Ireland in the autumn of 1689, but the old general, due to the Duke of Berwick's skilful military tactics in the field, failed to take Dublin before winter set in.

A further fillip to the Jacobite camp came in December. Lord Mountcashel escaped his captors and returned to Dublin, where he received a hero's welcome and a reception at the castle with King James presiding. His status as an escaped prisoner made him a marked man, though, and in the spring he sailed from Cork with the Irish Brigade (Irish troops that James traded for French ones), along with Rosen and Avaux.

In the meantime, following his stay in London, George Walker had returned to the north of Ireland, which was controlled by Schomberg's forces. Ezekiel Hopkins died in June 1690 and the bishopric William had promised Walker now looked set to become his. But before Walker could be invested, William, having determined to take personal command of his army (the failure to take Dublin had been unwelcome), sailed to Ireland and landed at Carrickfergus. Walker was there to meet him, and accompanied William on his march south to the Boyne.

In the middle of the battle fought on 1 July 1690 (12 July in the calendar that we use today*), at the ford near where Schomberg was dying and where the fighting was fiercest, Walker was shot

---

*Although this is wrong: it should be 11 July; the new calendar added ten, not eleven, days.

dead. His detractors, of whom there were many, saw his death as the just deserts of a clerical meddler thirsty for military glory. King William's alleged remark on being informed that the future Bishop of Derry had been killed at the ford – 'What was he doing there?' or, in some versions, 'What was the fool doing there?' – features prominently in several of the negative accounts against Walker subsequently given out. His supporters, of course, countered that this was unfair, and suggested he was probably there on an errand of mercy.

Walker's body was stripped by Scots-Irish camp followers and buried where it fell. Thirteen years later, his widow, Isabella, decided she wanted his remains brought home to the little church in Donoughmore. A man named Blacker, who had raised and commanded a group of volunteers at the Boyne, said he knew where the body was buried and promised he would fetch it back. He returned with a box containing a skull and a few bones and Mrs Walker paid him £20. The box was buried under the floor in the church, and when she died Mrs Walker was laid alongside it in her coffin. In 1838, during repairs to the church floor, the box was opened. It was found to contain a skull and two thighbones that 'both belonged to the one leg and there- fore could not have belonged to the same man'.

The Battle of the Boyne was also the end of Richard Hamilton's story, or at least the military part of it. He fought bravely, as well as brilliantly, was severely wounded and finally was taken prisoner. William, hopeful of intelligence from his illustrious prisoner, wondered, 'Is this business over or will your horse make more fight?'

Hamilton answered, 'On my honour, sir, I believe that they will.'

'Your honour, your honour,' William muttered.

Lurking behind this remark lay Richard Hamilton's recent history. He had been captured in England after William seized power. He had made peace with his captors and, on John Temple's recommendation, was sent to Ireland to turn Tyrconnell after promising to return to London if he failed. Once he got to Dublin, of course, he had reneged and so it was he came to be at the Boyne. William's muttered, 'Your honour', (if he ever did say it) was deeply ironic: honour was precisely what Hamilton, from William's perspective, did not appear to have. From this it was but a short skip to one of the principal pieties of the winning side. They were not only militarily superior, they were morally superior. Their word was their bond, while the word of their enemies was not.

Later, after the Williamite wars were over and the Jacobites had been vanquished, the victors would make great capital out of this distinction. In *Ireland Preserved, or the siege of Londonderry. A Tragic-Comedy written by a Gentleman who was in the town during the whole siege* (this might have been Mitchelburne, with help perhaps from George Farquhar, himself a native of Derry), an explicit connection was made between Hamilton's treachery and the suicide of his guarantor, Temple: 'The wretched youth against his friend* exclaims,/And in despair drowns himself in the Thames', went the damning couplet. At the root of Protestant woes, at least where Ireland was concerned, the Williamites believed there was only ever one cause: the Catholic talent for betrayal. It was an idea that went back at least to 1641.

---

*i.e. Richard Hamilton.

CHAPTER TWENTY-TWO

The End

Following the debacle at the Boyne, James left Dublin at sunrise on 2 July 1690 and moved south. When he reached Kinsale he wrote to Tyrconnell, whom he had not seen since they had parted company on the battlefield of the Boyne, when he had reconfirmed him as his Lord Deputy. Then James embarked on one of the ten French frigates that had been waiting for him and sailed away from Ireland, never to return.

For Tyrconnell, who knew that William and his army would shortly be rolling into Dublin (James's last order was that the city must not be burned to prevent this), it was necessary to find a new base. He fled west, arriving in Limerick on 6 July, the day that William entered Dublin. With characteristic energy and élan, Tyrconnell immediately set about reorganizing and consolidating the Jacobite forces, atomized at the Boyne.

William arrived before Limerick on 7 August, and at dawn the following day he summoned the garrison to surrender. The commander was the Marquis de Boisseleau, one of the French officers who had come to Ireland with James back in March 1689. He owed his command in Limerick to Tyrconnell, who by now had moved on to Galway. Boisseleau declined William's request and the Williamite forces began to lay siege to Limerick. It soon became clear to the defenders that unless some sort of diversionary manoeuvre could be effected they would have to capitulate.

Patrick Sarsfield, who had received his first military commission from Charles II, secured Tyrconnell's permission to ambush William's siege train, currently wending its way from Cashel, which, once it was *in situ*, would tip the balance the besiegers' way. Five hundred troopers intercepted the train at Ballyneety and overcame the escort with ease. Then they stuffed the considerable number of cannons with powder, buried the mouths in the ground and blew them up. The explosions were heard in Limerick.

This disaster placed William in a quandary. The fighting season was drawing to a close. His army in Flanders had been defeated earlier in the month at Fleurus and the French navy had prevailed during an engagement off Beachy Head. There were matters abroad of more importance than Limerick that required his immediate attention. So, on 30 August, William raised the siege and some days later he returned to England, leaving a considerable force behind under the Dutch General, Baron van Ginkel.

Two weeks later, Tyrconnell, having handed over the military administration to the Duke of Berwick, sailed to France. He needed a massive amount of manpower and the support of the French if the Jacobite project in Ireland were to succeed, because a new menace had just arrived. John Churchill, then Earl of Marlborough, had landed at Cork with the intention of capturing the Munster ports and thereby disrupting communication between Ireland and France. His arrival added an interesting personal dynamic because his sister Arabella, sometime mistress of James II, was the Duke of Berwick's mother. Marlborough would therefore be opposing forces commanded by his nephew. Furthermore, Marlborough's wife Sarah was the sister of Tyrconnell's wife Frances. Though this was an international war, it also bore many of the characteristics of an aristocratic power struggle.

Tyrconnell, in France, was able to effect little on behalf of the Jacobite cause in Ireland. At a personal audience with Louis XIV, all he could extract was the promise of supplies, some money and some officers. His trip was more successful personally, though, as he managed to offload the blame for all that had gone wrong in Ireland on to others' shoulders. Also, at his farewell audience at Versailles on 3 December 1690, Louis presented him with a gift of his own portrait in a magnificent diamond box. James proved equally generous, making Tyrconnell a Knight of the Garter – replacing the Duke of Grafton, recently killed fighting in Cork – and finally awarding him the full title of Lord Lieutenant. Now Tyrconnell was 'as great as his king could make him', as the author of *A Jacobite Narrative* observed with barely disguised contempt.

The new Lord Lieutenant returned to Ireland in December 1690 to find the Jacobite command structure divided by intrigue. Berwick had had several notables either arrested or removed from their respective offices on suspicion of abetting the enemy. Tyrconnell reversed these decisions, knowing that Berwick had to return to France. Indeed, he brought the orders to this effect with him.

The Jacobites and Williamites met in battle again at Aughrim on 12 July 1691. Each army numbered about twenty thousand men and the Jacobites were again defeated. Though Protestants would always view the Boyne as the key moment in their struggle with the Catholics for control of Ireland, for the latter Aughrim would become the seminal encounter. In the future Catholics would remember this battle as the point when they definitively lost and the Williamites won. News of the great disaster, as Aughrim was subsequently characterized among the losers, was brought to Tyrconnell at Limerick. He was 'struck with a deep wound of sorrow, and the more because the battle was lost so unexpectedly'.

Following his victory at Aughrim, Ginkel marched his troops to Galway, and the city capitulated on 22 July. Next he turned his attention to Limerick. Inside the walls, Tyrconnell rallied the troops and worked hard to ensure good relations between the Irish and French forces who were now cooped up together. The Lord Lieutenant knew they had to resist only until winter set in. Then the Williamites would have to withdraw and the Jacobites would have six months to reorganize, re-provision and, most importantly, secure more help from France.

But the Lord Lieutenant's body now let him down. On 10 August he was the chief guest at a dinner party given by a French lieutenant-general and friend, Monsieur d'Usson:

> He and company were very merry but at night, upon his preparing to go to bed, he found himself indisposed. The next day his malady increased. Remedies were applied, yet to no effect. On the third day, observing his weakness to be great, he settled his worldly affairs, and took care for his conscience . . . On the following day, his excellency grew speechless, and on Friday . . . being the fifth day of his sickness, he expired.

He was buried at night in Limerick Cathedral. For the author of *A Jacobite Narrative*, this was the true end of the Jacobite project in Ireland. When Tyrconnell fell so soon after Aughrim, the Catholic nation went with him, 'for there was no other subject left able to support the national cause'.

However, Limerick remained an awkward city to take. Ginkel therefore opened discussions with Sarsfield, the new Jacobite commander. Clearly the civil articles were going to be the most complex parts of any agreement. The Jacobites, their eye clearly on the future, demanded the restitution of estates to Catholics, liberty of worship, full civil rights and their own parochial organization. The Williamites promptly declined, but this was the position from which negotiations proceeded. There was, of course, a fundamental point that demanded clarification before anything could be decided: to whom would the terms, if and when agreed, apply? The Jacobite military remnant who negotiated them or the Irish Catholic community they represented? The Jacobites insisted, correctly, on the latter, and Ginkel and his negotiators agreed. But as the treaty was published and enacted, this was forgotten and omitted (which perhaps is one source of the abiding Irish distrust of treaties negotiated with the English).

The document was signed on 3 October 1691. The military provisions provided for the surrender of the city of Limerick and the counties of Limerick, Clare, Kerry, Cork, Sligo and Mayo, the release of prisoners and the transport to France of such Jacobites as wished to fight for Louis XIV. To the astonishment of many Williamites, twelve thousand soldiers and their dependants, were transplanted rapidly to France, where they would subsequently play a significant role in French military affairs. However, this Irish diaspora, while forming an important bridge between the continent and Ireland, would also, by virtue of their existence, cause problems at home. With so many Irishmen fighting for the enemy, Louis, how could any Catholics be considered loyal in future?

The civil articles, commonly referred to as the Treaty of Limerick, did not mention religious freedom or give any details on the position of priests. However, the first article did guarantee Catholics the liberties of religion they had enjoyed under Charles II, or as was 'consistent with the laws of Ireland', although exactly what this entailed was unclear. The subsequent articles did not cover those who had already surrendered or those who had opted for French service, only those Jacobites who were still resisting: an enormous group. According to the articles, if they took the Oath of Allegiance to William and Mary, they were guaranteed a pardon, their property and the rights to practise professions and to bear civilian arms.

This wasn't everything the Jacobites had hoped for, but it was not as bad as it might have been. It was certainly in spirit – if not

in letter – and by the standards of the day a generous and accom-
modating deal. Unfortunately, it was hardly signed before the
trouble started. Appalled Williamites, who had not been party to
the negotiations, condemned the document as too lenient.
Jacobites, meantime, cried foul, as the spirit of the agreement
was vitiated by double dealing and sharp practice. The fair copy
sent from Limerick to London omitted the first clause regarding religious toleration. The contemporary explanation – that
hasty transcription was to blame – failed to convince. The clause
was reinserted by Letters Patent, but by then it was too late. The
losers believed it had been left out deliberately and felt
aggrieved. The victors, especially those who had not been party
to the negotiations, saw this as yet one more example of Catholic
chicanery.

Those in this second camp formed the majority in the Irish
Parliament. They were always bound to be touchy on conces-
sions to Catholics, anyway, and when they ratified the treaty they
left out the clause about Catholic rights as under Charles II. This
signalled the onset of the systematic destruction of the Irish
Catholic Jacobite polity. First, in 1697, the clergy were assaulted
with an edict that allowed priests and bishops to be banished.
Then several Acts were passed that sanctioned the seizure of
Jacobite property which they had retained under the treaty. In
the eighteenth century there followed a series of penal laws.
These would reduce even further the tiny number of Catholic
landowners still hanging on (about a seventh of the land was in
the hands of such proprietors at the start of the century), and
consolidate the monopoly of power held by the Protestant
minority, the so-called Ascendancy.

For the Protestants the settlement delivered an entire country,
while for the Catholics it subsequently represented the moment
when they finally lost it all. Given that this was how the situation was viewed, one might expect that the clients of the
winning side – those, for example, who had held Derry for
William and provided sanctuary for his supporters – would be

showered with rewards. It was their resistance that helped deliver the settlement.

And, indeed, some were the recipients of official largesse. Captain James Hamilton, the nephew of Richard Hamilton who had arrived at Derry aboard the *Deliverance* in March 1688, became Baron Mountcastle and Viscount Strabane. The boatswain's mate on the longboat and his eight fellow-crew members each received £10 for their work at the boom. The widow of the *Mountjoy*'s master received from William a diamond chain that he tied around her neck himself and a pension on which she was able to retire to Ashbrook, outside Derry.

But for the citizen army who had borne the heat and burden of the siege there was the opposite of generosity. Charles Fox, the Paymaster of the Forces, reported that the eight Derry regiments, from the dates of their commissions to the end of the siege, were owed £74,786 18s. 2d. His meticulous accuracy was not as impressive as it might at first appear, though, for it transpired that this sum was only in respect of the officers, not the rank and file.

It was fifteen years before a House of Commons committee discovered, in 1705, that the ordinary soldiers had been left out. The sums were done again, and the total debt due to the garrison was set at £134,958 3s. 3d., of which less than £10,000 had been paid by that stage. It should be emphasized that this figure was merely wages: it did not take into account what soldiers and officers spent from their own pockets on horses, weapons, arms and accoutrements.

The ex-soldiers of Derry appointed Colonel Hamill of Lifford as their agent to pursue their claims. After several years of fruitless endeavour, he handed the matter over to his brother William, who was resident in England, and he pursued the matter for several decades but gained nothing other than debts and a spell in jail for his pains. Colonel Mitchelburne, who had lost his entire family in the siege, endured much the same fate. When he went to London in 1709 to advance his own claims for compensation, he was promptly imprisoned in the Fleet for debt. Happily, the sums due to him 'at length were paid, but in a manner far short of the merit of his brave actions and great services'. Unhappily, Mitchelburne's limited success in recouping some of what he was owed was the exception. His comrades did not succeed. With the war successfully concluded, it was felt unnecessary to remunerate them. For the majority of the garrison – who, like the majority of the refugees, were Presbyterian – the non-payment of what they were owed was part of a larger pattern of systematic, shabby, mean-spirited mistreatment. This came in the form of a series of legislative actions calculated to inhibit and stunt their economic development (which Nationalists, as Presbyterians have often grimly observed, have preferred to forget).

The inhibition of 'Irish' (Presbyterian) industry (notwithstanding that Presbyterians were the backbone of the Ulster plantation) was a practice with a pedigree that went back at least to 1660, thirty years before the siege of Derry. For instance, there were the amendments to the Navigation Act that prevented Irish shipping trading with the colonies. And there were the laws that prohibited the importation into England of a range of Irish-produced foodstuffs, especially beef, but also mutton, pork, bacon, butter and cheese. Not being able to export their produce to England, the Irish, especially the Presbyterians in the north, had switched to wool production and had prospered. Now, after the Williamite wars, when they had held Derry and Enniskillen for the Crown, they had to watch as the business they had created was eliminated. The Irish Woollen Export Prohibition Act of 1699 prohibited the export of Irish-manufactured wool to any country in the world. The Irish were told to switch to linen – and some in Ulster did with notable success – but for many nonconformists it seemed the fruits of their industry were unwanted.

On top of this, the Toleration Act was passed by the Parliament in England but was not extended to Ireland. Instead, in 1704, the

Irish Test Act was passed, which required every person holding civil or military office under the Crown to take the sacrament in his parish church. If he refused, he was debarred from serving. This was a test that no honest Presbyterian could pass – at least, not if he wanted an untroubled conscience. In Derry alone, out of a corporation of thirty-eight members, ten aldermen – six of them former mayors – and fourteen burgesses resigned rather than take the sacrament in a church where normally they would not worship.

For Ulster's Presbyterians, the Old World, and the part of it called Ireland, lost its lustre. They began to emigrate in their thousands to the New World, where they were free to practise their religion and enjoy the fruits of their industry. One such was James McGregor, the lookout in the Cathedral on 28 July who saw the *Mountjoy* and the *Phoenix* and fired the gun to signal that the relief was coming. After the Williamite wars he became the Presbyterian minister of Aghadowey, but in 1718 he went to America with a great number of his congregation. He founded Londonderry in New Hampshire, in memory of the city he had defended. When he died in 1729, 'his remains were borne to the grave in that new Derry beyond the seas by those who had been fellow defenders in the memorable siege of the city by the Foyle'. He was succeeded by the Reverend Matthew Clerk, also a veteran, whose temple wound, sustained in the siege, had never healed.

The haemorrhaging of Presbyterians continued through the eighteenth century. No doubt at the time it appeared to have benefits. Nonconformists were habitually troublesome, to conformists, at any rate, and administrators in England and Ireland heaved a sigh of relief as they flooded across the Atlantic. But 'The resentment which they carried with them continued to burn in their new homes and in the War of Independence England had no fiercer enemies than the grandsons and great-grandsons of the Presbyterians who held Ulster against Tyrconnell.'

The years following the siege saw many unlikely narratives being lived out by the protagonists. Certainly the most unexpected must be the strange story of Colonel Robert Lundy. In September 1689 he was in prison in London, facing extradition to Ireland and the prospect of a trial in his old command post, but that possibility was quashed by no less a figure than George Walker. There was still the possibility of a trial in England,* but if the witnesses were not in Derry, it was hardly likely they would be in London. Months of limbo followed, until, on 12 February 1690, Lundy was granted bail. For a few years he disappeared from view, but he had only one trade – soldiering – so it was inevitable he would re-emerge from obscurity sooner or later. On 10 August 1704 he applied to the Lord High Treasurer for an advance on his pay for his equipage in Portugal and was awarded £108. He was a soldier of the Crown currently fighting for the Portuguese army. Over the following years, he might have fought in Hesse. He might also have helped with the successful defence of Gibraltar against the French and the Spanish in the War of the Spanish Succession. He was certainly taken prisoner, probably at Almanza, on 14 April 1707, and spent twenty-six months in captivity before being exchanged for twenty French prisoners. He arrived back in England in June 1709, and two months later petitioned for the arrears of his pay lost when he was a prisoner-of-war. In Treasury papers of the time he was described as 'Colonel Lundy, Adjutant General of the King of Portugal's forces in the Queen of England's pay'. He died in July 1717.

More than three hundred years after the event, Governor Lundy's career in Derry remains an enigma. Was he a defeatist, an incompetent or a traitor? If the first, he could equally be called a realist who wished to make some accommodation with the enemy because he knew just how bad Derry's position was. Incompetence, the second charge, is the direction Macaulay leans towards, believing Lundy's conduct could be

---

*Lundy petitioned the House of Commons for this on 22 October 1689.

'attributed to faint-heartedness and to poverty of spirit'. He was just a weakling, Macaulay believed, contradictory, pusillanimous and vacillating, whose dithering and panic inspired only distrust.

The third alternative – that Lundy was a closet Jacobite – Macaulay discounts, although this was certainly the opinion of Lundy's contemporaries. Walker, for instance, claimed Lundy signalled to Hamilton when it was safe to cross the Finn; Mackenzie stated that Lundy's 'pernicious intentions' explained the loss of the key to the Ferry Quay Gate, as well as the missing gunner and the unloaded cannon, on the night of Murray's putsch. Both writers, it has to be said, twisted the facts to fit their accusations: for example, Lundy was still in Derry when Hamilton swam over the river at Cladyford. He could not have given a signal. On the evidence of Lundy's two clerical contemporaries, the argument that Lundy was a traitor does not stand up.

And there the matter might rest, except there was also the account given by Captain Kinaston. This was not a prejudiced report but apparently Lundy's own confession as relayed by an impartial witness after an interview. The only trouble here is this 'confession' was made when the Jacobites were about to storm the walls. It was perfectly possible Lundy was just a very frightened man who hoped, by what he said to Kinaston, to ingratiate himself with the enemy he thought would be in control of the city in a matter of days if not hours. And Lundy's subsequent actions were certainly not those one would expect of a Jacobite: once he was spirited out of Derry he did not cross to the Jacobite lines as he might easily have done; he fled to Scotland. But that leaves the conundrum of why King James behaved throughout his interview with Kinaston as if he knew all about Lundy's loyalty to him and the Jacobite cause. Perhaps he was improvising in an attempt to glean more information. We shall never know.

What is undeniable is that the siege of Derry as a narrative gains far greater resonance with Lundy cast in the role of the great betrayer. He adds so much as a 'traitor' that, had he not existed, it would have been necessary to invent him. In a way, maybe that is what happened.

A hundred years to the day after the apprentices had locked the gates, on a bright, dry Thursday morning at dawn, drums were beaten, bells were rung and Derry's cannons were fired. A flag, crimson like Mitchelburne's, was hoisted on the Cathedral. 'If a magistrate or military officer had interfered . . . a mob of all denominations would have pelted him with stones.'

This denominational unity was not as unlikely as it seems. First, over a century, the previous bitterness had dissipated somewhat. A coalition of progressive forces from the Catholic, Protestant and Presbyterian traditions was starting to coalesce in the face of English (or British) obduracy. These were heady times throughout Ireland, in Derry as much as anywhere else, though there were still signs of ancient enmity, too.

At half-past ten a vast procession formed in Ship Quay Street, headed by the Corporation. The clergy followed, Catholic alongside Protestant. Other participants included officers of the Royal Navy, the 46th Regiment, the Volunteer Corps (a local militia), tradesmen, schoolboys and the 'Merchants' Apprentices, preceded by the great-grandson of Colonel Adam Murray, who carried his gallant ancestor's sword. The orange ribbons - mandatory wear – apparently 'had a very happy effect . . . It is scarcely possible to do justice to the beautiful and august appearance exhibited at this stage of . . . so respectable a body of free citizens commemorating the heroic achievements of their ancestors, in the very spot which was the scene where they were performed.' Derry, thought this writer, was as dear to the inhabitants of the British Isles as Marathon was to the ancient Greeks.

The procession ended at the Cathedral, where the Very Reverend Dean Hume took as his text for the sermon Joshua, 4:24: 'That all people of the earth might know the hand of the

Lord, that it is mighty; that ye might fear the Lord your God for ever'. The sermon was followed by 'a selection of sacred music . . . from the Oratorio of *Judas Maccabeus* . . . [including] that fine air, so well suited to the occasion, "'Tis Liberty, dear Liberty Alone'". From the church, the congregation went to the Meeting House for an oration from a Presbyterian minister, the Reverend Black, 'which at once evinced his knowledge of English history and his ardent zeal for liberty'.

Mercifully, after the hours of sermons, there was now some spectacle. HMS *Porcupine*, 'covered over with a variety of the most splendid colours', appeared in the harbour 'to do honour to the festival'. Such a large ship of war had never before been seen in Derry's harbour. Twenty-one guns on the ramparts fired and the ship replied with an equal number. It was 'a lively representation of that memorable event, THE RELIEF OF LONDONDERRY'.

However, 'The first procession had scarcely terminated when another of a different kind commenced. Some of the lower class of citizens had provided an effigy representing the well known Lundy, executed in a humorous style'. The effigy was 'repeatedly exposed . . . to the insults of the zealous populace' and then 'burned in the market place with every circumstance of ignominy'.* There was a moral lesson in this. Such was the destiny of traitors that they deserved 'perpetual infamy' and the 'everlasting . . . detestation [of] even . . . the meanest of people'. The ceremony instructed the attentive mind of this universal truth. It's a moot point whether Lundy deserved to be at the service of such a lesson, but the population needed a hate figure, latched on to him and has never let go since.

The Apprentice Boys of Derry (a Protestant political society founded in 1814 and named after the original thirteen apprentice

---

*After the erection of the Governor Walker Memorial Pillar on the city walls in the nineteenth century, the ceremony was relocated there. When the IRA blew up the memorial, it was relocated again, this time to the steps of the courthouse.

boys) have long since taken charge of making the effigy and burning it. Over the years it has grown. Lundy effigies sixteen feet high and nearly a ton in weight are not unknown. Traditionally dressed in a black uniform with gold epaulettes and a cocked hat (a folk version of the Governor's uniform), and laden with firewood,* the giant figure traditionally bears – lest there should be any misunderstanding – two inscriptions: on the front 'LUNDY THE TRAITOR'; and on the back 'THE END OF ALL TRAITORS'.

If you attend the ceremony on or around 17 December in Derry,† you will not encounter any doubters. Lundy's allegiance is crystal clear: he was a Jacobite. The original defenders knew it, the generations who followed knew it, and those who carry on the tradition today know it. Colonel Robert Lundy worked tirelessly to pass the garrison of Londonderry to the Jacobites and deserves nothing in memory but execration and obloquy. To find the source of this degree of hatred we must go back to 1688.

Closing the gates against the Earl of Antrim's Redshanks was treason because they were the king's troops, and Lundy came to the city thereafter as the king's representative in a deal brokered by Mountjoy. But Lundy, according to the defenders' narrative – forged in conflict then and reinforced by endless conflict since – was a closet Jacobite who would have surrendered the city. He was the chosen instrument of Jacobite conquest, insinuated into the city after the Redshanks were seen off, and far more dangerous than Antrim's rabble. He orchestrated defeat at the fords and came perilously close to delivering the city to the enemy.

Once he fled, all became clear: his treachery was rumbled and

---

*When Lundy fled, disguised as a common soldier, he carried tow, the cord necessary to fire a gun at the time, popularly known as 'match'. But the effigy-makers, assuming match meant a bundle of tree branches used for starting fires, have always given their figure firewood. Though this is only a detail, it is yet another item in a long list of misunderstandings that has affixed itself to Lundy

†Held on this date rather than 7 December because of the adoption of the Gregorian calendar in the mid eighteenth century.

the defenders enjoyed the marvellous and intoxicating delights of
vindication. Slamming the gates might have looked like treason
in December 1688, but Lundy's defection (which betrayed his
true intentions) showed them they had acted correctly. But there
was still the matter of the four months between the closing of
the gates and Lundy's departure. To the Protestant Irish – loyal,
respectful of authority, law abiding – this was always a problem,
and it was here the ritual burning of Lundy's effigy had its
roots. When the effigy was burned, it represented the banishing
of uncertainty and resolved the crisis of conscience that had occured
in those four months. The course of 'No Surrender' had been
right. That was what the revellers of 1788 discovered and that was
what those who have participated in this ritual of purgation ever
since have known, too.

The original celebration in 1788 continued at half-past two,
when the gates were ceremonially shut. The Jacobites' captured
colours were then paraded to the Diamond. A *feu-de-joie* was
fired there, with the guns on the ramparts and aboard the
Porcupine joining in. At four o'clock everybody who was anybody, including 'the Clergy of the Church of Rome', sat down
to a plain but plentiful dinner in the Town Hall. Toasts were
drunk to William of Orange, to which, of course, 'no man was
idiot enough to object'. In spite of the overcrowding – there
were nearly a thousand people present - 'decorum and compla-
cency' prevailed. 'Religious dissensions . . . seemed to be buried
in oblivion, and Roman Catholics vied with Protestants in
expressing, by every possible mark, their sense of the blessings
secured to them by the event they were commemorating, and
the part which they took in the celebration of this joyful day was
really cordial.' This might be a slight exaggeration, but the
Catholics were certainly present and did not object to anything.

In the midst of the toasting, the company discovered they had
a unique guest. He was a man said to have been 'born a short
time before the investment of the city' who was then nursed in

a cellar throughout the siege. The company 'gazed with intense interest upon the venerable old man, who had breathed the same atmosphere' as Walker, Mitchelburne and Murray. They promptly organized a subscription to protect this veteran 'from the icy grasp of poverty'.

As dusk fell there were new pleasures. The 'ingenious Mr Black' (presumably the reverend who had spoken earlier) had arranged a set of transparencies all over the city that glowed in the falling darkness when light was shone through them. In Ferry Quay Street there was an image of the gates being shut. In Butcher Street there was Walker with sword and Bible, and Adam Murray with General Maumont's body at his feet. In Bishop Street 'The genius of Londonderry [was shown] fixing the imperial crown upon the head of KING WILLIAM, and trampling on a figure representing despotism'. Whatever the truth, the opinion in the city was clearly that Derry's resistance had delivered William his crown.

The day ended with a firework display, but the celebrations were far from over. The following day 'the carcass of an ox, decorated with orange ribbons, was drawn at noon through the principal streets to the Diamond'. It was later cut into pieces and distributed with bread and beer to the poor. The festival finally concluded that evening with a ball and supper at which 'God Save the King' was

> sung in full chorus . . . [with] joy . . . strongly felt and
> universally diffused . . . Thus terminated the festival.
> Judicious in its origin, respectable in its progress, and happy
> in its conclusion. The event and its commemoration, it may
> be said, were worthy of each other. No religious
> animosities, no illiberal reflections on past events poisoned
> the general joy and triumph. The genuis of Ireland seemed
> to preside, repressing in the Protestants all irritating marks of
> exultation, and exciting in the members of the Church of
> Rome the feelings of thankfulness for the deliverance of

their persons and properties from the shackles of a lawless
and intolerable despotism.

This non-sectarian celebration of the siege, however, was
short lived. The spirit that made it possible died with the brutal
suppression of the 1798 rebellion and the Act of Union that followed. By the time John Graham came to write his *History of the
Siege of Derry* in 1829, the country was already poisoned. The
behaviour of Roman Catholics at the 1788 event, he wrote,
was 'in strong contrast with the brutal ignorance of the agitators
of the present day who load the name of their deliverer with
obloquy, and consider the honours paid to his memory as an
insult to their religion'. These 'agitators' were the followers of
Daniel O'Connell, the leader of the crusade for Catholic emancipation, which reached its climax when Graham was writing.
With hindsight, we can see that the idea that Catholics really
ought to have seen William of Orange as their saviour was ten-
dentious. But this infelicity aside, Graham still has something
important to say. When he was writing, the Williamite celebrations had assumed their dual nature: for Protestants they were an
occasion for joy and delight; for Catholics, they were a cause of
anger and offence.

To understand this process by which the celebrations took
on a darker hue, the best place to start is topography. The
problem for the planters who built Derry was location. Dowcra
and others sited it where they did because, with the bog on the
west and the Foyle on the east, the piece of high ground on
which the city arose had good defences, theoretically. But it
was on the wrong side of the river. Being on the west, it was
always going to be a tiny bastion of plantation marooned in an
almost entirely Catholic hinterland. Had it been located on the
east, in a Protestant environment, the story would have been
very different.

The fault line where the two traditions were most in conflict
was on the city's west, along the stretch of wall from Bishop's

Gate to Butchers' Gate, where the city's defences met the bog, later the Bogside. This was where the most serious attacks during the siege where launched, which was only logical: there was no river here. This was where Mitchelburne's flag flew. And this was the side that continued, as those within the walls saw it, to be the location of the principal threat to their integrity, because this was where, when the city expanded in the eighteenth and nineteenth centuries, the Catholics who couldn't live inside the walls were concentrated. So it was no accident that the Apprentice Boys' Governor Walker Memorial Pillar was erected on the Royal Bastion in the 1820s. In this location, it became the stone equivalent of Mitchelburne's 'Bloody Flag' (incidentally, the society's emblem, as well as its colour). It towered over the Bogside and reminded the Catholics there not just of their earlier defeat but, more pertinently, of their present situation: those in the city who identified with the defenders in the siege would continue to resist Catholic encroachment.

As the nineteenth century rolled on two developments – one political, one technological – created the perfect circumstances for the conflict that has lasted into the present. The first was the rise of the Fenians (a revolutionary movement committed to Ireland's independence, achieved, if necessary, through violence). The second was the development of the railway system in Ireland. It had been one thing for local Derrymen to re-enact the closing of the gates in the early nineteenth century. It was quite another for thousands of strangers, Orangemen, to travel over from the east of the province to participate. As they continued to do so, conflict with the Catholic majority around Derry escalated, and not just at the celebrations of the shutting of the gates (in December) and the relief of the city (in August). In July 1868, for instance, after street disturbances following processions celebrating the Battle of the Boyne, Apprentice Boys gathered at the Walker Monument and fired salvoes of broken crockery into the Bogside. Then in December, a Catholic procession invaded the Waterside, the largely Protestant district on the east bank, their band playing 'The Wearing of the Green' (a song that celebrates Irish revolutionary resistance). The procession was fired on from the Waterside. In February the following year, Catholic processions forced their way past police cordons at Butchers' Gate and Bishop's Gate despite missiles raining down on them like hailstones. Two months later, the arrival of Prince Arthur provoked even more serious rioting. A Protestant and a Catholic procession met the prince, they each played 'God Save the Queen', but then both launched into their own party tunes, much to the other's fury. In the evening Catholic crowds invested the city and surged to the Diamond, where some demanded an Irish republic and carried green flags. Rioting and shooting followed as Protestants attacked them. The traditional Catholic route of retreat, through Butchers' Gate and back to the Bogside, was blocked by the police, greatly encouraging those Protestants on the attack. Three died in the fighting that followed and dozens were injured. A subsequent commission of inquiry reported:

> Sad as the results were, we can only express our surprise that they were not worse. The constabulary fired a volley in a crowded street; conflicting mobs not only assailed each other violently with stones, but revolvers were freely used by each body against the other . . . Surely it is a matter for rejoicing that a riot of such a character caused the loss of only three human lives.

In 1883 the whole sorry business was repeated. The Nationalist Lord Mayor of Dublin came to deliver a speech on 'Franchise'. A procession formed, and, despite the efforts of the police, who wanted it to go west to the Bogside where the Nationalist Party headquarters and Nationalist League premises were situated, it went east. Meanwhile, the Apprentice Boys, who had intended to hold a meeting of protest on a platform at the Walker Memorial, changed their minds and determined on direct confrontation. They formed a procession and, headed by a band, set off bearing Union flags and their traditional colours of crimson. They moved to the Diamond and seized the Town Hall, then fired on the Catholic procession as it approached. The Catholics returned fire, and both sides hurled slates and stones. By nightfall, there was serious rioting outside Bishop's Gate. Another commission of inquiry was amazed that this time 'only two persons received wounds of a serious character'.

The partition of Ireland in 1921–2, which crudely established the Catholic-majority Free State of the south and the Protestant-majority Northern Ireland in six of Ulster's nine counties, was supposed to put an end to all of this. But in Derry Catholics were the majority, although the Protestants had most of the power and the money. In the tiny houses of the Bogside and Creggan, for the first fifty years of Stormont rule, the old rage smouldered. Irish history never created the circumstances to smother the fire, so, in the 1960s, the flames took hold again.

In Derry in the early autumn of 1968, the Civil Rights Association gave notice of a march that was to follow a traditional Protestant route: from the Waterside Station on the east bank, across the Foyle by the Craigavon bridge to the Diamond, where the war memorials stood. Local Unionists objected to this route, and some even threatened a counter-demonstration. More ominously, the Apprentice Boys of Derry served notice of an 'Annual Initiation Ceremony' involving a march of their members from the Waterside Station to the Diamond, and then on to the Apprentice Boys Memorial Hall, close to the Walker Memorial.

The Stormont Minister for Home Affairs, William Craig, prohibited all marches either within the Waterside ward or within the city walls. A long meeting of those involved on the civil rights side decided to proceed, although the Civil Rights Association accepted Craig's restrictions. The following day, surrounded by police, the procession – hundreds, rather than thousands, strong – set off from Waterside Station. The new route

led uphill along Duke Street through a Protestant quarter of the
city. A police contingent waited for the marchers at the top of
the hill and there was light skirmishing between the two groups.
One of the leaders of the protest, Gerry Fitt (then Westminster
MP for West Belfast), was clubbed and carted away in an ambulance. This was followed by a sit-down protest by the marchers,
loud singing of 'We Shall Overcome' and speeches. Some of
those who now addressed the crowd advised dispersal but others,
insisting on the right of the people of Derry to march in their
own city, did not. These counsels for and against moderation
were then interrupted by the police, who ordered dispersal
through a loud hailer. This was followed by a spontaneous surge
of protesters against the police lines, to which the police
responded with a series of baton charges. They began to drive
the protesters down the hill, where a second police line had
been established. Dozens suffered head wounds where they had
been hit with batons, many of them young girls. They were
taken to Altnagelvin Hospital by ambulance. 'Derry, as dusk
gathered,' wrote Liam de Paor in his prescient account published a year or two after the event, 'was electric with tension,
and with a feeling that something had been done that could not
be undone.'

Northern Ireland's slide into the 'Troubles' had begun. It
remained only for the military to be introduced, thus ensuring
the conflict had all the appurtenances of a proper civil war. This
came about during the following year, in the aftermath of
Derry's celebration of her relief. The political atmosphere
throughout the Province, at the time, was bad owing to accelerating agitation for civil rights and clashes between activists and
the police. Relations had not been as bad since 1922, just after
partition. Given this climate, it was widely predicted that if
the Apprentice Boys went ahead with their annual procession on
the city walls to celebrate the lifting of the siege, the Catholic
population, who by now abhorred the ceremony, would react.
Government requests to the Apprentice Boys to cancel, however,

went unheeded. As the marchers processed through the city centre, Catholic protesters threw volleys of stones and the march broke up in disorder. The police attempted to drive the stone-throwers beyond the walls and back to the Bogside, but they were rebuffed with more stones and petrol bombs. The police were issued with steel helmets and shields but they still could not drive back the protesters.

Meanwhile, as the rioting ran on, diversionary attacks were launched in Belfast to prevent police reinforcements going to Derry. Sub-machine-guns were used in this city, and a child was killed by a bullet that came through the wall of his home. The violence was now at an altogether new level: it was epic, apocalyptic.

Television cameras obligingly recorded the carnage, and footage was beamed into living rooms throughout Ireland and Britain. The images from Derry after forty-eight hours of con-frontation showed buildings blazing and bedraggled policemen with torn or burned tunics huddling in alleys or doorways. The scene gave every appearance of a cataclysmic struggle that had been lost by the authorities – as was the case. The Northern Ireland government now felt obliged to ask for assistance. They needed the army, and the Labour government in London acceded to their request. This in turn led to the suspension of the Stormont Parliament and the transfer of authority to Westminster. The crisis in Ulster that had been fermenting since at least 1922 had finally come to a head.

Years of misery followed. Thousands of people died, yet many in Ulster continued to celebrate the great events of their past, causing offence in the process. In Derry, however, and within the narrow confines of the celebrations of the siege, the story has a more optimistic aspect. The celebrations of the three hundredth anniversary in 1990 successfully integrated the perspectives of the two traditions. First, Shaun Davey's 'Relief of Derry Symphony' was performed in the Guildhall. Then the audience spilled outside

to witness a pageant (created by Andy Hinds) that told the story of
the siege through the personal histories of an English Protestant
family and an Irish Catholic family. During the narrative, both
sides lose a family member, but Hinds wanted to do more than
show that the suffering was equivalent; he wanted to convince the
citizens of Derry that there was hope. In its third movement,
Davey's symphony contained a song about the mysterious white
horse that some defenders believed they had seen in the sky, which
they took to be a sign of their survival. At the pageant's culmination, the song, 'The White Horse', was reprised, first by the singer
who had sung it in the Guildhall, then by a choir of children, then
by a choir of adults. Finally, a white horse led by a young girl
appeared, followed by young children carrying white lanterns.
They led the audience to the waterfront, where, in the distance, a
massive white horse was illuminated against the sky. Fintan
O'Toole wrote that this gave a 'sense of the religious and the
political merging, the sense of a city celebrating and lamenting its
own founding events, the public enactment of terror and forgive-
ness'.

In the mid–1990s Northern Ireland's enduring Troubles were
curtailed, if not finally ended, by the Belfast (or Good Friday)
Agreement, which initiated devolved government and power
sharing. It may not have been entirely successful, but the level of
violence has declined sharply. However, there was still trouble:

A direct descendant of Captain Thomas Ash, a diarist quoted
frequently in this narrative, lives today at Ashbrook, the family's
ancestral home just outside Derry. His name is John Beresford
Ash. In the late 1990s, after the paramilitary cease-fires and the
Belfast Agreement had ushered in a future of acceptance and for-
giveness, he was visited by strangers reading from a different
hymn sheet. They were fire bombers, and they came three times
in ten months. The last time was on the night of 12 June 1998.
John Beresford Ash was asleep in bed with his wife when they
were woken by a crash:

We followed our by now set routine. As I came down the main staircase, I could see there was a tremendous glow of fire but this time it was outside the house not in. I flung open the door and to my absolute amazement saw five little fires in a semicircle about ten yards from end to end. I immediately realized what it was. We'd recently had a family photograph taken outside our front door for my sixtieth birthday that had been in the local papers. There were five of us there, my three daughters and my wife and myself. I assumed this represented the five of us being burned.

In Ireland the past is not dead. Indeed, as William Faulkner said, 'It is not even past yet.' But one has to set the experiences of the Ash family against the celebrations in Derry in 1990. There are many bitter, vengeful people in Ireland whose anger has its roots in what happened far in the past. But there are others who believe in acquiescence, accommodation and compromise. In the end they must prevail.

NOTES

If the author cited has more than one book listed in the bibliography, the specific work is also cited. Otherwise, only the author's name, followed by the page number where the quote appears, is given.

3 Uncivil War

19 'many thousands were preparing . . .' Hickson, Vol. I, 95.
22 'English Dogs!' ibid., Vol. I, 170.
23 'How sweetly they do fry . . .' ibid., Vol. I, 170.
25 'A plague on this book . . .' ibid., Vol. I, 190.
25 'and the plantation lands . . .' ibid.

4 War and Cromwell

28 'We of the city . . .' Milligan, *Walls*, 68-9.
28 'The miseries that . . .' ibid., 69.
29 'the monthly achievements . . .' ibid., 68.
29 'stately buildings, strong . . .' ibid., 70.
29 'cruel murderers and thirsty . . .' ibid.
29 'many artificial and exquisite . . .' ibid.
29 'a well-wisher . . .' ibid., 71.
32 'an hot-headed . . .' Macrory, 100.
32 'put to death rebels . . .' ibid.
33 'making as many several pictures . . .' Fraser, 340.
34 'cruelties which they . . .' Carlyle, Vol. II, 169.
34 'been lately acquainted . . .' ibid.

5 Richard Talbot's Rise to Prominence

38 'a little black man . . .' Petrie, 66.

42   'innocent papists . . .' Sergeant, Vol. I, 119.
45   'Colonel Richard Talbot, who had notoriously . . .' ibid., 252.
45   'His Majesty should . . .' ibid., 253.

6 The Reign of James II

53   'Clarendon's nomination as governor . . .' Sergeant, Vol. I, 298.
53   'everybody here knows . . .' ibid., 301.
54   'with full power . . .' ibid., 314.
55   'We have here a great . . .' ibid., 320.
55   'when he should be dispatched . . .' ibid., 322.
55   'rogues and old Cromwellians . . .' ibid., 323.
55   'with a thousand . . .' ibid., 326.
55   'Whether my Lord . . .' ibid.
56   'It is impossible . . .' ibid., 327.
56   'he could not imagine . . .' ibid., 330.
56   'it would appear . . .' ibid., 335.
57   'to make projects for Bills . . .' ibid.
57   'By the discourses he . . .' Petrie, 148.
58   'feuds and animosities . . .' ibid., 151.
58   'no great trouble . . .' ibid., 153.

7 The Closing of the Gates

64   'a brave soldier . . .' Macaulay, 12.
69   'To my Lord, this deliver . . .' Stewart, 64-5.
72   'Norman and the rest . . .' Walker, 2.
73   'divers of those . . .' Mackenzie, 6-7.
74   'the younger sort . . .' Walker, 2.
75   'Bring about a great gun . . .' Mackenzie, 9.

8 Confusion and Clarification

77   'we could not determine . . .' Witherow, *Diaries*, 61-2.
78   'If the supreme Majesty . . .' Dwyer, 142.
78   'My Lord, your doctrine . . .' Macrory, 130.
81   'publicly threatened . . .' Mackenzie, 12.
82   'our rabble . . . had shut . . .' ibid., 84.
82   'We cannot but think . . .' ibid., 85.
82   'younger and more inconsiderate . . .' ibid., 86.
82   'The next day . . .' ibid., 86-7.
83   'we then blessed God . . .' ibid., 87.
83   'we have resolved . . .' Milligan, *History*, 40.

86   'inflamed by the news . . .' Macaulay, 12.
86   'the chief Protestants . . .' ibid., 40.
87   'The Governor had already . . .' Walker, 2-3.
91   'What, my Lord . . .' Macrory, 127.
92   'and by that error . . .' Gilbert, 41.
92   'Londonderry proved . . .' ibid.

9 Diplomacy and Skulduggery

95   'to remove the said . . .' Gilbert, 43.
95   'a wise and sensible . . .' ibid.
95   'to go in his . . .' ibid.
95   'in all likelihood . . .' Macrory, 139.
96   'Let the people fall . . .' Witherow, *Derry and Enniskillen*, 49.
98   'hearing that a vessel . . .' Sergeant, Vol. II, 406-7.
100   'the Papists in Dublin . . .' ibid.
101   'you will be able . . .' ibid., 419.
101   'not being willing . . .' ibid.
101   'I have been . . .' and subsequent quotes, all ibid., 652.
102   'generally tainted with . . .' ibid., 654.
102   'If, sir, . . . your Majesty . . .' ibid., 653.
102   'a note of the things . . .' ibid., 416.
105   'to all gentlemen . . .' ibid., 424.
105   'the property of the unhappy . . .' Graham, *Siege of Derry and Defence of Enniskillen*, 43.
105   'necessary evils' ibid.
106   'with good reason, apprehensive . . .' Walker, 3.
106   'a young brisk zealous Protestant . . .' Witherow, *Derry and Enniskillen*, 54.
107   'where unto we are . . .' Dwyer, 146.
107   'of whose sincerity . . .' ibid., 147.
108   'were untrained . . .' Witherow, *Derry and Enniskillen*, 55.
108   'still do persist . . .' ibid., 387.
108   'any violence to women . . .' ibid., 389.
108   'with all imaginable . . .' Sergeant, Vol. II, 425.
109   'the country Irish . . .' Walker, 47.
109   'immediately enter upon . . .' ibid., 47-8.
110   'the Irish army . . .' Witherow, *Derry and Enniskillen*, 65.
110   'we are resolved to . . .' Mackenzie, 91.
112   'that the garrison at Dungannon . . .' Walker, 4.
114   'So considerable a . . .' Mackenzie, 94.

114 'ordinary vigour . . .' ibid.

115 'You are, without delay . . .' Walker, 43–4.

115 'and for the defence . . .' ibid., 44.

115 'wind and weather permitting . . .' ibid.

115 'to land the said . . .' ibid., 50.

115 'of further and greater . . .' ibid.

116 'to make the best . . .' ibid.

116 'to our trusty and well-beloved . . .' Macrory, 165.

10 James in Ireland

118 'a Protestant Magistrate, one Brown . . .' Graham, *Siege of Derry and Defence of Enniskillen*, 47.

118 'Brown had been in arms . . .' ibid.

119 'unclean birds of prey . . .' Macaulay, 14.

119 'whatever power he . . .' ibid., 15.

120 'the flight became wild . . .' ibid.

120 'were not altogether pleased . . .' Mackenzie, 19.

120 'advisable to quit . . .' ibid., 21.

120 'Immediately after the conference . . .' Graham, *Siege of Derry and Defence of Enniskillen*, 59.

121 'lest the townsmen . . .' Mackenzie, 21.

121 'in case the forces . . .' ibid.

121 'For the wiping of which aspersion . . .' Walker, 41–2.

122 'was much wondered at' Mackenzie, 22.

123 'the Committee of Derry . . .' ibid.

123 'absolutely refused . . .' ibid.

123 'The King . . . did him an honour . . .' Sergeant, Vol. II, 426–7.

124 'All along the road . . .' Gilbert, 46–7.

124 'James made his public entry . . .' Graham, *Siege of Derry and Defence of Enniskillen*, 53–5.

127 'one of three guns . . .' and subsequent quotes, Mackenzie, 23.

128 'never have troops marched . . .' Macrory, 152.

11 Fear and Loathing

130 'unwilling to stay . . .' Mackenzie, 28.

130 'to rescue the whole . . .' ibid., 94.

131 'That a mutual engagement . . .' ibid., 97.

131 'shall have the old houses . . .' ibid.

131 'That all persons of this garrison . . .' ibid.

131 'a pair of gallows shall . . .' and subsequent quotes, ibid., 98.

131 'stand by each other . . .' ibid., 28–9.

132 'Mr Walker receiving intelligence . . .' Walker, 5.

133 'some discontents appear[ed] . . .' Mackenzie, 29.

133 'all . . . that can or will fight . . .' ibid., 29–30.

133 'be ready to fight . . .' ibid., 30.

133 'that harrows should be . . .' Walker, 40.

134 'pressing him to . . .' Mackenzie, 30.

134 'The same day several . . .' ibid.

134 'frequently intersected by torrents . . .' Macaulay, 17.

135 'several fords where . . .' ibid.

135 'Everything else was rock . . .' ibid.

135 'They had taken everything . . .' Milligan, *History*, 113–14.

135 'for the soldiers are great . . .' ibid., 112.

135 'I shall do my utmost, Sire . . .' ibid., 113.

135 'to a military eye . . .' Macaulay, 20.

136 'with great resolution . . .' Mackenzie, 30.

137 'about thirty dragoons of . . .' and subsequent quotes, ibid., 32.

138 'But there was no . . .' ibid.

138 'was so ill placed . . .' ibid.

138 'The enemy perceiving this . . .' ibid., 32–3.

138 'fired briskly on the . . .' Gilbert, 45.

138 'But Gov. Lundy . . .' Mackenzie, 33.

139 'Gentlemen, I see you . . .' Walker, 54.

139 'You are all cut off . . .' Milligan, 86.

139 'Derry was his . . .' Witherow, *Derry and Enniskillen*, 94.

139 'gave order to . . .' Mackenzie, 33.

140 'expecting the Irish would take that way . . .' and subsequent quotes, ibid.

140 'This halt gave opportunity . . .' Gilbert, 46.

141 'Gov. Lundy being come . . .' Mackenzie, 34.

141 'Hearing you have taken . . . Witherow, *Derry and Enniskillen*, 97–8.

142 'orders and directions . . .' Mackenzie, 98.

142 'I am come back much . . .' Witherow, *Derry and Enniskillen*, 98–9.

143 'if the men . . .' ibid., 99.

143 'affairs were in great confusion . . .' ibid., 99.

143 'come next morning to town . . .' ibid.

143 'Since the writing of this, Major . . .' Witherow, 99.

144 'They called to the sentries . . .' Mackenzie, 37–8.

144 'did not agree with . . .' Dwyer, 15.

144 'stand by his men . . .' ibid.

145 'none were admitted . . .' Walker, 55.

145 'further succours of money . . .' Witherow, *Derry and Enniskillen*, 96.

145 'enemy was near their gates . . .' , Mackenzie, 36.

146 'Those of the Council . . .' and subsequent quotes, Mackenzie, 36–7.

147 'Col. Lundy, to delude . . .' and subsequent quotes, Mackenzie, 36–7.

12 Murray's Coup

148 'it was recommended . . .' and subsequent quotes, Walker, 7.

149 'out to the King . . .' Walker., 8.

149 'that he should not march . . .' ibid.

149 'they in the city . . .' Mackenzie, 38.

150 'to send to King James . . .' ibid.

151 'amuse the garrison . . .' ibid., 39.

151 'soon exposed them . . .' ' ibid.

151 'on the town as betrayed . . .' ibid., 37.

151 'madness . . . to stay behind . . .' ibid.

151 'The common soldiers . . .' ibid., 39.

151 'This day some . . .' ibid.

152 'were refused entrance . . .' ibid., 38.

152 'had before been very active' ibid., 38–9.

152 'Major Crofton . . .' ibid., 40.

152 'thought fit not to insist . . .' ibid.

153 'that none should dare to fire . . .' Walker, 8.

153 'of so considerable an army . . .' ibid.

153 'and dare the rebels . . .' Gilbert, 62.

154 'he would conceal no longer . . .' Mackenzie, 41.

154 'This discovery . . .' Walker, 9.

154 'opposed the enemy's . . .' Mackenzie, 32.

154 'having observed Col. Lundy's . . .' ibid., 38.

155 'resolved to sell their lives . . .' ibid.

155 'how little the Council . . .' ibid., 40.

155 'encouraged the men . . .' ibid., 42.

155 'could not be kept in any order . . .' Walker, 8.

156 'in much disorder . . .' ibid.

156 'violent humour . . .' ibid.

156 'for what had passed . . .' Mackenzie, 41.

156 'That he should immediately . . .' ibid., 42.

156 'the messenger being . . .' ibid.

157 'with some difficulty . . .' ibid.

157 'the people took an occasion . . .' Gilbert, 62.

157 'The multitude having eagerly . . .' Mackenzie, 43.

158 'treated as favourites . . .' and subsequent quotes, Milligan, 129.

159 'He assured them . . .' and subsequent quotes, Mackenzie, 43.

159 'away from an army . . .' and subsequent quotes, ibid., 44.

160 'The Council were resolved . . .' and subsequent quotes, ibid.

160 'for a while appear . . .' ibid., 45.

161 'there to expect the arrival . . .' Milligan, 126.

161 'gentlemen left us . . .' Walker, 9.

161 'who was dangerously sick . . .' ibid., 10.

161 'for the soldiers . . .' ibid.

13 The Siege Begins

163 'but he modestly . . .' Mackenzie, 46.

164 'to make an excuse . . .' Milligan, *History*, 127.

164 'the rabble . . .' Macrory, 222.

166 'so enraged . . .' Mackenzie, 47.

166 'Sir, The cause . . .' Milligan, *History*, 130.

167 'so that on the least . . .' Walker, 11.

168 'candles were to be lighted . . .' Milligan, *History*, 163.

168 'and lodged in four . . .' ibid.

168 'a salmon and a half . . .' ibid.

168 'we had no persons . . .' Walker, 12.

169 'to receive and protect . . .' ibid.

169 'that no such terms . . .' Simpson, 116.

170 'came thither to frighten . . .' Milligan, *History*, 136.

171 'there was not in the camp . . .' Gilbert, 65.

172 'stone by stone' Macrory, 217.

172 'the greater part of the officers . . .' ibid.

174 'till we plainly told him . . .' Walker, 13.

175 'My folly in undertaking . . .' Sergeant, Vol. II, 404.

175 'People discoursed today . . .' ibid., 405.

175 'the cold magnanimity . . .' quoted in Gray, 79.

14 The Fighting Begins

177 'as many as pleased . . .' Walker, 14.

178 'to relieve Colonel Murray . . .' ibid.

180 'The besieged, having made . . .' Mackenzie, 50.

180 'great grief to the enemy . . .' Walker, 15.

183 'were maintained by the store . . .' Mackenzie, 52.

184 'the bombs played hotly . . .' Graham, *Siege of Derry and Defence of Enniskillen*, 132.

185 'heard that Colonel Cunningham . . .' Witherow, *Two Diaries*, 1.

185 'arrived here one Stevens . . .' ibid.

186 'embark with some regiments . . .' ibid., 1–2.

186 'with all possible diligence . . .' Milligan, *History*, 190.

190 'four or five colours . . .' Mackenzie, 55.

190 '300 or them . . .' Walker, 16.

191 'reckoned the best soldier . . .' Witherow, *Two Diaries*, 67.

191 'very negligently . . .' Walker, 16.

192 'an English dependency . . .' Foster, 144.

193 'no other test . . .' Bagwell, Vol. III, 224.

193 'relieving such as have been injured . .,' Sergeant, Vol. II, 443–4.

15 Grinding on

195 'On 2 May the . . .' Hamilton, 25–6.

197 'have several times beaten . . .' Witherow, *Two Diaries*, 2.

198 'and the four French officers . . .' and subsequent quotes, ibid., 3.

199 'was taken in by the besieged . . .' Walker, 2nd edn, 12.

200 'without orders to parley . . .' Witherow, *Two Diaries*, 68.

200 'they may want provisions . . .' Milligan, *History*, 191.

201 'will have all his troops killed . . .' ibid., 194.

201 'the enemy's want . . .' Walker, 16.

201 'Captain Noble and others . . .' Mackenzie, 54.

201 'We were informed . . .' ibid.

201 'this proved the justness . . .' Witherow, *Two Diaries*, 63.

202 'After the placing of these camps . . .' Mackenzie, 57.

202 'with a design . . .' ibid.

202 'the besieged found it impossible . . .' Walker, 18.

203 'not to keep faith . . .' ibid., 17.

203 'was troubled in his conscience . . .' ibid.

203 'denied they were concerned . . .' ibid.

204 'From 10 May . . .' Mackenzie, 60.

207 'dispatches of the enemy . . .' Simpson, 125.

207 'From other parts . . .' Witherow, *Two Diaries*, 71.

208 'Several people came . . .' Witherow, *Two Diaries*, 7–8.

208 'One of the difficulties . . .' Witherow, *Derry and Enniskillen*, 136.

208 'About the end . . .' and subsequent quotes, Mackenzie, 61–2.

209 'to prosecute him . . .' ibid., 62.

209 'the government of . . .' ibid.

209 'the meetings of this Council . . .' ibid.

210 'we had liberty enough . . .' Witherow, *Two Diaries*, 73.

210 'the great and small guns . . .' ibid., 72–3.

210 'to secure the breast work . . .' ibid., 72.

211 'could not enjoy their rest . . .' Walker, 19.

213 'fair play' Gilbert, 76.

213 'a loud huzzah . . .' Walker, 18.

214 'three of these bold men . . .' Walker, 19,

215 'grabbed them by the hair . . .' Mackenzie, 59.

215 'also did good service . . .' ibid.

216 'preserve their own bodies . . .' Walker, 19.

217 'You see here . . .' Gilbert, 77–8.

217 'contrary to every kind . . .' Milligan, *History*, 210.

217 'a general despondency . . .' ibid.

217 'In a word . . .' ibid.

16 'In the Cup of Joy, Bitterness is Sometimes Mingled'

218 'plowed up our streets . . .' Walker, 19.

219 'The bombs, by throwing down . . .' Mackenzie, 63.

220 'Both these people . . .' ibid.

221 'were very thick . . .' ibid., 10.

223 'got out most of her guns . . .' ibid., 12.

223 'all her shot-holes . . .' ibid.

223 'her rigging spliced . . .' ibid.

224 'many more by shattering . . .' ibid., 76.

225 'gave us at the present . . .' Mackenzie, 64.

225 'Upon the appearing . . .' ibid

226 'were resolved to march away . . .' Witherow, *Two Diaries*, 77.

226 'to know if anyone . . .' ibid., 15.

227 'the terror was soon over . . .' Mackenzie, 64.

227 'the enemy now began . . .' Walker, 20.

227 'oppose the ships . . .' Mackenzie, 64.

227 'when we saw . . .' ibid.

227 'This morning . . .' Witherow, *Two Diaries*, 21.

228 'In the cup of joy . . .' Simpson, 128.

228 'with the intent . . .' Walker, 22.

228 'to rob the fish houses . . .' Mackenzie, 67.

228 'that the enemy received . . .' Walker, 23.

229 'they were so terrified . . .' and subsequent quotes, Mackenzie, 67–8.

230 'A sort of Council . . .' and subsequent quotes, ibid., 65

231 'Governor Baker . . .' ibid.

231 'The rabble of our garrison . . .' Witherow, *Two Diaries*, 77.

231 'would not hear of money . . .' ibid., 79.

231 'and made a fire of it . . .' Mackenzie, 64.

231 'Mr Walker's own lodging . . .' ibid., 85.

231 'though indisposed . . .' Mackenzie, 65–6.

233 'how little they . . .' and subsequent quotes, Walker, 23.

233 'That Crimson Flag . . .' Milligan, *History*, 372.

17 Nastier and Nastier

235 'Several debates . . .' Witherow, *Two Diaries*, 15.

235 'the several obstacles . . .' ibid., 16.

235 'they were neither pressed . . .' ibid.

235 'continue here in Lough Foyle . . .' ibid., 18.

235 'which if desperate . . .' ibid.

236 '(it being the advance ship) . . .' ibid.

236 'ordered the gunners . . .' Mackenzie, 660.

236 'we lost the benefit . . .' Walker, 23.

237 'Are those brave fellows . . .' Lucy, 39.

239 'He told us . . .' Witherow, *Two Diaries*, 80.

239 'an account of the ships . . .' Mackenzie, 69.

239 'the fevers, flux . . .' ibid., 66.

239 'in the kindest manner . . .' Graham, *Siege of Derry and Defence of Enniskillen*, 193.

239 'more alarming to them . . .' ibid.

240 'he found that his clothes . . .' Simpson, 166.

240 'was resolved, however . . .' ibid.

241 'charged the Chevalier . . .' Witherow, *Derry and Enniskillen*, 159.

241 'a man of good sense ' ibid.

241 'being in hazard . . .' Mackenzie, 69.

242 'if we have not a speedy supply . . .' Dwyer, 88.

242 'the booms across the river . . .' ibid.

242 'our case calls for help . . .' ibid., 90.

243 'resolved to raise . . .' ibid.

243 'but one small . . .' ibid., 91.

244 'either one or both . . .' Witherow, *Two Diaries*, 20.

244 'we have fished' Macrory, 272.

245 'General Rosen has no power . . .' Walker, 50

245 'free liberty of goods . . .' ibid., 51.

245 'it will be in the King's . . .' ibid., 50.

245 'upon horse flesh . . .' ibid., 25.

246 'it did no other harm . . .' Witherow, *Two Diaries*, 81.

246 '(being so sworn to do) . . .' Mackenzie, 69.

246 'he was in the enemy's camp . . .' ibid.

247 'called over to us . . .' ibid., 70.

247 'unanimously resolved to eat . .' Walker, 25.

247 'a young madcap . . .' Witherow, *Derry and Enniskillen*, 161.

247 'We were often told . . .' Walker, 25.

247 'had missed its aim . . .' Graham, *Siege of Derry and Defence of Enniskillen*, 201.

248 'they thundered upon them' Walker, 24.

248 'so many shots . . .' Witherow, *Two Diaries*, 82.

248 'Angel, mounted on a snow-white horse . . .' Graham, *Siege of Derry and Defence of Enniskillen*, 202.

248 'his death was a sensible loss . . .' Walker, 25.

249 'greatly beloved . . .' Witherow, *Two Diaries*, 82.

250 'There is no doubt . . .' Witherow, *Derry and Enniskillen*, 180.

251 'for the gathering together . . .' ibid., 166.

251 'have orders to give . . .' ibid., 167.

253 'the disturbance given us . . .' ibid., 168.

253 'yet we expect no mercy . . .' ibid., 170.

253 'whereof our lives . . .' and subsequent quotes, ibid., 171.

18 Threats Fail, Kirke Demurs

256 'they were weary of . . .' Witherow, *Two Diaries*, 22.

257 'Our men at first . . .' Walker, 27.

258 'warmed with a new rage . . .' ibid.

258 'the prisoners might have Priests . . .' ibid.

260 'barbarous Muscovite . . .' Macrory, 286.

260 'Trusty and well-beloved . . .' , Witherow, *Derry and Enniskillen*, 176.

261 'regard [to] your project . . .' ibid.

261 'in which we have . . .' ibid.

261 'full of benevolence . . .' ibid., 177.

262 'before the enemy . . .' ibid., 176.

262 'between your Majesty's . . .' ibid.

263 'have the honour . . .' Milligan, *History*, 273.

264 'Captain Richards had landed . . .' ibid., 279.

267 'using reproachful language . . .' Mackenzie, 102.

268 'as if the Devil . . .' Witherow, *Two Diaries*, 89.

268 'thrusting and thronging . . .' ibid.

271 'mentioned Major-General Kirke's . . .' Mackenzie, 75.

271 '4,000 horse and 9,000 foot . . .' ibid.

273 'blessed be God . . .' Witherow, *Two Diaries*, 91.

19 Desperate Times

275 'Be good husbands . . .' Walker, 22.

276 'to rectify and set right . . .' Witherow, *Two Diaries*, 95.

277 'if after all . . .' Milligan, *History*, 301–2.

277 'kept his bed . . .' Witherow, *Derry and Enniskillen*, 194.

277 'it being extremely bare . . .' ibid.

20 At Long Last, Relief

281 'Seeing that Derry . . .' Witherow, *Derry and Enniskillen*, 196.

282 'saluted him by some great names . . .' Walker, 30.

284 ''Tis truth they . . .' Dwyer, 114.

286 'that if we followed these orders . . .' Witherow, *Two Diaries*, 40.

288 'for we only reckoned . . .' Walker, 33.

289 'if they came not now . . .' Witherow, *Two Diaries*, 99.

290 'the most dreadful to the besieged . . .' Walker, 33.

290 'struck such a sudden terror . . .' Mackenzie, 79.

291 'he died by the most enviable . . .' Macaulay, 44.

292 'A day to be remembered . . .' Witherow, *Two Diaries*, 98–9.

293 'Early this morning . . .' ibid., 49–50.

21 Aftermath

299 'to congratulate . . .' Walker, 35.

299 'to give the necessary . . .' Witherow, *Two Diaries*, 52.

299 'the Major-General . . .' ibid., 53.

300 'The Governors treated . . .' ibid.

300 'on the nature . . .' ibid., 102–3.

301 'prevailed on to go . . .' Walker, 35.

301 'upon pretence . . .' Mackenzie, 81.

301 'that a great many . . .' ibid., 84.

303 'upon suspicion of treasonable . . .' Macrory, 190.

303 'That Colonel Lundy . . .' ibid., 191.

304 'most material witnesses . . .' ibid., 192.

304 'he had a faction . . .' ibid.

304 'most of the houses . . .' ibid., 326.

305 'Mr Walker receiving . . .' Walker, 5.

305 'Mr Walker took his post . . .' ibid.

305 'Mr Walker found the gates . . .' ibid., 6.

305 'Mr Walker found it necessary . . .' ibid, 14.

305 'a spy upon the whole . . .' ibid., 12.

305 'there were eighteen . . .' ibid., 11.

305 'were equally careful . . .' ibid.

306 'several non-conformist ministers . . .' ibid., 58.

306 'Mr Walker will be . . .' Dwyer, 73.

306 'Mr W. allows . . .' ibid., 74.

307 'a long-winded paraphrase . . .' Macrory, 332.

309 'What was he doing there . . .' ibid., 339.

309 'both belonged to the one leg . . .' Witherow, *Derry and Enniskillen*, 334.

309 'Is this business over . . .' Lucy, 76.

310 The wretched youth . . .' Macrory, 140.

22 The End

313 'as great as . . .' Gilbert, 126.

313 'struck with a deep wound . . .' Gilbert, 148.

314 'He and company . . .' ibid., 155.

314 'for there was no other . . .' ibid.

315 'consistent with the . . .' Foster, *Modern Ireland*, 151.

318 'at length were paid . . .' Witherow, *Derry and Enniskillen*, 347fn.

319 'his remains were borne . . .' Milligan, *History*, 321.

319 'The resentment which they carried . . .' Froude, Vol. I, 392.

320 'Colonel Lundy . . .' Milligan, *History*, 147.

321 'attributed to faintheartedness . . .' Macaulay, 20.

321 'pernicious intentions' Mackenzie, 45.

322 'If a magistrate or military officer . . .' Graham, *Siege of Derry and Defence of Enniskillen*, 282.

322 'had a very happy . . .' ibid., 283.

323 'a selection of sacred . . .' ibid., 284.

323 'which at once . . .' ibid.

323 'covered over with a variety . . .' and subsequent quotes, ibid., 284–6.

325 'the Clergy of the . . .' and subsequent quotes, ibid., 286–7.

326 'gazed with intense . . .' and subsequent quotes, ibid., 287–8.

326 'sung in full chorus . . .' ibid., 289–90.

327 'in strong contrast . . .' ibid., 287.

329 'Sad as the results were . . .' Stewart, 74.

330 'only two persons . . .' ibid., 75.

331 'Derry, as dusk gathered . . .' Paor, 170.

333 'sense of the religious . . .' O'Toole, 5.

334 'We followed our by now set routine . . .' Taylor, 28.

BIBLIOGRAPHY

Bagwell, Richard, *Ireland under the Stuarts*, 3 vols (1909–16; reprinted Holland Press, London, 1963)

Bryant, Arthur, *King Charles II* (Longmans, Green & Co., London, 1932)

Burton, Richard, *The History of the Kingdom of Ireland* (Machell Stace, London, 1811)

Clarendon, Edward, Earl of, *The History of the Rebellion and Civil Wars in Ireland* (London, 1720)

Colby, R. E., *Ordnance Survey of the County of Londonderry, Volume the First* (Hodges & Smith, Dublin, 1837)

Cromwell, Oliver, *Oliver Cromwell's Letters and Speeches*, 5 vols, ed. Thomas Carlyle (Chapman & Hall, London, 1849)

Dwyer, Reverend Philip, *The Siege of Derry in 1689* (London, 1893). [Contains Walker's reply to his critics, *A Vindication of the True Account of the Siege of Derry in Ireland* (London, 1689]

Foster, R. F., *Modern Ireland, 1600–1972* (Allen Lane, London, 1988)

Fraser, Antonia, *Cromwell: Our Chief of Men* (Weidenfeld & Nicolson, London, 1973)

Froude, James Anthony, *The English in Ireland in the Eighteenth Century*, 2 vols (Longmans, Green & Co., London, 1872)

Gilbert, John T., (from a Jacobite text written by an unknown author) *A Jacobite Narrative of the War in Ireland, 1688–1681* (Dublin, 1892; reprinted Irish University Press, Shannon, 1972, with introduction by J. G. Simms)

Graham, Reverend John, *A History of the Siege of Londonderry and the Defence of Enniskillen in 1688 and 1689* (William Curry, Dublin, 1829)

—— *Ireland Preserved; or the Siege of Londonderry* (Hardy & Walker, Dublin, 1841)

Gray, Tony, *No Surrender!* (Macdonald & Janes, London, 1975)

Hamilton, Andrew, *The Actions of the Enniskillen-Men: from their first taking up arms in 1688 in defence of the Protestant religion, their lives and liberties, to the landing of Duke Schomberg in Ireland* (London, 1690; reprinted Castlepoint Press, Scotland, 2001)

Hickson, Mary, *Ireland in the Seventeenth Century; or the Irish Massacres of 1641–2*, 2 vols (Longmans, Green & Co., London, 1884)

Killen, W. D., *Mackenzie's Memorials of the Siege of Derry Including his Narrative and its Vindication* (C. Aitchison, Belfast, 1861) [Contains Mackenzie's *Dr Walker's Invisible Champion Foiled: or An Appendix to the late Narrative of the Siege of Derry* (London, 1690)]

Lucy, Gordon (ed.), *Lord Macaulay on Londonderry, Aughrim, Enniskillen and the Boyne* (Ulster Society, Lurgan, 1989)

Macaulay, Lord, *The Story of the Siege of Londonderry as contained in his 'History of England'* (sold in aid of the fund for the rebuilding of the Apprentice Boys Memorial Hall, Londonderry, 1937)

Mackenzie, John, *A Narrative of the Siege of Londonderry* (London, 1690). [Contains Walker's *A True Account*]

Macrory, Patrick, *The Siege of Derry* (Hodder & Stoughton, London, 1980; OUP Paperback, 1988)

Milligan, Cecil Davis, *History of the Siege of Londonderry 1689* (H. R. Carter Publications, Belfast, 1951)

—— *The Walls of Derry* (Londonderry Sentinel: Part 1, 1948; Part 2, 1950; reprinted as single vol. Ulster Society, Lurgan, 1996)

Moody, T. W. and Martin, F. X. (eds), *The Course of Irish History* (Mercier Press, Cork and Dublin, 1967)

O'Donovan, John (ed.), *A narration of the services done by the army employed to Lough-Foyle under the leading of me, Sir Henry Dowcra, Knight, reproduced in the Miscellany of the Celtic Society (or Irish Historical and Literary Association)* (Dublin, 1849) [Contains passages from the *Annals of the Four Masters* that cover the same ground as Dowcra's]

O'Fáolain, Sean, *The Great O'Neill* (Longmans, Green & Co., London, 1942; paperback edn Mercier Press, Cork, 1981)

O'Toole, Fintan, 'No Doubts in Derry' (*Irish Times Weekend Supplement*, Saturday, 12 May 1990)

Paor, Liam de, *Divided Ulster* (Penguin Special, London, 1970; reissued Pelican Books, London, 1971)

Petrie, Sir Charles, *The Great Tyrconnel: A Chapter in Anglo-Irish Relations* (Mercier Press, Cork and Dublin, 1972)

Sergeant, Philip W., *Little Jennings and Fighting Dick Talbot: A Life of the Duke and Duchess of Tyrconnel*, 2 vols (Hutchinson & Co., London, 1913)

Simpson, Robert, *The Annals of Derry Showing the Rise of the Town from the earliest accounts on Record to the Plantation under King James 1st–1613 and thence of the City of Londonderry to the Present Times* (Hempton, Londonderry, 1847; reprinted North-West Books, Limavady, 1987)

Stewart, A. T .Q., *The Narrow Ground* (Faber & Faber, London, 1977; rev. paperback edn, 1989)

Taylor, Peter, *Loyalists* (Bloomsbury, London, 1999)

Temple, Sir Charles, *The Irish Rebellion; or, An History of the attempts of the Irish Papists to extirpate the Protestants in the Kingdom of Ireland, together with the Barbarous Cruelties and Bloody Massacres that ensued thereupon* (London, 1646)

Walker, Reverend George, *A True Account of the Siege of London-Derry* (London, 1690) [Contains Mackenzie's *Narrative*]

—— *Walker's True Account of the Siege of Derry* (James Hempton & Co., Londonderry, 1937) [Corrected edn containing additional phrases; indicated when cited]

Witherow, Thomas, *Derry and Enniskillen in the Year 1689* (William Mullon & Son Belfast, 1913)

—— *Two Diaries of Derry in 1689, Being Richards's Diary of the Fleet and Ash's Journal of the Siege* (William Gailey, Londonderry, 1888)

York, James, Duke of, *The Memoirs of James II, His Campaigns as Duke of York 1652–1660*, trans. A. Lytton Sells from the Bouillon manuscript (London, 1816; reprinted Indiana University Press, 1962)

INDEX

Reference is generally made to Derry rather than Londonderry.
Abbreviations have been used as follows:
JII (James II); RL (Robert Lundy); WO (William of Orange *also* William III.
Followers of James II are referred to as Jacobites, those of William of Orange as
Williamites.
Ranks are usually the latest quoted in the text.

CIVITAS VICTORIA

Printed by Edw. Serin
and are to be Sold at his
House in Stephens
Greene Dublin.

CHURCH

LAND

SMITHS

PROPOR
TION THE